Praise for
The Trouble with Markets

"This challenging and provocative book is essential reading for every corporate executive and business owner. It poses fundamental questions about what it is that makes a market economy tick and it tackles the thorny ethical aspects of the role of business in society. After you have read it, your thinking about business in society will never be the same again."
John Connolly, Senior Partner and Chief Executive, Deloitte LLP

"Roger Bootle is one of the best interpreters of modern capitalism around. This account of the crisis and what it means is as important as it is accessible."
Will Hutton, Executive Vice Chair, The Work Foundation and author of the bestselling *The State We're In*

"Compelling prescriptions from an economist unusually able to speak with authority – because unlike most of his peers, Bootle spotted that the boom was unsustainable."
Robert Peston, BBC Business Editor and author of *Who Runs Britain?*

"This book will stand out in the explosion of financial crisis literature. Roger Bootle is one of the top, practical economists in the financial world but he is not afraid to tackle the bigger, deeper questions around the future of capitalism, the role of markets and government."
Vince Cable, MP, Liberal Democrat Shadow Chancellor of the Exchequer and author of *The Storm: The World Economic Crisis and What it Means*

"In his last book, *Money for Nothing*, Roger Bootle predicted with great accuracy the property crash and subsequent financial crisis. In *The Trouble with Markets*, he offers us a way out of the almighty mess that excessive debt created. It should be made compulsory reading for all policymakers."
Jeff Randall, *Sky News* business presenter and *Daily Telegraph* editor-at-large

"Roger Bootle knows how markets work, and also when they don't work. Everyone who wants a real understanding of the strengths and weaknesses of the market economy should read this book."
John Kay, *Financial Times* **columnist and author of**
The Long and the Short of It

"A brilliant book that puts markets in stunning perspective. Once again, Roger Bootle tackles, head on, some of the toughest economic questions of our time. An extraordinarily penetrating and absorbing analysis."
Sir Brian Pitman, Former Chairman, Lloyds TSB Group and
Senior Advisor to Morgan Stanley

"Roger Bootle's *The Trouble with Markets: Saving Capitalism from Itself* impresses with its style, substance and courage. I hope that the Lucases read and respond, the young quants listen and learn and the CEOs and risk managers comprehend and implement it."
Prof. Dr. Norbert Walter, Chief Economist of Deutsche Bank Group and
CEO of Deutsche Bank Research

The Trouble with Markets

Saving Capitalism from Itself

Roger Bootle

NICHOLAS BREALEY
PUBLISHING

LONDON · BOSTON

First published by
Nicholas Brealey Publishing in 2009

3–5 Spafield Street
Clerkenwell, London
EC1R 4QB
Tel: +44 (0)20 7239 0360
Fax: +44 (0)20 7239 0370

20 Park Plaza, Suite 1115A
Boston
MA 02110, USA
Tel: 888 BREALEY
Fax: (617) 523 3708

www.nicholasbrealey.com

© Roger Bootle 2009

ISBN 978-1-85788-537-8

British Library Cataloguing in Publication Data
A catalogue record for this book is available from the British Library.

Printed in the UK by Clays Ltd, St Ives plc
on Forest Stewardship Council certified paper.

FSC
Mixed Sources
Product group from well-managed
forests and other controlled sources
Cert no. SGS - COC - 2061
www.fsc.org
© 1996 Forest Stewardship Council

Contents

Preface

The origins of this book go deep in my own history. Working in and around the City of London for 30 years has been a splendid vantage point from which to observe the financial markets. For much of that time my desk has been in, or just next to, one or other of the "dealing rooms," the vital organs of the financial markets.

I have worked as a dealer in the money markets, as an adviser to an investment bank, and as chief economist for two stockbroking firms, a merchant bank, and one of the largest commercial banks in the world. I have written extensively about the financial markets, first as an academic at Oxford, then as a City economist, and more recently as the author of three books, as a columnist on three of Britain's national newspapers, and as an adviser to one of the largest global accountancy businesses. I now make my living primarily by running a consultancy firm, Capital Economics, which advises clients around the world, most of whose business is in some sense financial.

I have always felt ambivalent about the financial markets. On the one hand, their efficiency, energy, and single-mindedness in the pursuit of success are admirable. On the human level, they have provided employment to many splendid individuals of both talent and integrity, some of whom I have been privileged to work with. And they have brought out the good in millions of people blessed with drive and native wit. At the macro level, in my own country, the UK, they have brought prosperity to many, as the wealth they have created has spread far and wide. As so many of Britain's traditional sources of wealth have declined, the City's success has shone like a beacon. And, by and large, the markets have been good to me. Indeed, you could say that in a minor way I too have been, and to some extent still am, on the financial markets gravy train that I criticize in this book.

On the other hand, I have been troubled by the increasing dominance of markets over business relationships, liquidity over commitment, and greed over public purpose. I have been even more troubled by the realization that as the markets' success seemed to grow, it became more and more widely believed that they offered a blueprint for how society at large should be organized.

This book is the third part of a trilogy. My thoughts on the major economic issues before us have been developing between books. So, in the process of addressing the major questions about the future of the market economy, *The Trouble with Markets* also attempts to build on my earlier work and to tie up some of the loose ends left dangling by the two earlier volumes.

The Death of Inflation, published in 1996, argued that the world faced a future of low inflation accompanied by high rates of economic growth and low unemployment. Soon after the book first appeared, the immediate flow of news seemed to support its central thesis. No one knew, though, how long this happy state would continue and there were plenty of critics who argued that it was very temporary. At times they appeared to be right – and from a perspective some way into the future, they might yet be right. In the event, with some qualifications, the era of low inflation lasted at least until 2006.

But now, with central banks and governments pouring money into the system by the squillion, many people think that a return to much higher inflation is just around the corner. By contrast, this book argues that, despite the huge risks and challenges, the low inflation era will last a good many years yet. Indeed, deflation is the greater threat.

What *The Death of Inflation* did not foresee was that as the forces that produced low inflation gathered strength, darker clouds would appear, partly as a direct result. The rise of China and the associated processes of globalization may have helped to keep inflation low, but they also helped to produce a world of abnormally low interest rates, accompanied by the free flow of finance, which fueled a bubble in asset markets, especially real estate. Ironically, what so many people regarded as a threat, namely the rise of China, was actually a source of prosperity, whereas what so many rejoiced in as the source of prosperity, namely rising house prices, was actually a snare and a delusion.

This was the essential message of *Money for Nothing*, published in 2003. The book's fate was the exact opposite of *The Death of Inflation*. At first, its warnings seemed surreal and its cautionary advice fell on deaf ears. Indeed, as property prices carried on rising, to many people the book must have seemed off the wall.

It is very common for bubbles to inflate much further than any fundamentals-based forecaster can imagine. That is, after all, why they are bubbles. This is exactly what had happened with the dot-com boom and it is what happened with the subsequent property boom. As property prices went up and up, *Money for Nothing*'s strictures on house prices were widely disregarded. Yet house prices have now fallen heavily in America, Ireland, Britain, Spain, France, and Denmark.

In retrospect, while *Money for Nothing* was too early in its warnings of a housing disaster, much of the book has now been vindicated. Not only has the property bubble burst but, just as the book warned that it would, this bursting has endangered the whole financial system.

The weakness of *Money for Nothing* was not that it failed to foresee future events, but rather that it failed to see their full ramifications. Although it caught a glimpse of the disasters yet to come, it did not envisage their full consequences. Now we are drowning in them. *The Trouble with Markets* tries to provide both life jackets to keep us afloat and a rescue boat to take us back to dry land.

Although it does have things to say about the immediate economic outlook, this is not a book of forecasts. As I argue in Chapter 2, there are good reasons to believe that the world will be afflicted by the effects of the crisis of 2007/9 for some considerable time. Nevertheless, it is possible that the global economy could surprise everyone by its powers of rapid recuperation, just as it surprised on the downside. Indeed, by the time you are reading this, things may seem to be back to normal. However, the challenges that this episode poses for the structure of capitalist societies will remain vital – as will the various measures and remedies that I propose in Part III.

The plan of the book is straightforward. In Chapter 1, I examine the origins of the financial crisis of 2007/9 before moving on to the economic consequences in Chapters 2 and 3. Chapter 2 tries to answer the question of how serious things will be by looking at the past. Chapter 3 tackles the question of whether the system will fall into a period of deflation or whether, as many people fear, the depression will end in a prolonged burst of high inflation.

In Part II, I examine the deep causes of the crisis – the trouble with markets. Chapter 4 asks which bits of the market system work well and which do not, and why. In Chapter 5 I use this framework to analyze the failings of financial markets in particular. Chapter 6 tackles the weaknesses of the international financial system, concentrating on China.

While Parts I and II are devoted to causes and consequences, Part III is devoted to cures. I start, in Chapter 7, with how individuals should manage their finances. I should say, though, that it isn't a road to riches I lay out there, but rather a guide to survival. Chapter 8 is the system-wide equivalent, discussing what measures governments and central banks need to take to get us out of the mire. Chapter 9 looks beyond the immediate crisis to discuss the shape of the world once the problems are over, and what steps need to be taken to reform the system to ensure that nothing like it happens again. In the Conclusion I draw together what all this implies about how we should regard the capitalist system.

Acknowledgments

In writing this book I have accumulated large debts of gratitude. Many of the people who have helped considerably cannot be acknowledged individually: the thousands of traders, investors, and market operators I have encountered, if not known, over the years, whose attitudes and behavior have fascinated, enlightened, and sometimes infuriated. They have provided the book's raw material – the substance of "the market," its people and its views. For this, I offer my thanks. For what I write about some of what they have said or done, I offer my apologies.

At the opposite end of the spectrum from these nameless thousands, I must offer my thanks also to the midwife who assisted at the birth of my son Alexander. She influenced me more than she could have imagined. Having just come from a City meeting about the award of bonuses, I found myself watching her go about her business, and being intrigued by the issues of motivation, purpose, and reward. I asked myself whether she was incentivized by the prospect of a huge bonus. If not, why not? These thoughts planted a seed that led to the birth of this book, albeit rather more than nine months later.

Steve Clarke of Reuters provided inspiration and stimulus, as he did with *Money for Nothing*. Much further back in my life but of great importance still, my inspiration has come from my wonderful teachers at Oxford, to whom I owe so much: Max Corden, Tony Courakis, the late Sir John Hicks, Vijay Joshi, and Peter Oppenheimer. If they do not agree with the extremely critical remarks I make in Chapter 9 about modern economics, I hope that they will at least forgive me.

In addition, many people have helped me enormously by giving advice, information, and critical comment, and by reading drafts of the book, in whole or in part. I would single out George de Nemeskeri-Kiss, Marian Gilbart Read, and Christopher Smallwood.

I was fortunate to be able to present the core of my thesis at a meeting of The Accumulation Society and benefited greatly from the discussion there. I am most grateful to the Society's members for their comments. In addition, I organized a lively gathering of a few economists, bankers, and corporate executives, and was delighted to receive invaluable comments from Philip Booth, Richard Delbridge, Guy Heald, William Keegan, John Llewellyn, Gavin Morris, Derek Scott, and Jack Wigglesworth. I am grateful also for the comments I have received on my developing ideas at seminars and gatherings organised by Deloitte, to which I act as economic adviser.

At Capital Economics, most of my colleagues provided assistance in some shape or form, but I am particularly grateful to Paul Ashworth, Paul Dales, Kevin Grice, John Higgins, Julian Jessop, Jonathan Loynes, Jennifer McKeown, Ben May, Vicky Redwood, Ed Stansfield, and Mark Williams. Samuel Tombs and David Rees helped considerably by acting as my research assistants, while Faith Elliott and Samantha Howard-Carr performed sterling work managing the typescript.

As with my previous books, my children cannot be said to have helped, but at least this time they did not hinder my efforts! I am grateful to them, and to my beloved Alya, for putting up with many absences and much absorption in yet another bout of extended writing. I suspect that they will know this book as *The Trouble with Roger: Saving Daddy from Himself*.

None of the above individuals is responsible for any sins of commission or omission in the text. As always, responsibility for these rests with the author alone.

Roger Bootle
September 2009

Part I

The Great Implosion

1

How on Earth Did We Get Here?

The markets, the markets,
The markets know best.
They take all the money...
And damn all the rest. Anon

In September 2008, under the Swiss/French Alps, an experiment took place that could have imperilled the world. By dint of a phenomenal feat of engineering, an enormous machine, the Large Hadron Collider, occupying a subalpine tunnel 27 kilometers long, was ready to smash atoms together at enormous velocities. Many of the world's best scientists were engaged on the project. They hoped that this collision of atoms would reveal the origins of the universe.

Critics argued, though, that this experiment could spell the *end* of the universe, as everything could be sucked into a gigantic black hole. Across the globe, people of a more nervous disposition waited anxiously. As you who are reading this know full well, the world survived; in fact, the result was something of a damp squib. Mind you, five years of further experiments are to follow – and heaven knows what thereafter.

By contrast, above and beyond the subalpine tunnel, it seemed that the financial world had *already* been sucked into a black hole. The value of complex financial instruments, designed by some of the world's best "*rocket* scientists," collapsed. Some large banks went bust, others were saved only by gigantic injections of public money, financial markets hovered on the brink of meltdown, house prices fell, share prices tumbled, and hundreds of millions of people shuddered over their future. At the worst point, about 60% of the world's stock-market wealth, equivalent to two years of America's GDP, had evaporated – a sum of about $30 trillion, or if you like your noughts, $30,000,000,000,000. So no wonder that people were terrified about their savings and their pensions, their homes and their jobs. The financial structure cracked and buckled. Nothing seemed certain or secure.

The 1930s had seen the Great Depression and the 1970s the Great Inflation. The 1990s had seen the Great Moderation. This was the *Great Implosion.*

Yet, before the events of 2007/9, the world economy had apparently been strong. Indeed, people had talked about a transformation in economic prospects. Globalization and new technology had radically improved the outlook for economic growth. Meanwhile, improved economic management and more placid conditions had supposedly brought an end to economic instability.

Accordingly, the trouble with markets hit people like a blow to the solar plexus. While the world survived the acute crisis in 2008/9, when at one point it seemed that the whole financial system might collapse, we can't relax over financial markets. At least five years of further tests lie ahead.

Do markets work?

Despite the trillions of dollars lost, and despite the worries of millions of people, more than this – much, much more – is at stake. For this crisis has delivered the killer blow to an idea that has underpinned the structure of society, framed the political debate, and molded international relations for decades. It is simply the idea that *markets* work and governments don't.

From the events of 2007/9, it seems plain that the financial markets have *not* worked to promote the common weal, and they have caused, rather than absorbed, chaos and instability. Ironically, they have had to be bailed out by governments. Meanwhile, it seems that the fortunes "earned" by bankers high and low were not really earned but expropriated from the rest of us. If the system can produce such wealth-destroying success for some, how can it work for our overall benefit? And if the financial markets are like this, then what about the rest of the market system?

The trouble with markets is that not all markets are the same. Some work well, some barely work at all. And financial markets are special – and especially powerful, for both good and ill. Although all markets need some oversight, the need in the world of finance is of an altogether different magnitude.

You do not readily find pyramid selling schemes or major fraudsters in the world of soap-sud manufacturing or the retailing of ladies' underwear.

This is not because there is anything inherently superior about making washing powder or selling underwear compared to the world of finance, nor because the people working in the former are necessarily more upstanding than those working in the latter. The difference is that the businesses of soap-sud manufacturing and underwear distribution are so rooted in the real, material world that it is nigh-on impossible to use them to turn base metal into gold, or to create money out of nothing.

Equally, the consequences of a manufacturer or retailer going bust are seldom drastic for the economic system as a whole, even if the businesses are extremely large. By contrast, the failure of even a small financial company can endanger the whole financial system. For finance is intangible. It is built on trust. Once confidence is shattered, the whole edifice can collapse, as the events of 2007/9 attest.

How on earth did we reach the current ghastly position? My answer to this question is a tale of greed, illusion, and self-delusion on a massive scale. It not only reveals the truth about markets and economies, but also shines a torch on the nature of society – and on human nature itself.

The meltdown

This answer has two parts: the historical events that led to the collapse of 2007/9; and the underlying causes. The history can be quickly told.[1] Over the previous decade, clever investment bankers had invented a whole alphabet soup of new financial instruments: CMOs, CDOs, CDSs, and heaven knows what else. They talked about a transformation in the financial world, mirroring the supposed transformation in the real world, thanks to new financial instruments and the advent of financial engineering. Never mind the technological revolution, this was a *financial* revolution.

The result was an explosion in the availability of finance – especially mortgage finance. The consequence of that was an upsurge in property prices almost everywhere. As part of this financial revolution, banks lent more and more money on mortgages, including to people in America who, in the past, would have had little or no chance of getting loans. And with good reason: on past form they seemed to have little or no chance of paying the interest, never mind repaying the capital. The bankers joked that these were NINJA borrowers: no income, no job, and no assets. But they kept lending.

Clever investment bankers then packaged these mortgages up as securities and sold them on to banks and other financial institutions, who might trade them with other banks. Still cleverer investment bankers split these packaged mortgages into segments, distinguished by different levels of riskiness. The most risky carried the highest return, the least risky the lowest. The idea was that potential investors could choose from the list – as if from a menu – according to their tastes and tolerance for the mixture of risk and return.

However, these collateralized debt obligations (CDOs) were potentially lethal. If only 1% of mortgage holders defaulted then the worth of the most risky category could fall to zero. Even so, lots of institutions that seemed to be safe and secure bought these instruments. The result was that when the American housing bubble burst, apparently staid, boring Landesbanks in Germany could be brought down by the defaults of NINJA borrowers in trailer parks in Arkansas. This was the result of a decade of technical progress in the world of finance.

Worse than this, because these instruments were traded, when it began to be evident that there was a serious problem with CDOs, no one knew where these instruments were held; if you like, where the bodies were buried. Once the markets woke up to how serious the problems were, and how difficult it was to track down these troubled assets, confidence collapsed.

The problem then fed on itself. The market for trading these instruments evaporated, so their market value fell – if there was a market for them at all. Many of the assets on banks' books were so complex that it was almost impossible to know what they were reasonably worth. And in the panicky conditions of 2007/9, many of them seemed to be worth next to nothing. This meant that the value of banks' capital was uncertain. In other words, it was impossible to be sure that banks were not already bust – or likely to go bust very soon.

Consequently, banks began to be worried about other banks' credit-worthiness, and so became reluctant to lend to each other. A crisis of confidence about *solvency* morphed into a crisis about *liquidity*. (When there are not firm prices for buying and selling an asset in large quantities, the market is said to be illiquid.) But illiquidity undermined solvency. For banks that were dependent on loans from other banks, the drying up of liquidity spelt doom. This was what brought down Britain's Northern Rock and threatened to bring down the whole financial system – until governments and central banks intervened.

The perilous position of the banking system caused the banks to reduce their ordinary lending.[2] With reduced access to finance, individuals and businesses curtailed their expenditure, which reduced GDP and in the process impaired the value of all assets in the system, including the ones sitting on the banks' books, thereby causing the banks to cut back lending still further, and so on and so forth.

From meltdown to slump

Soon the consequences spread out from the financial system to engulf pretty much everyone. People and companies unable to get finance cut back on their purchases of big-ticket items. Manufacturers and retailers, anxious about working capital, cut back on their stocks. Companies unable to get trade finance were unable to export. The result was a collapse of world trade unparalleled since the 1930s. In some countries exports fell by 40%. Industrial production went into freefall everywhere.

Simultaneously, the usual mechanisms of recession started to crank up: consumer confidence collapsed and consumer spending slowed or, in some countries, fell. Unemployment rose. Something that began in the world of finance came to engulf the whole economy. By the middle of 2009, it was impossible to find a single major country in the world that had not felt the consequences.

And further worries lurked in the shadows. For much of the postwar period, the west's pension systems – whether of the pay-as-you-go or the funded variety – have been an accident waiting to happen. For countries with the former, including most of continental Europe, what kept the show on the road was the growth and structure of the population, which ensured that there were plenty of workers to be taxed to pay for the retired. For countries with the latter, such as the US and the UK, what kept the system going was strong equity markets. Now, with equity markets depressed and estimates of average longevity ever increasing, in almost all western countries pension systems are under threat. For some people, particularly in the US and the UK, the solution is to put off retirement until later and later. For others it is simply to wait and worry – and in the meantime to curtail unnecessary spending.

For those relying on the state for their pension the worry is increasing, because the Great Implosion has engulfed the public finances. While the recession has eaten into tax revenues, governments have poured huge amounts of money into bailing out and supporting the banks, leading government borrowing to balloon.

As the Great Implosion developed, the large, passive rise in the public deficit and governments' ability to use discretionary increases in spending or cuts in taxes to bolster demand were part of the solution. In some countries they are now rapidly becoming part of the problem. Debt has increased so much that there is a widespread fear that what the developed countries face is an unpalatable choice between default, inflation, or savage cuts in government spending, accompanied by huge rises in taxes. What is more, how all this pans out will depend closely on what happens to governments' "investments" in the banks. At the extreme, you could now regard the UK government as a very large bank with a business in public administration on the side.[3]

Indeed, many people fear that, as taxpayers, they will be paying for the bankers' mistakes – and their bonuses and bailouts – for decades to come. Accordingly, they are afraid that for all of us not on the financial markets gravy train, the future is extremely bleak. I take a much more optimistic view, which I explain in Chapter 8. Nevertheless, either the fear of the policies needed to put the public finances right, or the reality of them, threatens to be a leading cause of extended economic depression. And even if the world economy continues to recover in 2010 and the years beyond, the threat of more pain to come – and the scars left from the damage already done – will linger for many a long year.

What caused it all?

Now the causes. This crisis is the result of the interaction between eight powerful factors: the bubble in property; the explosion of debt; the fragility of the banks; the weakness of risk assessment; an error of monetary policy; the super-saving of China and a number of other countries; the complacency and incompetence of the regulators; and the docility of outside assessors. Behind this concoction of immediate causes lies a deeper underlying cause, which I will come to in a moment.

The property bubble

First, the bubble. There have been bubbles throughout financial history. Indeed, the last 25 years have been dominated by a series of bubbles. In October 1987, the US equity market fell by as much as 20% in a single day, although neither the financial system nor the economy even wobbled. In the late 1980s, there was a mammoth bubble in Japanese property and shares. A subsequent bubble in emerging markets culminated in the Asian/Russian crisis of 1997/8. The immediately affected countries were devastated, but the west sailed on regardless.

That is not quite what happened in the next bubble, the dot-com boom, which burst in 2001. This time the US economy did fall into recession and the world economy shuddered. Moreover, for a time the financial system trembled, although more because of the events of September 11.

After the dot-com collapse the party moved on – to property, both residential and commercial, and to an associated bubble in risk and credit instruments. Just as that bubble was getting close to its bursting point, another was still inflating, in commodities. Now that bubble has burst as well.

Although the world survived all of these earlier bubbles – albeit with a little bit of luck – some of the associated financial shocks were very serious. In Asia, Japan's banking and financial collapse shook the foundations of the system and of Japanese society itself. The financial convulsion that the smaller Asian economies went through in 1997/8 resulted in drops in GDP almost as large as those that America endured in the Great Depression.

The American banking system was almost brought to its knees in the 1980s over the collapse of savings and loan associations. They had lent for long periods on fixed rates of interest but borrowed for short periods, thereby obliging them frequently to renew their funding and putting them at risk from higher interest rates. When interest rates went up sharply they were bust and had to be bailed out at massive cost to the US taxpayer. The Latin American debt crisis of 1982 resulted in the US banking system itself being effectively bust. It was rescued by a cut in interest rates, which helped to generate an increased spread between the interest rate earned on banks' assets and the rate paid on their liabilities.

In 1998 came the failure of a hedge fund, Long Term Capital Management (LTCM). A bailout was organized by the Federal Reserve, the US central banking system, using private money. Again interest rates were cut sharply. After the event, then Chairman of the Fed Alan Greenspan said that if LTCM had been allowed to fail the whole financial system would have been endangered.

Funny that no one seemed to draw the implications – least of all Alan Greenspan. If the failure of a hedge fund that until then scarcely anyone had heard of could bring such danger, then what would happen if the bursting of a major bubble were to put at risk the core of the financial system? That is exactly what the property bubble did. It was international, rather than being confined to one country. Property prices were inflated more or less everywhere, from Florida to Florence, from San Francisco to Scunthorpe.

Moreover, property was not an asset class like black tulips, which had been the subject of a bubble in Holland in the seventeenth century; or the British South Sea stock, whose bubble inflated and burst in 1720; or Australian mining shares, which experienced bubbles in the 1960s. While these were spectacular bubbles when measured by the size of the increase in the price of the asset, the asset class in question was small in relation to the overall stock of assets, and small in relation to the economy. By contrast, property, the subject of the mid-noughties bubble, is the biggest asset class of all.

History suggests that financial systems can usually withstand collapses of the equity market fairly readily, because equities are not normally financed by money borrowed from banks. Property is different. When property prices tumble, the banking system, and with it the whole of the financial system, is undermined. The last decade's rise in house prices and, linked to this, commercial property prices was quite simply the greatest bubble in the whole of financial history. Scarce wonder that when it burst the world trembled.

Debt and the fragility of the banks

Even so, in a different state of the world, the bubble might have burst without the same scale of ill effects. The second factor underlying the collapse of 2007/9 was the perilous fragility of the financial system in general and the banking system in particular. For the bubble had inflated at a time when major western economies were hooked on debt.[4]

In the world of *low* finance, that is to say the everyday affairs of ordinary folk, indebtedness was extremely high. Huge mortgages – sometimes 125% of the value of the property purchased, and six or seven times earnings, often "self-certified" earnings at that – spoke of a system drunk on debt. There had been a boom in ordinary consumer credit, credit card debt, store credit, anything to promote tomorrow's spending today. After all, as borrowers could readily assure themselves, credit takes the waiting out of wanting.

Meanwhile, in the world of high finance, the flurry of innovation had made the financial system much more complex, and in the process much more vulnerable. The theory was that sophisticated finance, using the new instruments, would transfer risk to those most able to bear it and this would make the system more robust. The reality was that risk was transferred to those who were least able to understand it. In the process, this made the system more fragile. This was all too reminiscent of what had happened in the Lloyds insurance market in the late 1980s, when insurance risks were reinsured and then the reinsurance was reinsured, and that was reinsured, with the result that it was nigh-on impossible to unravel where the true risk lay.

Meanwhile, old banking practices that relied on relationships had been overtaken by marketization. The banks' "treasuries" and "proprietary trading desks," the departments that placed big bets on the markets, were dominant. And where banks would once have been conservative and risk averse, holding a high proportion of liquid assets against the chance that something might go wrong, they now held very few. Never fear: the market would provide.

Indeed, in the good times it did. The trouble was, as many banks were soon to find out, in the bad times it did not.

Furthermore, the banks held this extraordinary mix of assets and liabilities with very little protection in the form of capital reserves. In order to maximize the "return on equity" – that is, the gains enjoyed by shareholders – these were kept to a minimum. Moreover, banks acted to reduce the amount of capital they were required to hold by moving assets "off balance sheet," into subsidiaries and financing vehicles whose capital requirements were lower, or even nonexistent. So, not only the banks' customers but the banks themselves were highly geared, some borrowing as much as 40 times their capital. Their capital holdings were a fair bit lower than they had been in the early 1990s, when the ratio of capital to total assets at US commercial banks had been more than 1:20. However, they were amazingly low compared to the more distant past. In 1900 the ratio of capital to assets had been more like 1:6, and in the middle of the nineteenth century it was 1:2.[5]

This change did not occur by accident. The success of banking activity should be judged by the return on banks' assets. But the profitability of the banks, and the effectiveness of their managements, have in fact been judged by their return on *equity*. The banks were caught between two sorts of competitive pressure: competition drove down the return on assets (i.e., squeezed the margins on lending and other activities) while it also drove up the target return on equity. In the words of Andrew Haldane from the Bank of England, "Caught in the cross-fire, high leverage became the only means of keeping up with the Joneses."[6]

Outside the banks, debt held sway as well. Private equity businesses grew like topsy on a sea of debt and "leveraged" the companies they bought up to the eyeballs. Meanwhile, investors borrowed billions to invest in hedge funds, who then borrowed billions more to invest in assets.

So the whole financial system was a gigantic inverted pyramid of debt, resting on a tiny base of capital.

Risk management

It is not as though the banks were unaware that they were running big risks. On the contrary, they used mathematical risk management techniques, and employed armies of "risk managers." One of the large banks subsequently taken over by the British government reputedly employed 400 of them.

The problem is that it was a particular definition of risk that they were managing. The prevailing way of measuring risk was to look at the variability of prices over some past period. The results were then expressed in the language of formal statistics. If an event had occurred 1% of the time in the past, it was assumed that there was a 1 in a 100 chance that it would occur over an equivalent length of time in the future.

When you describe the procedure in simple English, it seems scarcely credible that banks were relying on measures formed in this way to assess their exposure and vulnerability. For a start, often the periods over which the movement of asset prices would be assessed were extremely short. And, as none other than Alan Greenspan put it, "Probability distributions estimated largely, or exclusively over cycles that do not include periods of panic will underestimate the likelihood of extreme price movements."[7]

Moreover, the assumption of the mathematical models was that the variability of these prices was accurately described by the so-called normal distribution, which is sometimes known as the bell curve because a graph of it has a bell-like shape. In fact there was no good reason to believe that this was necessarily true. Lurking out there in the unknown future, ready to trip up the unwary, there could be some improbable but high-impact events, what Nassim Nicholas Taleb has called Black Swans. Indeed, as we now know, there were.[8]

Most extraordinarily, the "quants" borrowed this method of measuring risk from the physical sciences, without thinking whether it applied to human affairs. It doesn't. Instead, human affairs are interactive. As George Soros puts it, they are characterized by reflexivity.

Most importantly, as regards the future, what we face is not *risk*, as described by some probability distribution, but pure *uncertainty*, a distinction made clear eons ago by the economists Knight and Keynes. In the language of Donald Rumsfeld, the world is full of unknown unknowns. As the mathematician Paul Wilmott puts it: "Following the formulas was like relying on your seatbelt to drive crazily: it's not going to save your life."[9]

While all this nonmeasurement of "risk" was going on in the dealing rooms, in the boardrooms the results were being passed through in a state of glazed noncomprehension. What did Sir Thingummy Whatnot or Myron C. Hamburger III know about "sigma events"? Could Dame Nod-it-Through seriously be expected to know her onions about complex derivatives? They and their similarly noncomprehending colleagues would have been better advised to sack at least half the risk managers and replace them with people who knew something of economic and financial history and could communicate in plain English. But they didn't.

Monetary policy errors

Overseeing all this, of course, were the policymakers in central banks and treasuries, whose job, you would think, is to keep the system safe and sound. It is easy to pin the blame for what went wrong on them, and some of the blame does indeed rest at their feet. But Alan Greenspan and his equivalents in the other major central banks were operating in a particular global context and in pursuit of particular policy objectives, under a particular policy regime. It is my contention that the real villain in the piece has been not any particular individual, but rather the interaction between the policy regime and the global context.

In fact, for most western central banks, ensuring financial stability was not their primary task at all. Getting and keeping inflation low was the primary task assigned to them. (In the US this ranked equally with maintaining growth and employment.) They did not see their role as the prevention of bubbles. Accordingly, in their deliberations about monetary policy, asset prices played no more than a supporting role – except on the downside. Fed Chairman Greenspan was particularly sensitive to those downside risks. He was always ready to reduce interest rates to counter stock-market weakness. At one point, after the events of September 11, 2001, he cut rates to 1% and kept them there for an extended period.

Greenspan did openly worry about bubbles, as when he inveighed against "irrational exuberance" in the stock market. But he subsequently decided that (a) it wasn't certain that there was a bubble; (b) if there was, there wasn't a great deal the Fed could safely do about it; (c) the way to react, if it was a bubble, was to allow it to burst and then clear up the mess afterwards.

This view, which subsequently became known as the Greenspan doctrine, was broadly accepted by other western central banks. If they were confronted with surging asset prices, the only real question for them, in the regime under which they operated, was what such increases implied for the outlook for aggregate demand (i.e., the total amount of spending in the economy) and consumer price inflation.

This whole approach to monetary policy was a response to recent history – both to what had happened and to what had not. The world economy and its financial system had teetered on the brink of *inflationary* disaster during the 1970s. By contrast, *financial instability* ensuing from asset bubbles had appeared not to be a serious matter since the 1930s; although the experience of Japan and Scandinavia in the 1990s ought to have suggested otherwise. Central banks focused on keeping aggregate demand on a path consistent with their objectives for inflation and employment. In the prevailing conditions of the time, the result was a prolonged period of low interest rates and a bias, fully perceived in the markets, toward even lower interest rates, which set up the conditions that led to the property bubble.

Of course, the policymakers might have thought that the policy of low interest rates with easy credit would keep the economies of the west growing steadily without stoking a bubble. It is just about possible to imagine that this could happen. But what we know of human nature, and financial history, cries out that the result will be a financial disaster. Those extending themselves will include the least creditworthy; the banks offering more credit will include the least well managed; the projects backed will include the most speculative; and asset prices will be bid up as "investors" seek the quickest way of making easy money.

With finance as cheap as central banks made it, and in conditions of easy access to credit and lax regulation, it was inevitable that bubbles would result. The central banks now bemoan what happened, but it happened as a direct result of the policies *they* pursued. They should have known better.

The global context

That said, given their mandate, in the prevailing conditions of the time it would have been difficult for them to have acted differently. Paradoxically, given the vast increase in debt, in global terms these were conditions of *savings* glut and consequently of incipient recession. When the dot-com bubble burst and the "new economy" boom subsided, western policymakers confronted a new underlying reality. Domestic demand was now weak, while the rapidly growing countries of Asia, led by China, were building massive trade surpluses, exporting far more to the west than they were importing from it. In 2007/8, a sharp rise in oil prices exacerbated these global trade imbalances. The countries of the west now had external trade deficits foisted on them from two sources.

The result was an acute policy dilemma for western governments and central banks: either accept the situation, or take action to replace the demand being sucked out with new demand injected in. If they had taken the first option the result would have been weaker economic performance earlier in the decade, rather than now. Arguably, though, that would have been better because, without the bubble, a period of economic weakness could have amounted to a normal recession, not one involving a banking collapse and a drop into depression.

Yet in almost all western countries this option was not seriously considered. The very upsurge of productive potential in China and other emerging markets that created large current account surpluses for such countries also delivered low inflation in the west. In the US inflation reached a low of just over 1%; in the eurozone it touched 1.7%; in the UK it fell to as low as 0.5%. Governments and central banks paying attention to inflation alone would have been encouraged to take expansionary measures. If they also acknowledged responsibility for real output and employment, what they had to do would have been even clearer. It was a no-brainer: domestic demand had to be boosted to offset the draining of demand by the super-savers.

Accordingly, the policymakers felt duty bound to keep people spending, by imposing a policy of low interest rates and letting the credit flow – and thereby letting the debt build up.

So this was a crisis that was born of the union of rampant finance capitalism and the super-saving of China *et al.* To be sure, the structures and attitudes of western finance could have produced a financial crisis without the intervention of the Chinese; indeed, they had managed to produce quite a few before the Chinese economy became an important player on the world scene. That said, it is difficult to imagine *this* crisis happening without the global imbalances unleashed by the rise of China.[10]

Regulatory somnolence

If the monetary policymakers had some sort of defense, what about "the regulators" who *were* supposed to focus on financial probity and stability? In practice, the regulatory authorities on both sides of the Atlantic were supine. The problem was not lack of regulation; there was regulation aplenty. The trouble was that it did not seem to affect the substance of what banks were doing. The regulators were engaged in an elaborate exercise in box ticking. The banks easily met their minimum capital requirements, yet when the troubles began in 2008, these capital cushions proved hopelessly inadequate.

Incredibly, the regulators even acquiesced in the practices by which banks reduced their capital requirements by moving business off balance sheet. And then, surprise, surprise, they were apparently taken aback when bank capital reserves proved to be inadequate.

Part of the reason for the regulatory mistakes was the run-of-the-mill incompetence that seems to bedevil many public agencies. Britain's Financial Services Authority (FSA) was apparently in constant close touch with the problems, but somehow contrived to do nothing about them. In the case of the UK, lax financial regulation was not only the result of incompetence. The authorities explicitly followed a policy of "light touch" regulation, because they wanted to maintain London's competitive position as a leading global center for financial services. In the event the regulatory system turned out to be more like "soft touch."

Over and above this conscious decision, not only in London but also in the US and throughout the western world, both regulators and banks simply did not understand or imagine what the future could possibly be like. They were lulled into a false sense of security by the complexity of financial models that neglected history and stifled imagination. In the event, the measurement of risk was a fiction and its regulation a sick joke.[11]

Private complacency

The failure of oversight was not confined to the public sector. Of all those who should have seen the crisis coming, surely among the front rank are the ratings agencies, that is to say the commercial organizations that are paid to assess the riskiness of bonds, all sorts of securities, and even countries. They didn't see it coming. More than that, by giving their AAA stamp of approval to the various fancy new derivative instruments that proliferated in the boom, they enabled banks and others to trade in them and hold them on their books with an easy mind. Like everyone else, the ratings agencies were taken in. It didn't help that they received the bulk of their income from the banks.

Nor did the armies of equity market analysts, paid small fortunes to analyze the stock market and its constituent companies, foresee the crisis. Going into 2008, ThomsonReuters found that analysts expected corporate earnings globally to rise by 11.8%, with a rise of 14.9% in the US. At the beginning of 2009 they were expecting a fall of 12.5% for the quarter, having anticipated a rise of 37% six months earlier. By May they were forecasting a fall of 37%.[12]

Nor, with the honorable exception of a few journalists, did the press rumble what was going on. Interestingly, those writers who perceived the perils of excessive indebtedness were, on the whole, not financial specialists. The specialist financial press, by contrast, seemed to be cheering on the party from the sidelines.

Bearing in mind the scale of the distortion of market values and economic activity, and the pervasiveness of the mindset that allowed this situation to continue, the word *bubble* seems increasingly inadequate to describe what led to the Great Implosion. This was a society-wide, mass delusion about the sources of prosperity, just as John Kenneth Galbraith said had gripped America in the 1920s.

An accident?

Why was it only in 2007/9 that disaster struck? What finally pushed the system over the edge can best be regarded as an accident. Nevertheless, that does not mean that the financial implosion can be regarded as truly accidental.

If there is one event that seems to have turned the crisis into a potential catastrophe, it is the collapse of Lehman Brothers in September 2008. There is a view that if only Lehman Brothers had not been allowed to go bust this would have been a comparatively minor crisis, with no devastating conse-quences, let alone a depression.

I don't accept this view, even though Lehman's collapse was critical in the chain of events that led to disaster. The point is that given the way the system was, there was bound to be a Lehman somewhere, sometime. The authorities felt that they could not bail out all institutions regardless. Not only were they worried by the moral hazard aspect, they were also concerned about what they saw as their limited resources. The appetite of the US Congress for financing bank bailouts was not unlimited. Something would have to be let go. If Lehman had been saved and the system had not imploded, the skeptics in Congress would have been emboldened to override the next bailout. At some point, some institution would have had to go – and thereby endanger the system – for Congress to be persuaded to put up more money.

It's the bean counters' fault

Some commentators have argued that the crisis of 2007/9 originated with other specific factors that could have been avoided – or at least corrected. One view is that the problems were caused, or severely exacerbated, by so-called mark-to-market accounting; that is, the continuous revaluation of banks' assets to market values. This had the consequence that when liquidity dried up and the market for complex, difficult-to-sell instruments evaporated, it was very difficult to put any value on these at all, with the result that the value of banks' assets was reduced, implying that the value of their capital (the difference between their assets and their liabilities) was depleted.

There is something in this – but not much. It is very difficult to believe that the essence of a problem as severe as the one confronting the financial system in 2007/9 can come down to a matter of accounting. After all, what in reality would be changed if banks were allowed to put higher values on these assets? Yes, their calculated capital ratios would be higher, but this would mean nothing. Who would believe them? Surely if banks were allowed to ascribe what values they liked to assets, confidence in the banking system would be undermined still more.

Interestingly, during the Japanese banking crisis of the 1990s, exactly the opposite argument was deployed about mark-to-market accounting. Then it was argued that insisting that banks *did* mark to market would help to boost confidence in banks because it would increase transparency. By the way, that didn't work either!

A variant of this view is that the real villain of the piece was the system that governed bank capital requirements, known as Basle II, which had the effect of allowing banks to lend on the basis of very little capital.[13] In the UK, the three banks to adopt it early were Northern Rock, Alliance and Leicester, and Bradford and Bingley, each of which subsequently faced extinction when the market turned sour and each of which was taken into public ownership.

But why was such a system of capital regulation established? And, bearing in mind its clear lacunae and deficiencies, why was it allowed to continue? It was as though the regulatory system performed no essential function and was there for decorative reasons only. It was, if you like, the fifth wheel under the coach. I will give you an explanation for official acquiescence in ineffective regulation in a moment.

"Subprime" lending the root cause?

Another reason offered by some observers for the financial crisis was that it was caused solely by reckless lending to the subprime sector. They claim that if only this had been effectively controlled in the first place, or contained once the crisis had broken, then this would have been a minor financial episode, rather than a global crisis. Some critics of governments' role in the crisis even argue that banks only lent to subprime risks under enormous pressure from the US government, including the threat of class action lawsuits against the financial services sector to force it to lend to the poor.

It is true that subprime lending is where the crisis began, as the fact emerged that massive losses would be incurred on the complex derivatives associated with the financing of such loans. However, subprime was merely an egregious manifestation of a much more widespread phenomenon: excessive lending to real estate, period. Without the subprime aspect the banks would have suffered huge real estate losses anyway, albeit probably a bit later and in different places.

Moreover, risky mortgage lending was part of a more general embrace of risk throughout the financial system. Wherever you looked it was the same story: credit freely available, dodgy credit risks able to get finance easily, and at rates not much higher than those ruling on "safe" loans.

One of my favorite examples of the headlong embrace of risk comes from the spread between the yields on emerging market government debt and US government debt, known in the market as "Treasuries." At the peak (or was it the *trough*?) in 2007, the markets required a premium of only 1¾% over Treasuries to lend to a basket of emerging market governments. Ten years previously they had required a premium of 12%. I use the word "basket" advisedly, as this group of emerging markets includes such luminaries of the investment world as Panama and Morocco.

Subprime happened to be the spark, but that is all. Attributing the disasters of 2007/9 to subprime is rather like saying that the First World War was caused by the assassination of Archduke Franz Ferdinand in Sarajevo in 1914. Given the state of the financial system, if the subprime crisis hadn't happened, something else would have.

After all, the asset whose failure caused most trouble for Lehman Brothers was not a sophisticated, "toxic" one at all, but rather excessive and extremely risky exposure to commercial property. And, for all the talk about new-fangled instruments, the factor that brought down the British mortgage lender Northern Rock was about the most old-fangled thing in banking: illiquidity.

Forget the litany of "if only" explanations. The foundation of this crisis was pretty simple and pretty general: excessive lending by banks to dodgy borrowers, combined with inadequate capital. Banks had been taking this risk for years, in the process putting in peril the whole financial system. The crisis could have come on several occasions in the past. It didn't happen then for a variety of reasons, but in essence these came down to luck. In 2007/9 the luck ran out.

A disaster unforetold?

If the disaster was bound to happen at some point, there is an obvious, highly pertinent question. Her Majesty the Queen is not known for her avid interest in matters economic and financial, but in 2008 she asked it: "Why didn't any-one see this coming?" In fact, they did. It is true that no one saw the whole caboodle, but many did see large parts of it. The trouble was that their warn-ings went unheeded.

There had been extensive disquiet about the rapid development of the financial sector and the huge rewards and incentives for risk taking that it generated, going back to the distinguished American economist James Tobin in the 1970s. The scale of international imbalances in trade and the precarious nature of the American economy, floating on a sea of debt and increasingly dependent on inflows of foreign capital, had long worried many serious com-mentators. The American economist Nouriel Roubini had been repeatedly issuing stern warnings. William White at the Bank for International Settlements warned that monetary policy was too loose because policymakers were paying insufficient attention to asset prices. And a few analysts, includ-ing yours truly, warned of the dangers posed by the huge bubble inflating in real estate, residential and commercial.[14]

There are several reasons why the Cassandras were ignored and the siren voices were listened to. But the fundamental factor was something deep in human nature – no one wanted to believe that the system really was that vul-nerable. The consequences of facing a financial collapse were too awful to contemplate and the consequences of trying to prevent one were, for those involved in the markets, almost as bad. Moreover, the realization that profit-seeking, self-interested institutions could produce such a destructive result was simply too threatening for the whole capitalist set-up. Better not to think about it and just carry on. Everyone did – until disaster struck.

The gallery of villains

So, as I have shown, there is an extended list of individuals and institutions responsible for the current mess. Yet there is another culpable group of people who usually escape scot free from all blame and responsibility. Indeed, I believe they are the ones who are ultimately responsible.

I refer to the economists – the long line of professors, thinkers, and teach-ers who at first propounded and then disseminated the *ideas* that underlay the disaster: the idea that the markets know best; the idea that the markets are "efficient"; the idea that there was no good reason to be concerned about the level and structure of pay in banking; the idea that bubbles cannot exist; the idea that in economic matters, human beings are always "rational"; the idea that if China and other countries wanted to save massively, we should simply lie back and enjoy it; the idea that central banks should be allowed no scope for judgment and should be controlled by tightly described rules; the idea that economic and financial history is another country.

These ideas came to dominate policy thinking, not just in the university on the shores of Lake Michigan where they mostly originated, and not only in universities and business schools throughout the western world, but also in central banks and chancelleries, in boardrooms and dealing rooms, and in the minds of investors and commentators. If you even questioned, never mind disputed, these ideas, you were regarded as a complete no-no. This was the dictatorship of the professoriat.

When thinking about proximate causes of the events of 2007/9, you could say that, like so much else in the modern world, this disaster was made in China. But if you are thinking about underlying causes, it was surely made in Chicago.

Now, I have nothing against this great city; indeed, some of my best friends are from Chicago. Really. And it has produced some fine economists. Equally, there have been other sources of malign intellectual influence, including the philosopher and novelist Ayn Rand, whose attacks on government intervention and eulogies to free markets had a major influence on both President Reagan and Alan Greenspan. The Nobel Laureate Paul Samuelson recently said of Greenspan: "But the trouble is that he had been an Ayn Rander. You can take the boy out of the cult but you can't take the cult out of the boy." According to Samuelson, "He actually had an instruction, probably pinned on the wall: 'Nothing from this office should go forth which discredits the capitalist system. Greed is good.'"[15]

Nevertheless, the ideas that Chicago University has fostered have a lot to answer for. It was prominent in the opposition to the Keynesian revolution in the 1930s; several of its professors led the way in the emasculation of Keynes' message in the 1950s and 1960s; it nurtured and produced Milton

Friedman, whose championing of monetarism, while lauding the stability and optimality of the free market system, seemed to cast Keynesian insights onto the scrapheap; and it was the home of those who propounded the efficient markets theory.[16]

The power of ideas

Economics has supplied quite a few bromides over the years. At one point some very distinguished economists pushed the theory of "rational expectations" and applied it pretty indiscriminately to models and markets, despite the rejection of it by psychologists and many empirical economists. In the late 1990s, others came up with the idea of the "New Paradigm," which seemed to underwrite the dot-com boom. Quite a few gave credence to the idea of an "end to boom and bust," which underpinned the outbreak of overoptimism in the markets and the onset of self-satisfied complacency by the politicians.

However, it was the *efficient markets theory* that really led people up the garden path: market practitioners, central bankers, regulators, and commentators. This theory holds that whatever information is available about the prospects for an asset is embodied in its current market price. The result is that, although markets might sometimes misprice assets, they do not do so systematically, and it is therefore impossible for individuals to beat the market by systematically opposing its judgments, or for policymakers to improve the performance of the economy by trying to alter the market prices that result from them.[17]

There is an apocryphal story about a professor of finance taking a stroll with one of his students. At one point the student exclaims, "Look, there is a $10 bill lying on the ground, let me go and pick it up." "Don't bother," the professor retorts. "If there had been a $10 bill there it would have been picked up already."

Belief in this theory led to an unquestioning faith in "the market." Markets are driven by selfish behavior. This is not a criticism, it is a description. But the result is supposed to be maximum efficiency, and hence prosperity for all. Never mind the selfishness: greed is good. Never mind the huge gaps in income and wealth this system causes: huge wealth at the top cascades down to those at the bottom. Never mind the sense of injustice: people get an income commensurate with their contribution, as measured by the forces of supply and demand. Never mind the apparent chaos and instability: the world is bound to be uncertain, and the market system absorbs and transforms uncertainty to deliver the best of possible outcomes in the circumstances. In short: never mind.

The message was clear: leave the markets well alone. Indeed, try to mimic their structure and behavior in those parts of society that had traditionally operated on different principles. Make all aspects of society more like the financial markets. And outside the gilded world of the developed countries, try to persuade the upstarts of the emerging world to adopt the same system. Open up their economies; marketize; let the financial markets have free rein. They, the developing countries, and we, the already developed ones, will be better off if they do.

What is wrong with the efficient markets theory?

In fact, the efficient markets hypothesis comes in mild and extreme forms. A rather weak definition was put forward by the distinguished financial economist Fischer Black:

> *We might define an efficient market as one in which price is within a factor of two of value, i.e., the price is more than half the value and less than twice the value. By this definition, I think almost all markets are efficient almost all the time.*[18]

On this definition, even I would subscribe to the efficient markets hypothesis! Indeed, I think it would be difficult to find many market skeptics who would not. But the extreme form of the hypothesis is that markets are efficient *all* of the time, and efficiency means price and "value" being virtually indistinguishable. It is surely remarkable that this strong form of what was initially advanced as a hypothesis gradually came to be widely believed, and then accepted as an established fact. Acceptance of this interpretation of "efficient markets" led to an absurd reverence for the markets and their assessments.

Yet, who are "the markets"? For anyone who has worked in the financial markets, reverence should not come easily. Financial markets prize quickness over insight, liquidity over commitment, information over knowledge. Peopled by, on the whole, clever, quick, devil-may-care young men on the make, who know little about anything outside their narrow purview, it is difficult to believe that their practices and their verdicts are the way to run a financial system, never mind a whole economy.

At the macro level, the major threat from the financial markets concerns bubbles. Since they take valuations to levels unjustified by a careful and balanced assessment of underlying financial realities, they can only occur if market participants are ignoring the available information. Why on earth should they do this?

Surely we know the answer: because people form unrealistically optimistic expectations of the future and then convince themselves that these are right because everyone else seems to be convinced. Bubbles are an example of crowd behavior. At times it is rational to do what everyone else is doing, regardless of the fundamentals. Are short or long skirts "better"? There is no sensible answer, but there is an answer to what is "in fashion." The efficient markets theory denies this perspective because it embodies a narrow view of rational behavior. So much the worse for the theory.

But this theory is the very opposite of a victimless thought crime. The trouble with the efficient markets theory is that it provides an incentive and an excuse for investors (and regulators) to do no serious analysis, thought, or due diligence, because they all believe that it will have been done already by "the market" – which consists, by the way, of other investors who have been similarly reduced to incapacity by the same theory.

Indeed, for the efficient markets theory to work, there must be many powerful players operating in the market who do *not* believe in it and, what is more, put their money at risk in the belief that it is wrong. Incredibly, this is the theory that has dominated the actions and, more importantly, the inactions of both market people and policymakers for three decades.

Political influence

Given the theory's deficiencies, it is surprising that so many people were taken in by the idea that the markets should be left well alone. As to why *governments* were taken in there is a less than edifying explanation, namely the political influence of the major financial firms. There has always been a significant flow of money, quite legitimately, from financial firms and the top people in those firms to political parties and causes, on both sides of the Atlantic. Such flows of money are bound to have their effect. According to one investigative report, over ten years the top 25 American originators of subprime mortgages spent about $370 million on lobbying and campaign donations to ward off tighter regulation of their industry.[19]

However, political influence went well beyond donations. The senior personnel of investment banking are very close to the levers of power. For example, Jamie Dimon, JP Morgan's CEO, sits on the board of directors of the Federal Reserve Bank of New York, which has been at the center of market support programs and bank bailouts. More importantly, many former senior bankers have taken prominent positions in government. In this respect one bank stands out – Goldman Sachs. President Clinton's Treasury Secretary, Robert Rubin, was from Goldman Sachs, as was President Bush's Treasury Secretary, Hank Paulson. And William Dudley, a former US chief economist of Goldman's, is President of the New York Fed and vice-chairman of the FOMC, the committee of the Federal Reserve system that sets interest rates. Around the world Goldman alumni are in positions of great power and influence.

Scarce wonder, then, that the interests of investment banks and investment bankers have received a favorable hearing. It is particularly striking that two supposedly left-leaning governments, namely President Clinton's in America and Tony Blair's in the UK, which you might otherwise have expected to be critical of the financial markets, in fact turned out to be star struck by them. Both had close links with Goldman Sachs.

A former Chief Economist of the IMF, Simon Johnson, has gone so far as to say that the interpenetration of the financial and political elites in the US is so great that it reminds him of the typical emerging market country that has to go cap in hand to the Fund. And the way in which key individuals with strong links to those in power manage to prosper, even amid general financial disaster, reminds him of what goes on in postcommunist Russia.[20]

Popular unease

There was also a broader reason for acceptance of the markets' behavior that affected both governments and ordinary people: their apparent success.

Handsome is as handsome does. Although the western financial system came very close to disaster on a number of occasions, it survived. Meanwhile, the top people in the markets made huge amounts of money, and even the foot soldiers did extremely well. The economies of the west prospered and, with some exceptions, ordinary people outside the financial markets did well too.

Furthermore, on a grand scale, the 1990s showed that the system of socialist economics did not work at all. The Communist Party might still rule in China, but as a way of running its economy what system did it espouse? Capitalism, red in tooth and claw.

The upshot is that although decent, ordinary people on ordinary incomes – teachers and train drivers, clerks and cleaners, car workers and teleworkers – might not like what they saw on Wall Street or in the City of London, they had better swallow hard and accept it. It was all for the best.

But now we know it wasn't. In fact, the system doesn't work. It is bust. The fortunes earned by the mega-winners have, at best, been like the fortunes won by lottery winners. What has been "earned" by them has been lost by someone else. And the losers have been all of us.

From causes to consequences

Enough about the causes. The purpose of this book is not the chronicling of a cataclysm but the charting of a course. The destination, after avoiding present and future disaster, is the realization of the enormous opportunities that lie ahead for humankind.

As I show in Chapters 2 and 3, even if the signs of recovery that appeared in the middle of 2009 prove to be reliable, there are several major challenges yet to be faced. Moreover, as I shall show in later chapters, just as with earlier critical episodes, the Great Implosion will continue to have major consequences for society long after the waters of history have closed over the factors that caused it.

2

How Bad Will It Be: Another Great Depression?

While the crash only took place six months ago, I am convinced we have now passed the worst and with continued unity of effort we shall rapidly recover. There is one certainty of the future of a people of the resources, intelligence and character of the people of the United States – that is, prosperity.

President Herbert Hoover, May 1930[1]

In 2009 it became clear that the financial crisis that began in 2007 had led to a *global* downturn of extreme proportions. At the very least, the world economy was experiencing its weakest growth for 60 years. Europe was as badly affected as the US, if not worse. Japan had returned to a state of deflationary recession; China had experienced a very sharp slowdown in growth; some Asian countries had been through a massive contraction in GDP; and many countries in Africa, Latin America, and emerging Europe had been plunged into turmoil. Unemployment had risen sharply in most countries, bankruptcies had soared, bad debts had multiplied, and trade had collapsed.

Mind you, by the time you read this, confidence may well have recovered sufficiently that imminent recovery appears to be assured. Indeed, it could be. But you should beware: events do not always move in straight lines. In the interwar period there were ups and downs. And, even if we can't forecast them accurately, we should be prepared for disappointments and nasty surprises now. Accordingly, even if the economy recovers a bit in 2010 and 2011, that does not necessarily mean that it's all over.

How can we gauge what is likely to happen next? We could be guided by the common view, or business opinion. But all along, people, both expert and ordinary, have failed to get the full measure of what has happened, continually looking on the bright side and expecting only a mild downturn, and then an early recovery. We could look to the economic forecasters for guidance.

But bearing in mind their lamentable record in foreseeing the Great Implosion, not to mention countless other major events, this would represent the triumph of hope over experience. Alternatively, we could see what financial market valuations seem to be implying. But that would be dangerous: stock markets have forecast ten of the last three recoveries.

I think the best way of assessing what may happen is to take a sober and critical look at the past. A reading of the historical evidence, which I am about to present to you, suggests that, even if the economy does show some signs of life after the intensity of the events of 2007/9, an early and complete recovery is unlikely, and the danger of a recovery petering out is considerable.

Past experience

There is a wealth of economic and financial history to guide us. In what follows I concentrate on experience in the west, not least because it is for western economies that we have the best data. Nevertheless, I am acutely conscious that much of Asia experienced an enormous economic contraction in the years following the financial crisis of 1997. That is a subject I take up in more detail in Chapter 6.

There have been economic fluctuations of sorts throughout human history. The Bible speaks of seven fat years being succeeded by seven lean. And right up to modern times there have been variations in the level of prosperity brought about by changes in the quantity and quality of the harvest. Theories evolved linking these variations with sunspots, or volcanic activity, which affected the amount of dust in the atmosphere and hence the amount of sunlight that got through to the earth. Disease has long been another source of fluctuations in prosperity.

All of these variations have been natural in origin; that is, they have been caused without human intervention, and humans have been powerless to prevent or correct them. Of course, data limitations make it difficult to draw certain conclusions, but it seems that in preindustrial times the main form of *man-made* variation came from war. Economic hardship originating from this source had in common with natural disasters the characteristic that they were both associated with physical loss: the destruction of crops and buildings and the loss of life, resulting in a reduced labor force. These economic downturns were what a modern economist might term "supply-side shocks."

The natural sources of fluctuation, as well as the devastation wrought by war, survive into modern times, although in developed western economies they are no longer the major cause of economic fluctuations. Since the Industrial Revolution and the development of a money-exchange economy, that cause has been not supply but demand driven – and man-made rather than natural.[2]

In the downswings, times are bad not because of the destruction of crops or buildings or labor, but simply because of a shortage of effective *demand*. All the real sources of wellbeing and prosperity are exactly as they were before, yet people are worse off. For this reason, such man-made downswings have always prompted feelings of puzzlement and bewilderment, even soul searching about the structure of society – just as is happening now.

The idea of the "cycle"

Even though such fluctuations are man-made, they may result from things outside the nexus of decisions that are made today and, as such, may be beyond our control. There is a view that man-made fluctuations constitute a *cycle*, a wave-like pattern in our affairs that we can perhaps understand but can only with difficulty correct.

Is our current suffering to be seen as the downswing of one of these waves? If we did take that line, we might view with more indulgence the people who stand arraigned for their contribution to our current plight. And we might also feel that there is little to be done to mitigate the results. Trying to stop the downturn of an economic cycle that is deeply ingrained in the system would be like trying to hold back the tide.

By contrast, I think the evidence is that the economic "cycle" is dead, if indeed it was ever alive. If there are regular cycles at work in the modern economy, their influence is overwhelmed by other factors such that the observed fluctuations do not correspond to a regular *cycle*. The downturn we are experiencing now can more readily be seen as the result of a lot of mistakes – for which key individuals and institutions are at least causally responsible, and perhaps even, in a moral sense, culpable. Relatedly, it is more plausible to envisage corrective action being effective and the recession being stopped in its tracks.

Super-cycle?

Over and above the short-term variations in prosperity that seem endemic in the market economy, there is the idea of a super-cycle, lasting perhaps 60 to 80 years, usually associated with the name of Kondratiev. Nicolai Kondratiev was a distinguished Soviet economist who fell out of favor with Stalin and was shot on the latter's orders in 1938. (In those days they knew what to do with underperforming economists.) His theories, which have some echoes in the ideas of Joseph Schumpeter and with the Austrian school of economics, have occasionally found favor in the west, particularly at times of serious crisis like the present. Can we usefully regard current events as the downswing of a Kondratiev cycle?

There is one part of the Kondratiev approach that does appeal to me and that is the generational aspect. When major shocks occur, or major mistakes are made, people often learn from them and adapt their behavior and reshape institutions accordingly – for a while. Then they forget. Eventually, they are replaced by others who never learned the lessons in the first place, which sets the stage for a repeat. Surely this has been an important aspect of the Great Implosion.

Beyond this, however, I am highly dubious about the idea of a super-cycle. For a start, there is very little data to go on to build up a convincing picture. If the modern, industrial economy can be thought to have begun somewhere around the year 1800 (and this in itself is a gross simplification, not least because experience was so different in different countries), and Kondratiev super-cycles last between 60 and 80 years, the world has undergone at most three super-cycles. This is a pretty slender basis on which to base a case for the existence of a super-cycle.[3]

I think that the notion of the "cycle" – ordinary or super – has received far too much attention. The best way to think of the variations in economic activity is, as the economist Ragnar Frisch once described them, as "variations in a series about its own mean," with normal or minor fluctuations, sometimes interrupted by shocks. What we are experiencing now is not a "cyclical" downturn but rather the result of one of these shocks – and a pretty enormous one at that.

Of previous man-made shocks, what we have come to know as the "Great Depression" is far and away the most significant. As the crisis of 2007/9

deepened, the ghastly thought started to take root that what we face is something like a repeat of the 1930s. Indeed, what happened to the world economy
from the beginning of the current downturn in April 2008 until June 2009
fully matched what happened over the equivalent period in the Great
Depression – and in some ways it was worse.[4] In the middle of 2009, as the
world economy seemed to be recovering, widespread fear of a repeat of the
Great Depression eased. Yet, even if recovery does continue into 2010 and
2011, both policymakers and ordinary members of the public would be ill
advised to put thoughts of the Great Depression aside – as a brief study of
the period amply testifies. After what proved to be a shallow and fragile recovery, at the end of the 1930s the US economy appeared to be slipping back
into depression – until it was rescued by the demands of war.

What made the Depression Great?

The Great Depression began in the United States in 1929, and lasted, with
some variation across countries, until 1939. But the seeds of what went wrong
were sown well before. In the US the preceding decade was known as the
"roaring twenties." This is very much a theme of the literature of the time,
most notably F. Scott Fitzgerald's novel *The Great Gatsby*. From 1922 to 1928,
share prices on the Dow Jones index rose by an average of 22% per annum
and by 200% in total. This boom had a major effect on mood and culture. As
John Kenneth Galbraith put it, "the American people [were]... displaying an
inordinate desire to get rich quickly with a minimum of physical effort."[5]

What subsequently befell the American economy during the 1930s can
only be described as a cataclysm. GDP fell by 30%, unemployment rose to
25% of the workforce, the price level dropped by 25%, house prices slumped
by 30%, and the stock market lost 80% of its value.

These developments were not fleeting either. It took the best part of four
years for US GDP to reach a trough. As it was, it was only in 1941 that output
regained the level at which it had stood in 1929. By 1938, one person in every
five was still out of work, and the stock market did not return to its previous
peak until 1954.[6]

Outside America

In Germany, things were not quite as bad as in America, but they were still pretty awful. The total peak-to-trough fall in real GDP was 16%, while in Germany's neighbor Austria the fall was more than 22%.[7] As with nearly everywhere else during this period, prices in Germany fell sharply – down by about 4% in 1930, 8% in 1931, and over 13% in 1932. And unemployment soared, rising from 1.9 million (13% of the workforce) in 1929 to 5.6 million (30%) in 1932. By 1933, however, the German economy was recovering strongly and, for reasons we needn't go into here, the later years of the 1930s saw some amazing rates of economic growth: over 6% in 1933, followed by 9% in 1934, then 7%, 9%, 6%, 8%, closing with 9% in 1939. By 1938 unemployment was down to only 2% of the workforce.

Italy suffered falls in GDP in 1929 and 1930, substantial rises in unemployment, and falls in the general price level. However, the pain was not as serious as it was in Germany and, like Germany, the second half of the 1930s saw strong growth.

In France, GDP fell by 3% in 1930, 6% in 1931, and 6.5% in 1932. The economy rebounded strongly in 1933, but this recovery turned out to be short lived. Growth turned negative again in 1934 and 1935.

Compared to the US and Germany, the UK got off lightly. Admittedly, unemployment rose from 7% to 15% and equity prices fell by 40%, but output dropped by only 5%. Sweden also escaped relatively lightly, enduring a fall in output of "only" 12%.

Explaining the differences

What might explain this international pattern? There were two reasons why the downturn was much less serious in the UK. The first is the starting point. It is notable that while the years leading up to the Great Depression were exceptionally good in the US, in the UK they were awful. From 1915 to 1921 GDP fell by a quarter, and from 1920 to 1928 the price level dropped by nearly 40%. While in the 1920s the unemployment rate fell as low as 1.8% in the US, in the UK the lowest it reached was just under 7%. So for the UK, the period of dreadful economic performance was not the 1930s, but the 1920s.

The second reason is macroeconomic policy. The key development came in 1931, when the UK left the Gold Standard, leading to a large fall in the pound. No longer having to maintain the fixed link to gold also gave the UK freedom to operate its own monetary policy. Interest rates were cut to 2% – where they remained, despite a brief flurry in 1939, for 20 years.

Fixed exchange rates were also the key to explaining much of the unusual distribution of economic pain across the world. Those countries that remained on the Gold Standard for longest were more affected than those that left early or did not adopt it in the first place. This was because membership of the Gold Standard meant that countries could not use lower interest rates to support economic activity, and instead had to mirror the deflationary policies being operated in the US. Meanwhile, they lost market share to those countries, such as the UK, which came off the Gold Standard early and enjoyed an increase in competitiveness as a result of a lower exchange rate.

Germany and Austria suffered more than others because they had very low gold reserves and weakened banking systems as a result of the First World War and subsequent reparations. Yet they rejoined the Gold Standard after the war ended. This meant that their economies were more vulnerable to any downturn in domestic or overseas demand, and to the usual panoply of problems that affected the banking sector in difficult times. One major reason Sweden emerged from the Great Depression earlier than most other countries was because it embarked on a Keynesian-style fiscal expansion.[8]

What caused the Depression?

Eighty years on from its beginning, the Great Depression still evokes enormous controversy.[9] There are no widely agreed answers to the crucial question of what caused it. And readers should beware: as with just about everything in economics, seemingly arcane disputes, even about history, are closely bound up with ideological battles of much wider significance. In this instance there is a keen dispute between monetarists and Keynesians, the first arguing that the Depression was caused by errors of monetary policy, and the second arguing that, in the context of great systemic fragility, it was caused by the earlier excesses of the private sector, leading to a collapse of confidence.

Even the name given to this period speaks volumes. The Great "Depression" seems to suggest a major psychological dimension. This fits with the broadly Keynesian interpretation of what went wrong. Monetarists prefer to call the episode the Great "Contraction," referring to the fall of the money supply. You will have noticed that I have called it the Great Depression and I propose to stick with that name; you can draw your own conclusions.

There are four leading candidate explanations for what happened, which I discuss in turn.

Falling asset prices

After having nearly quadrupled in the previous eight years, in October 1929 US share prices started to falter. By the end of 1929 they had fallen by 30% and within three years they were down by 80%, or $72 billion – equivalent to the loss of about 70% of one year's GDP.

It is still unclear how much the 1929 crash contributed to the subsequent collapse of the economy, which was already far from sound. In fact, the National Bureau of Economic Research suggests that it entered recession in August 1929, two months before the stock-market crash. Nonetheless, this does not necessarily diminish the significance of the crash. Galbraith wrote, "When a greenhouse succumbs to a hailstorm something more than a purely passive role is normally attributed to the storm. One must accord similar significance to the typhoon which blew out of lower Manhattan in October 1929."[10]

While most analysts focus their attention on equities, it is also important to consider what happened in other asset markets. Between 1925 and 1933 average house prices fell by 30%, placing a dent in household wealth and limiting the ability of banks to lend and borrowers to borrow.

Commodity prices also fell very sharply during the early Depression years. Over the 11 years from their peaks in 1920, oil and cotton prices fell by 80%. Of course, lower commodity prices boost consumers' real incomes; but they have the opposite effect on the real incomes of producers. At the time, the agricultural sector was a very important part of the US economy. The inability of farmers to service their home loans was a significant feature of the Depression. It led to an explosion of bad debts, which weakened bank balance sheets and led to large numbers of farmers swelling the ranks of the unemployed as they lost both their homes and their livelihoods.

What is more, falling commodity prices exacerbated deflationary forces. And deflation intensified the problems of the times, not least by raising the real value of household and company debts.

Monetary contraction due to bank failures

Milton Friedman argued that the Fed's decisions to raise interest rates and not to help the banks were crucial, as they led to thousands of bank failures, which caused the money supply to contract by 25%. Without this, he argued, the Depression would not have been so bad. Indeed, when asked whether the stock-market crash caused the Great Depression, Friedman said, "Whatever happens to a stock market, it cannot lead to a Great Depression unless it produces or is accompanied by a monetary collapse."[11]

It is certainly easy to see why he placed so much importance on the collapse of the banks. Over half of all US banks went out of business, or were taken over by other banks. Furthermore, from 1928 to 1933 the total deposits of US banks fell by $20 billion, or 30%.

The Fed appeared to believe that by weeding out the weakest players, bank failures provided a necessary prerequisite for a sustained economic recovery. Accordingly, it did not take any action to support the banks that were in trouble. In addition, at that time there was no deposit protection, so the system was extremely prone to runs on banks.

Ben Bernanke, the current Chairman of the Fed and formerly a distinguished academic who has made a close study of the Depression, also thinks that the behavior of the Fed turned what could have been an ordinary recession into a depression. Indeed, in a speech in 2002 (when he was a Governor of the Fed rather than its Chairman) he apologized on behalf of the central bank, saying, "We did it. We're very sorry. But... we won't do it again."[12]

In their weighty tome on the period, Friedman and Anna Schwartz[13] argued that the majority of bank failures were the result of a classic banking panic where "a contagion of fear spreads among depositors." In particular, they attached a lot of significance to the failure of the Bank of the United States in December 1931, which at the time was the largest bank ever to have failed and whose distinctive name "led many at home and abroad to regard it somehow as an official bank." In other words, they believed that the banks did not need to fail and that had the Fed or the White House stepped in to prevent the bank runs, the contraction in the money supply would have been less marked and the Depression more modest.

Even those disposed toward a Keynesian interpretation surely have to accept that there is much force in this. But what was the cause of the trouble besetting banks? Although Friedman and Schwartz argue that banks failed due to liquidity problems caused by bank runs, it is arguable that the primary cause of bank failure was insolvency, due to the falls in asset prices and the downturn in the economy. Nor is it obvious that the sharp falls in the money supply were purely due to reduced preparedness or lower ability of banks to lend. At a time when unemployment was soaring, at least some of the contraction in the money supply was because there was no *demand* for funds. Indeed, with the economy mired in deflation, there was little incentive to borrow, as the real value of debt was continually rising. Hence, the contraction in the money supply could be seen as a symptom of the Great Depression rather than its fundamental cause.

Fiscal policy errors

Two American Presidents also took decisions that contributed to the Depression. Both Herbert Hoover and his successor, Franklin D. Roosevelt, believed in a balanced budget. This meant there were no attempts to relieve the stress by a net increase in government spending and/or a cut in taxes.

In the popular imagination, Roosevelt is widely credited as bringing the US out of the Great Depression. This is wrong on two counts. First, the Great Depression did not end until the US started preparing for the Second World War. Second, although Roosevelt enacted various programs of increased state spending and direct state intervention in the economy, he did not follow Keynesian policies, since he funded this extra spending by raising taxes. In fact, given that the budget deficit would normally widen during an economic downturn, by seeking a balanced budget Roosevelt could be said to have run *contractionary* fiscal policies.

The lurch toward protectionism

In May 1929, the House of Representatives passed the infamous Smoot-Hawley Tariff Act, which imposed tariffs on imports into the US. Between

1929 and 1932, France, India, Australia, Spain, Switzerland, Canada, Italy, Cuba, Mexico, New Zealand, Denmark, the Netherlands, Belgium, Luxembourg, and Britain (on the advice of Keynes) all raised import tariffs. The result was that between 1929 and 1932 world exports fell by almost 30%.

The way this affected the world economy is not widely understood. Since keeping out imports boosts demand for your own country's output, protection cannot cause a world depression by directly reducing aggregate demand. As all countries cut back, demand by other countries for your exports is replaced by increased domestic demand for what used to be your imports. This is a zero-sum game. It will not collectively boost aggregate demand, but at least it will not depress it. Accordingly, it is as plausible to imagine full employment in a completely autarkic world (in which countries are economically self-sufficient) as in a fully integrated one. It is just that people do different jobs.

However, the move from a largely integrated world to a largely autarkic one did depress aggregate demand indirectly. First, a shift toward autarky implies lower real incomes, as the benefits of specialization are lost. This may readily persuade consumers to reduce their spending and may contribute to a fall in aggregate demand.

Second, the shift toward autarky renders large amounts of capital obsolete and large numbers of workers redundant. In equilibrium, their resources would have been redeployed and reabsorbed elsewhere. But the path to a new equilibrium was anything but smooth. The dynamic forces of closure, losses, redundancy, and unemployment would have been felt before the expansionary effects of new opportunities to replace imports and cater to domestic demand. This was enough to set in train the downward spiral of demand. There is an eerie echo here in today's circumstances. I take up this subject in Chapters 8 and 9.

An overall winner?

This is not the place to attempt a detailed weighing up of these four candidate explanations for the Great Depression. On this subject I have no academic axe to grind. I suspect that all four explanations have something to contribute. For me, the striking thing is that they all have resonance today.

The "Long Depression"

Economic history did not begin in 1929 and recessions did not first appear then either. Recessions were a frequent occurrence during the nineteenth century, although, in global terms, none of them was anything like as serious as the Great Depression. The recession that comes closest, at least in the imagination, is the one known as the *Long Depression*, which began in 1873.

Unlike other nineteenth-century downturns, the Long Depression dragged on for 24 years. On the face of it, however, the episode does not justify its name. For a start, the economy continued to grow. True, between 1873 and 1897 average GDP growth in Britain slowed to 1.9% p.a., from an average of 2.2% p.a. from 1830 to 1873. But that is hardly a lot to write home about. Elsewhere in Europe, indeed, average growth during this period of "depression" was faster than in the preceding 40 years; and it was faster than in the subsequent period, leading up to the First World War. This was also true for the US.[14]

So why the "Long Depression"? This episode is best seen as a prolonged period of depressed *prices* rather than of depressed output. A worldwide shortage of gold required countries that were adherents to the Gold Standard to restrict the growth of the money supply. As a result, prices in the UK were approximately 40% lower at the end of the Long Depression than they had been at its beginning. Deflation catalyzed the rapid unionization of the workforce and increased the bitterness of labor relations. Workers were dissatisfied with nominal pay freezes or cuts, even though falling prices meant that their real income was increasing at a faster rate. This increase in real wages led firms to lay off workers, causing unemployment to rise sharply.[15]

In the US, prices fell by about 30%. Farmers were particularly hard hit by falls in agricultural prices. The real value of their mortgage debt kept mounting while their incomes were falling. This is the background to the famous speech in 1896 by William Jennings Bryan, the Democratic candidate for President, against the evils of deflation and the Gold Standard. He ended with the famous cry: "You shall not crucify mankind upon a cross of gold."[16]

Moreover, for Britain there was another factor. The 1870s saw the US become the world's largest economy, pushing Britain into second place, and the last quarter of the nineteenth century saw convergence between Britain and Germany. Thus the "Long Depression" in Britain is best seen as "a twenty year period of doubts, self-questioning and disenchantment."[17]

Earlier recessions

The Long Depression was far from being the only recession of the nineteenth century. The recession that hit Britain in the mid-1820s bears some of the hallmarks of the period leading up to the current crisis: excessively loose monetary policy, a domestic stock-market boom, and an investment bubble. This led to a crisis of confidence in 1825, which culminated in the collapse of one of the largest banks of the time (Henry Thornton's) as well as several smaller banks. A full-scale collapse of the banking system was only prevented when the Bank of England began to act as a lender of last resort.

The 1840s saw the bursting of a speculative bubble in railway stock, akin to the IT boom of the late 1990s. The subsequent panic, when many railway investments turned sour, led to a series of bank failures and recession.[18]

In nineteenth-century America, all but two recessions were associated with financial panics and bank failures.[19] An investment boom in cotton, land, and canals in the mid-1830s, for example, was followed by a stock-market crash and banking panic in 1837. This resulted in the collapse of 343 banks, and led many US states to default on their debt payments.[20] Between 1839 and 1840, GDP contracted by 6.4%.[21]

In 1857, the failure of the Ohio Life Insurance and Trust Company led to the collapse of railroad investment corporations.[22] That year, the US stock market was 66% lower than its 1850 peak. The crash induced a contraction in US GDP of 8.7% between 1857 and 1858.[23]

The continental European experience in the nineteenth century was different from that of the US and the UK. Growth was more volatile, but internal conflict and war, rather than financial crises, were the main causes of downturns.[24]

Postwar economic cycles

Coming closer to our own time, in the postwar period most recessions have been fairly tame affairs. Until the Great Implosion, the eight most recent

American recessions lasted, on average, only 10 months, with real GDP contracting, on average, by only 1.7% and employment falling by 1.5 million. Recent UK recessions have been longer, but they have still been fairly pale affairs compared to what was experienced before the Second World War.

Until the Great Implosion, recessions in postwar continental Europe have also been pretty timid by historical standards, and generally less severe than those in the US and the UK. They have also been far less frequent. Indeed, in France, Germany, and Italy, output rose every year from 1950 until 1975. Just as in the nineteenth century, financial factors have not played an important role in causing instability.

On the basis of such postwar experience, we should be comparatively positive about our current difficulties. Indeed, if you are reading this soon after the book's publication, on the basis of postwar experience the recession may be nearly, or even completely, over.

But this postwar experience is almost certainly irrelevant. Postwar recessions were usually associated with rising inflation and with big increases in interest rates. By contrast, the essential element in today's events is the near-collapse of the banking system and the shattering of confidence in the whole financial structure. In most western societies, nothing like this has been seen since the 1930s. The current downturn seems more nineteenth century in character.

Japanese lessons

Not all postwar experience, however, fits the European and American pattern. The Japanese experience of the 1990s offers a more up-to-date reminder than the Great Depression of what can go wrong. This period in Japan is known as the "Lost Decade." As far as GDP was concerned, though, these years were far from being the total write-off this description implies. Between 1991 and 1996 the Japanese economy grew by just over 7%, slightly faster than Germany over the same period.

Nevertheless, if you look at what happened to asset prices, you can see why the period is believed to have been such a disaster. Between December 1989 and April 2003, Japanese equity prices fell by 80%. From peak to trough, Japanese land prices fell by about 70%. And in 2009, consumer prices were about the same as they had been in 1993, having been both higher and lower in the interim.

It is widely believed that the Japanese authorities made a hash of managing the economy. They were slow to recognize the seriousness of the situation and they were hesitant in implementing policy measures to deal with it. They did engage in a substantial Keynesian expansion, and this may well have prevented a still worse outcome. Nevertheless, Japan did not really get going again until the world economy took off (and then it fell back sharply when the world economy weakened). In addition, the authorities cut interest rates to zero and operated a policy of expanding the money supply, which is also widely believed not to have been very successful.

It is worth bearing in mind that the scale of the problems confronting the Japanese authorities could easily be said to be greater than those faced today, in that the bubble in Japanese asset markets in the late 1980s was much greater – and encompassed both property and equities.

But there is something about the Japanese experience that should cause you to worry. The Japanese ability to withstand the collapse of a massive bubble, and to bounce back into some sort of recovery, should be seen against the backdrop of a world economy that was, on the whole, strong. More especially, Japan was helped enormously by the emerging economic miracle on its doorstep, namely China. The world today does not enjoy that advantage. In a global downturn, there is no external source of demand to look to.

Scandinavian lessons

In many ways this is also the lesson to emerge from the Scandinavian experience of banking-induced recession in the 1990s.[25] The received wisdom about this period is that things could have been a lot worse, but for the speedy, sensible, and bold action of Nordic governments and central banks. It does seem that the Scandinavian authorities acted reasonably well in difficult circumstances to bring about the best of all possible results. Central banks moved rapidly to provide liquidity, while governments intervened both quickly and massively, nationalizing some banks and setting up "bad banks" to manage the troubled assets of the banks they had nationalized.

The Nordic governments plowed large sums of money into the banking system, estimated at the equivalent of 2%, 3½%, and 9% of GDP into the Norwegian, Swedish, and Finnish banking sectors respectively. After the crisis was over, all three governments were able to recoup a large proportion of their costs through the sale of assets acquired during their rescue operations. Accordingly, the estimated net costs to the taxpayer of the banking crisis are rather lower. Indeed, the Swedish government almost recovered the whole of its "investment" and the Norwegian government actually made a profit.

Given this record, it is all the more remarkable that governments and central banks in America and other European countries had not properly heeded these Scandinavian lessons when contemplating their own bank bailouts in 2007/9. When it comes to thinking about these lessons now, there are three key features to bear in mind. Most importantly, the Scandinavian economies were very small. They were able to gain competitive advantage against most of their neighbors by devaluing their currencies. Moreover, during the period in which they were trying to rehabilitate, by and large the world economy was strong. None of these advantages is open to the world today.

Comparisons with the Great Depression

So, of the various past episodes with which the Great Implosion can be compared, it is indeed the Great Depression to which the current experience seems closest. Both had their roots in large asset price bubbles and both involved catastrophic problems in the banking sector. Moreover, like the Great Depression, the Great Implosion is truly global.

Furthermore, there must be a risk that the world will again succumb to protectionism. Indeed, in 2009, coming on top of the stalling of the Doha trade talks that aim to lower trade barriers, it was alarming to see in President Obama's program for restoring the American economy a prominent place for the policy of "Buy American." There have also been protectionist stirrings in both China and the EU. And in the area of banking and finance the world has already turned in an isolationist direction, with large banks withdrawing from activity outside their home base and concentrating limited lending capacity on the domestic market.

For most of the postwar period the idea of bringing in protectionist poli-cies for macro reasons – that is, to boost aggregate demand – has seemed otiose. If there are unemployed resources, surely all the authorities have to do is to cut interest rates, raise government spending, or reduce taxes. But from today's perspective things don't look quite so simple. Interest rates are already virtually at zero almost everywhere, while concern about the size of government debt limits the scope for expansionary fiscal policies. There is still "quantitative easing" in the armory, and it can supposedly be pursued without limit. Nevertheless, so far it seems to be having little effect and there are growing worries about what it will ultimately do to inflation. These wor-ries are limiting both how far it will be pursued and the extent to which it will be effective. (I discuss these issues in Chapter 8.)

In these conditions, you can readily see how protection may seem attrac-tive. After all, for any individual country protection definitely would result in a rise in aggregate demand – provided that it could avoid other countries retaliating. Of course, it would *not* be able to do this, but history is full of examples of countries taking actions that prove to be ultimately self-defeating.

Differences from the 1930s

Thankfully, there are some significant differences between the Great Depression and how the Great Implosion has evolved to date. For a start, the greater size of the state has proved to be stabilizing. There is a larger chunk of the economy where expenditure is not automatically cut due to lack of finance or loss of confidence, and indeed there is more automatic cushioning of private-sector spending as the public deficit expands passively in response to lower tax payments and higher benefit spending.

Over and above these passive responses, policymakers have also been proactive. Indeed, one conclusion of the meeting of the G-20 in November 2008 was that governments should use Keynesian-style policies to support eco-nomic activity. And they have. The governments of the US, Japan, Germany, China, France, and the UK have all announced significant fiscal expansions.

Moreover, those in charge of monetary policy have slashed interest rates aggressively. More than that, they have acted to continue expansionary monetary policy once rates have hit near-zero, through quantitative easing. And policymakers have been quick to prevent banks from failing and depositors from losing their money. Furthermore, the dangers of protectionism are now much better understood – at least by governments.

More to come

So, on the basis of past experience, how deep and how long should we expect this downturn to be? If we know anything, it is that we do not know the future. Even as I write this, I wonder whether the gloomy and fatalistic consensus view could be overdoing the dangers and the downside potential. By the autumn of 2009, with the world economy apparently recovering, this looked a distinct possibility. Perhaps we will look back in a few years' time and wonder how we could all have been duped into a state of exaggerated pessimism. After all, the fall of commodity prices experienced in 2008/9, as long as it is sustained, will bring a massive boost to real incomes in most of the developed west. Meanwhile, enormous stimulatory action has been undertaken by central banks and governments alike. At some point asset prices will have fallen far enough, and at some stage these stimulatory actions will have a marked effect. Common opinion, both expert and popular, may be just as bad at anticipating the recovery as it was in spotting the downturn in the first place.

Although I think this scenario is possible, I do not think it is likely. Because it began in the housing market, it will be tempting to believe that once that sector stabilizes, the crisis, if not over, will at least be past its worst. However, it would be wrong to assume this blithely. Although the stabilization of house prices is a necessary condition for recovery, it is not a sufficient one. The game has moved on.

Recessions are like the plague. The Black Death that ravaged Europe in the 1340s did not hit every city simultaneously. While it was raging in Milan, across the Alps in Geneva people thought they were safe, but within a few weeks Geneva was consumed by it too. Meanwhile, in Paris things continued as usual – for a while. By the time the time the plague was raging in Paris, it was finished in Milan, but London was yet to fall. By the time London had succumbed, Geneva was clear.

Similarly, by the time house prices have stabilized everywhere, other stages of the crisis will still need to be worked through. The housing market collapse weakens banks; the weakening of banks reduces bank lending and weakens companies; the weakening of companies causes them to shed labor, which causes unemployment to rise; high unemployment weakens consumer incomes and consumer confidence, which leads to reduced demand; reduced demand weakens companies, which weakens banks, and so on, and so forth.

Who knows what further financial problems lie ahead? It is quite possible that even after the huge government bailouts of the banks in 2008, yet more public money will need to be poured in as they need to be recapitalized all over again. Moreover, with the exception of the American giant AIG, there have so far been no insurance company failures, although it is surely possible that several significant insurance companies will yet go under.

Similarly, there has been no major pension fund element to the crisis so far. For many companies in the US and the UK, what happens in the pension fund can overwhelm what happens in the business. British Airways, for instance, has been described as a huge pension fund with a small airline business on the side.

As if private-sector financial fragility were not enough, this crisis has exposed the fragility of government finances. For the first time in two generations, there is a real possibility of a developed western country's government defaulting on its debts. What is more, this danger even applies to countries that not long ago would have been regarded as unimpeachable – the US and the UK. This is limiting the extent of fiscal stimulus and may even lead to early fiscal tightening.

Moreover, even without a reversal, there are doubts about how effective stimulatory monetary policy will continue to be. Bill White, former chief economist of the Bank for International Settlements and a trenchant critic of the central bank policy of cutting real interest rates even lower to keep the game going, is pessimistic. He thinks that the effect of this policy has been to keep drawing prosperity from the future – until the future arrives. "It does the job for a while but moves in interest rates have to be even more violent to achieve the same effect. My worry is that we may have reached the point where the policy ceases to work altogether."[26]

What makes this situation so dangerous is the obvious friction between countries that, if the system is to be saved, will have to cooperate. Yet there is no clear, widely agreed model of what the future world should look like. Not so long ago, in his famous book *The End of History*, Francis Fukuyama thought that the future would be one of liberal, democratic capitalism, holding sway everywhere unopposed.[27] He was wrong. But what is the new vision to take its place? No one seems to have one.

From past lessons to future experience

It is already clear that for the world as a whole, the Great Implosion is the worst downturn of the postwar period. Whether it turns out to be worse even than that will depend largely on how effective the policymakers' actions are in bringing countervailing forces to bear. The fact that by the autumn of 2009, the danger of an imminent collapse into another Great Depression seemed to have been averted, the economy had stabilized, and even shown some early signs of recovery, was in large part due to the implementation of some of the policy measures that I discuss in Chapter 8.

But we cannot be sure how effective those policies will continue to be, for how long they will be sustained, or when they will be reversed. If we know anything, we know that events like the Great Depression, the Japanese "Lost Decade," and the Great Implosion bring about major policy *mistakes*. Looking back, it is often easy to see those mistakes as plain as a pikestaff. At the time, they are anything but. There is still plenty of scope for major mistakes now.

For my money, the aspect of the current situation that will present some of the most serious challenges, and over which the policymakers will be most liable to making a mistake, is something that played a major part in the events of the Great Depression of the 1930s, the "Long Depression" of the nineteenth century, and the Japanese "Lost Decade" in the 1990s – namely, the threat of a progressive fall of the price level, which we know by the term *deflation*. The problem is now all the more intense, and the dangers all the greater, because at the time that the deflation threat is most pressing, many people and institutions fear its opposite: inflation.

From Inflation to Deflation – and Back Again?

We are convinced that we don't have to prepare for deflation because we don't see deflation coming.

Wim Duisenberg, President of the ECB, June 2003

The *Death of Inflation* was a great title for a book, even though it caused some confusion. As a new author, I remember proudly entering my local branch of a major chain of bookstores, expecting to find the book prominently displayed, only to discover that it was not displayed at all. I was dismayed. Eventually I found it – in the fiction department, murder mystery section.

Not only was the title arresting, but it lent itself easily to extending the metaphor. Who killed it? Was it murder or suicide? Is it dead or merely sleeping? If it is merely sleeping, is it asleep like Monty Python's dead parrot? Or if it is dead, is it dead in the manner of Dracula, ready to spring back to life?

In the aftermath of the Great Implosion, that is exactly what many people think we face before too long – if you like, the rebirth of inflation. After all, although it took some time to develop and the Second World War intervened, the Great Inflation of the postwar period can be seen as the direct result of the Great Depression of the 1930s.

I believe that the era of low inflation that began in the early 1990s has much further to run. The collapse in aggregate demand that I described in the last chapter is creating excess capacity in the economy. In the US, this excess capacity (which economists often refer to as "the output gap") is on a scale unseen since the 1930s. And in many other OECD countries the output gap is of a similar, or even larger, size. In classic fashion, excess capacity is putting prices and wages under intense competitive pressure. Even when the economy recovers, this slack will take some time to be used up; the economy will need to grow for several years above its long-term sustainable rate for the slack to disappear. In fact, for the reasons I gave in the last chapter, I doubt that the economy will easily grow even at its sustainable rate for several years.

In that case, the slack will continue to increase, and downward pressures on prices and wages will intensify.

Monetary and fiscal policy will, of course, be deployed to try to ameliorate this difficult situation. In Chapter 8 I lay out my suggestions for how we can extract ourselves from this mess and get the economy back on an even keel. However, so great is the shock to the system and so severe the shattering of confidence caused by the Great Implosion that I suspect policy will be only weakly effective at best.

Meanwhile, the structural changes I first identified in *The Death of Inflation* are continuing, with the result that prices and wages are much more downwardly flexible than they were for most of the postwar period. There are five main forces:

1 In the domestic economy, things have become more competitive. The ideological changes of the early 1980s led to a series of measures that, in America and the UK, and later spreading to other countries, boosted competition. Unions were tamed; nationalized industries broken up or privatized; and private corporations re-energized to become more competitive.

2 These effects have been compounded by technological change. The internet connects markets. It provides information and it overcomes distance. It is the digital equivalent of the railroad, motor car, and aircraft revolutions rolled into one. It undermines local monopoly by spreading information and globalizing the marketplace.

3 Meanwhile, on the global stage, the rise of China and the associated processes of globalization have provided the western world with a series of favorable price shocks, as more expensive western production is replaced by cheaper Asian goods.

4 Moreover, the knowledge that other producers with much lower cost bases abound, and that they could appear at any moment on your patch, has altered the wage- and price-setting behavior of both workers and companies. They have become less keen to pass cost increases on, and more keen to keep prices competitive so as to win and keep business.

5 The consequence of these changes is that expectations of inflation, which are a key determinant of what inflation turns out to be, are now easier to subdue and easier to keep down.

In *The Death of Inflation* I argued that as a result of these factors, central banks would find it surprisingly easy to get and keep inflation low. They could still blow it, of course, as has happened in Zimbabwe, but western central banks following normal procedures would find keeping inflation low a doddle. The consequence would be a long period not only of low inflation, but of low inflation accompanied by rapid growth and low unemployment.

Broadly speaking, this is indeed what has happened. And now the Great Implosion has clobbered aggregate demand and shattered confidence. The upshot is that, as I argue later in this chapter, deflation is now a more realistic possibility that at any time since the 1930s.

Inflationary challenges

Nevertheless, during the crisis of 2007/9, to many observers and commentators it seemed as though the thesis of *The Death of Inflation* was fundamentally wrong. The crisis produced four separate reasons to think that inflation might be on its way back: much higher government borrowing; big increases in the money supply; the lure of inflation as a way out; and the prospect of much higher oil and commodity prices, implied by the continued rapid growth rates of China and much of east Asia.

The outlook for inflation is of tremendous importance for the economy and for the political landscape; as well as for investment prospects, which I discuss in Chapter 7. Indeed, if inflation did pick up sharply in the years ahead then central banks might feel obliged to raise interest rates smartly. This could easily snuff out whatever recovery has by that time begun. So the inflation outlook is a critical issue to get right. I have put my cards on the table. Now I must address the four counter-arguments laid out above.

Public borrowing to create inflation?

As the bailouts of banks rumbled on, so the scale of public borrowing reached heights hitherto scarcely imaginable. It looks as though in 2009 borrowing will be not far off 13% of GDP in the US, 10% in the eurozone, and about 15% in the UK. Isn't all this public money poured into the system bound to be inflationary?

It is ironic that so many market analysts should think that increased public borrowing will be inflationary, because a strand of popular economics, in wide circulation in the market and outside, is that increases in public borrowing will have no effect on demand. Unless you believe that the boost from increased public borrowing is being given in conditions of full employment – which, *ex hypothesi*, it isn't – or that the increase of demand through public borrowing has some inherent inflationary quality – which it manifestly doesn't – then saying that it will have no effect on demand and that it will be inflationary are in blatant contradiction. Never mind: why let a contradiction stand in the way of a good rant?

Yet if you suppose that increased public borrowing *will* lead to an increase in aggregate demand, isn't that bound to be inflationary? Well, yes, if you mean "compared to the situation that might exist if borrowing had not been driven up to provide support," because that situation could easily have involved a fall into deflation.

But not necessarily inflationary compared to the position that the economy has just been in. There has been an extraordinary destruction of wealth from the fall of house prices and equity prices. Moreover, largely related to the weakness of property prices, there has been a massive destruction of high-powered wealth – that is, bank capital – and therefore a collapse of the ability to lend. Banks have been forcibly merged, taken over, and subject to injections of public capital and control. On top of this, public confidence has been shattered, creating not the sort of anxiety that features in neat surveys of economic conditions, but the sort that leaves you with an uncomfortable feeling in your gut and stops you from sleeping at night.

The increase of public spending and borrowing will, of course, tend to lead to increased aggregate demand and therefore tend to increase inflation, *compared to what it would otherwise have been*. But if the support package exactly offsets the factors making for the downturn, then the economy – and inflation – will simply end up back where they were to start with. Moreover, because of anxiety about public debt, I think it is unlikely that government support will be on a sufficient scale to return aggregate demand to normal any time soon. Accordingly, the net impact of all this is likely to be *dis*inflationary, because it will tend to reduce aggregate demand.

Long-term consequences

So the argument that increases in public borrowing must be inflationary in the short term doesn't stand up to close scrutiny. There is, however, a legitimate question about what happens later. Suppose that when private-sector spending recovers, the stimulus from extra public spending and borrowing remains. That is not such a silly proposition. Governments find it difficult to cut spending and to raise taxes. Accordingly, it is reasonable to entertain the idea that they will fail to face up to the job of stabilizing the public finances. Therefore, at some point private-sector spending could recover while demand from the public sector was still strong, thereby creating a surge in aggregate demand. Before long, rising inflation would be the inevitable result.

This is a legitimate concern, but in fact there is a wealth of evidence showing that when push comes to shove, governments *can* take the tough action to reduce borrowing and bring debt under control. The borrowing of governments during the Second World War was of gargantuan proportions. In 1946, the UK's debt-to-GDP ratio was 250%; by the mid-1970s it was below 50% of GDP. In the US, the peak figure was 108% of GDP in 1945; by the mid-1970s it was down to 25%. Nor is this the only example. After fighting another existential war, this time against Napoleon, in 1819 the UK's debt-to-GDP ratio peaked at over 260%, but by the outbreak of the First World War in 1914 it was down to 26%.

In the US, fears about the public deficit have been a recurrent theme of recent commentary about the future. When President Clinton was first elected in 1993, fears about the government deficit were particularly strong. In the event, Clinton turned the deficit into a surplus, which in 2000 reached 2.4% of GDP, and the debt ratio fell from 48% of GDP in 1992 to 33% in 2001.

It is a similar story in countries that have faced the need to borrow huge sums to recapitalize their banking system. Finland faced such a task in 1991. The banking system was effectively bust and the government borrowed a total of 9% of GDP to recapitalize it. In 1993, the Finnish government borrowing requirement was just under 10% of GDP. Yet by 1998 the budget had bounced back into surplus, and inflation stayed low. True, in 2007/8 inflation rose to a peak of 4.7%. But this was no worse than was experienced by other developed countries in reaction to the surge of commodity prices, and inflation has subsequently subsided.

It was a similar story in Japan. The cyclically adjusted budget deficit rose to 7.4% in 2000. However, by 2007 a combination of expenditure restraint and tax rises had brought it down to 2.6%. And this was despite the economic recovery being feeble by western standards. Over this period, consumer prices were stable to falling.

Moreover, in 2009, even as governments were announcing expansionary fiscal packages, the worries were mounting that public debt was too high. In the UK, the opposition Conservative Party, which was hoping to win power in 2010, was planning cuts to public spending and increases in taxes to bring public borrowing under control. In the US, alarm about the public finances was not far behind, and there was a similar situation in Germany. Before too long, governments in much of the western world will be tightening fiscal policy in pursuit of lower deficits.

In view of this history, and of the prevailing ethos in society and among the political class in the west, it is more likely, I suspect, that governments will seek to repair the public finances too quickly, thereby extending the period of weak economic growth.

Monetary incontinence

This is all very well, but it relates only to fiscal policy. Another key characteristic of the period after the banking collapses of 2008 was the huge sums of money – hundreds of billions of dollars in each large monetary area – poured into the monetary system by central banks. According to a certain breed of monetarist, it is inevitable that these injections will be inflationary.

I disagree. The key is that there are different sorts of money. The money that is pumped out by central banks, unsurprisingly, is central bank money; that is to say, the liabilities of the central bank. And, with some qualifications, we can say that the central bank can potentially expand this pretty much without limit.[1]

Central bank money is exchangeable into notes (which are also the liability of the central bank). Because of this, a policy of expanding the central bank balance sheet by buying assets, which is known in the jargon as quantitative easing, is often referred to as "printing money." Isn't this bound to be inflationary? Not necessarily. In this case extra central bank deposits, or notes, are not being dished out *gratis*, but rather are being exchanged for other assets in the system.

More importantly, no one responds directly to the supply of central bank money. The man in Peoria, Illinois, does not jump up and down at the news that central bank money has just risen. He does not say to his wife, "Dora, do you know our share of the central bank money stock has just risen by $500? Let's go out for dinner." Indeed, strange though it may seem, he does not even know what the central bank money stock is, never mind what his share has risen by!

Broad money

Central bank money is the small change of the monetary system. The bulk of the money supply consists of the liabilities of private commercial banks. If the central bank money stock has any relevance at all to spending behavior, it is through its effect on other parts of the financial system, to which the man in Peoria's behavior will more reasonably be responsive; namely, his stock of money deposits and the availability of credit.

So what will be the result of central banks increasing their balance sheets massively? The monetarists see some magical, invincible result, as central bank money spreads its way through the system. In normal times there is indeed a reasonably stable relationship between the supply of central bank money and private bank money.[2] Give the banks more central bank money, therefore, and you could expect to see a surge of bank lending and asset purchases as they seek to reduce their holdings by buying income-earning assets.[3]

But we are not in normal times. If banks are afraid that if they lend money or buy assets they will lose all of it, why should they invest or lend it in the first place? OK, a zero return on deposits at the central bank is not good, but it is better than minus 30% or minus 100%. Accordingly, in these conditions, the relationship between central bank money and private bank money breaks down.

I suppose it is possible that, in the extraordinary circumstances ruling after the Great Implosion, under public control or influence, the banks will be cajoled into keeping their lending at their pre-Great Implosion pace, thereby maintaining growth of the money supply and preventing any collapse of aggregate demand from this source. Although this is possible, it is surely unlikely. Private-sector banks are going to be cautious to an extreme.

Meanwhile, the banks under public control will face an uncomfortable dilemma. Their lords and masters may want them to carry on lending to support the economy, but they will also want to get their money back. Caution is likely to be the order of the day.

This is not mere theoretical surmising: it is exactly what happened in Japan earlier in the decade. The Japanese central bank injected huge amounts of money in an attempt to boost the money supply. At one point the stock of central bank money was up by 36% in a year. The Bank of Japan's balance sheet increased by 60% in three years. Nevertheless, the effect was to boost the Japanese money supply by only 7%.

Again, there is a qualification relating to the later years. If banks are left with a huge supply of liquidity when the economy recovers, then surely lending will take off again and inflation will pick up. Yet there is no need for this to happen. In principle, it should be easy for central banks to take central bank money out. All they have to do is to sell the assets they have accumulated, and thereby reduce the size of their balance sheets. There are some practical difficulties with such a policy, which I discuss in Chapter 8. Despite these, however, there is no reason to believe that a resurgence of inflation cannot be prevented.

Actually wanting inflation

This is all very well, but as the international financial crisis rumbled on, an increasing number of people came to believe that governments, and even some central banks, would in the end *choose* inflation. Moreover, this would be a "good thing." In fact, some people came to think that it offered the only way out. Could they be right?

It is certainly possible that governments and central banks, or at least some of them, could choose inflation as the lesser evil. Presented with a choice between continual depression, default, or inflation, some would surely choose inflation. If that were the choice, they might even be right.

But that is not the choice. There is a way out of our current predicament that does not require or imply a return to high inflation, as I lay out in Chapter 8. In some countries in the west, there may need to be a program of expenditure cuts and tax rises. In general, however, that will not be necessary.

Sustained restraint on government spending combined with economic growth will bring government deficits sharply lower and stabilize the ratio of public debt to GDP below panic levels. Sustained near-zero interest rates and quantitative easing in the west, combined with expansionary policies in China and much of the rest of Asia, can generate the recovery on which all this depends, without leading inexorably to higher inflation. And, as and when inflation looks like picking up again, these policies can be sent into reverse.

The "inflation is good" school misses two further tricks. As soon as the financial markets got the slightest whiff of the idea that governments saw inflation as the way out, you would not see the government bond yield for dust. The result would be that the cost of financing the government's deficit would skyrocket. So, far from overcoming the constraints imposed by the huge government debt burden, unleashing inflation could cause them to come much closer. Without too much imagination, in these circumstances you could readily envisage the position becoming intolerable – with default the only way out.

There is something else. For the last 30 years, the policy establishment on both sides of the Atlantic has fought tooth and nail to get inflation low and keep it there. They have done this because they have believed that inflation, and the associated high level of interest rates, does untold harm. They have not changed their view. Accordingly, if they were consciously to unleash inflation on the system they would believe that they were damaging the economy – effectively undoing the good work of the last 30 years. And in the process of hobbling the economy, they would worsen the problem of the public finances.

In summary, consciously opting for inflation is not something that this generation of policymakers is going to do lightly. Resisting inflation is in their blood. Of course, this could change. In particular, the political fallout from the financial collapse could yet bring about a stronger constituency in favor of inflation. However, the evidence of the past is that such changes take some considerable time to work their way through. The reason is probably generational. Policymakers, doubtless like the rest of us, often have a searing experience that colors their approach to the world. The current generation still recoils from the inflationary upsurge that happened in the 1970s. At some point, they may be replaced by a new generation that recoils from the aftermath of the Great Implosion. But not yet.

Resolving an important theoretical dispute

This leaves two further arguments, both of which are associated with a theoretical dispute reignited by *The Death of Inflation*; namely, whether real factors such as the rise of China can have any bearing on the inflation rate, as distinct from on relative prices.

Central banks and commentators, even many of those steeped in monetarist analysis, now seem to be signed up to the view that they can. Indeed, they talk about the possible waning of the favorable part of the China effect, combined with the growing unfavorable part – the upward pressure on oil and commodity prices – leading to higher inflation. This is deliciously ironic. To many of these erstwhile monetarists, my thesis that real factors could affect the inflation environment originally seemed heretical to the point of economic illiteracy. Now it seems to be the conventional wisdom.

Nevertheless, not everyone is converted. So before discussing what the outlook for China and commodity prices implies for inflation, I feel I must try to resolve a theoretical dispute that I sense needlessly divides opinion.[4] I am no physicist, but as I understand it, in physics there is a chasm between the laws that seem to apply at large size and those that apply at small size. At large size, Einstein's theory of relativity holds sway, with Newtonian physics still giving a pretty good approximation of the truth. But at the subatomic level, the weird world of quantum mechanics gives the answers. Physicists are in search of a grand unifying theory that will bring these two aspects of our understanding together.

I feel there is a similar dichotomy in monetary affairs. It is very striking that so many of the conclusions of monetary analysis are derived from thinking about *major* changes in the monetary environment. And, I have to say, I have next to no quarrel with monetarist analysis of major inflationary changes. Hyperinflations are all monetary phenomena, certainly in the respect that they could not get going or continue without big increases in the money supply, and often also in the sense that the primary, originating cause is an increase in the money supply.

At very high levels of inflation, what does it matter if a surge of cheap imports from China reduces the price level by 2%? Or a wave of privatization or enhanced competition alters wage- and price-setting behavior? These factors are easily obliterated in the flood of monetary incontinence.

However, matters are altogether different at low initial rates of inflation. Shocks to the price level can then have a major effect. Meanwhile, in systems where money supply is a fuzzy and variable concept, the quantity of money, whatever it is, can readily adjust to changing demand. So, monetary changes can sometimes be the result of changes in the economy, rather than always the other way round.

The competitive climate

Accepting that the real factors I have outlined can affect the inflation rate, and have done so in the last 20 years, is the tide of institutional and structural change still running strongly in the direction of low inflation? The picture is mixed. Countries aplenty have followed the US/UK's lead in deregulating and privatizing. The result is that the competitive environment continues to be sharper. But the supply of new, favorable price shocks from this source has all but run dry.

On the technological front, there is probably much more still to go. Although the majority of people in western societies are internet enabled, a large minority are not. The consequence is that society cannot move to a footing where it is assumed that everyone is online, with adverse implications for the savings of resources and the efficiency of markets.

On globalization too the answer is nuanced. There is no doubt in my mind that the process has a very long way to go. China's price level remains way below the level in the west, and there are all sorts of areas of production where China is not yet a factor but will be some time in the future. Moreover, there are still umpteen countries that have not yet followed fully the globalization route taken by China. The possibilities offered by Africa becoming a fully fledged member of the world economy are enormous.

The upshot is that exposure to foreign sources of supply will continue to have a favorable effect on the western price level for many years to come. But that is not the same as keeping the *inflation rate* down. Imagine that replacing European production with Chinese production delivers a downward shock to the price level of 1%, and thereby immediately lowers the inflation rate by 1%. To keep inflation at this reduced level, 1% lower than it would otherwise have been, it is not sufficient for there to be a continuing supply of such favorable price shocks. What is required is that such favorable price shocks continue *at the same rate, year by year*. Any slackening in the pace of such shocks would cause the inflation rate to rise.

It would not be surprising if the rate of exposure to favorable price shocks were now slowing. If that is right, the central banks will have to work harder to keep inflation down. They can still do it, of course, but it will not come so easily.

How easily will depend greatly on what happens to firms' and households' expectations of inflation. Here the picture is quite promising. Expectations of inflation understandably underwent an upward push in 2008 after the upsurge of inflation itself, but they didn't rise that far and they quickly came down again, both in financial markets and among the general public. Moreover, as retailers will readily attest, consumers retained their eye for a bargain. The increased sensitivity to prices that retailers first noticed when inflation fell to low levels in the 1990s endured; the same applies to business purchasers.

The upshot is that before the financial crisis of 2007/9 hit, I reckoned that the economy was set for a continuation of the low inflation conditions that I had first identified in the early 1990s. Other things being equal, even after aggregate demand has recovered from the shock delivered by the Great Implosion, low inflation should continue. But will other things be equal?

Higher oil and commodity prices
One major factor that may not be equal is oil and commodity prices. The surge in prices in 2007/8 set the alarm bells ringing. Could this merely be a foretaste of what is to come?

The widespread inflationary panic unleashed by the oil and commodity price upsurge of 2008 should not, I suppose, be surprising. People who should look forward, in fact start by looking back. The past that western consumers – and commentators – so vividly remembered, and feared, was the two oil price shocks of the 1970s, which saw oil prices rise by 300% and 180% respectively. In both cases the world economy was brought to its knees. In 2008 people naturally assumed that it would be third time unlucky.

But they were wrong. What was remarkable about inflation in 2008/9 was not how high it reached but rather how low it remained. Oil prices doubled in a year. Agricultural prices and metal prices doubled in two years. The result was that inflation in the OECD area rose by only 3%, from a low of 1.7% in August 2007 to a peak of 4.7% in July 2008.

There are two reasons why the inflationary response was so different from the 1970s. The first is that although the percentage rise in the price of oil was about as serious as in the 1973/4 oil shock, oil is simply not as important in our economies as it was. Over the last three decades, the ratio of oil consumption to GDP has fallen by about a half in the advanced OECD countries, and by about a third in the rest of the world. Admittedly, the rise of China and other countries in the east has distorted this picture a little, by transferring heavily energy-intensive production to the east. However, even if you measure oil consumption in relation to world GDP, the result is substantially the same. Moreover, the evidence is that in all economies, the amount of oil consumed in the production of an extra dollar of GDP is continuing to fall.

The second reason is that, as I argued above, the competitive conditions are utterly different. The forces that helped inflation to come down and stay down in the 1990s also prevented it from rising much in response to the commodity price surge of 2008/9.

The commodity price threat may still re-emerge at some point, and there are plenty of people who think that energy Armageddon has only been postponed rather than forestalled altogether. (I will deal with the outlook for commodity prices in more detail in Chapter 7.) Suffice it to say here that as and when the commodity price threat does re-emerge, just as in 2007/8, it will not cause a lasting increase in overall inflation.

The deflation danger

So in a nutshell, despite the widespread alarm about the inflationary danger, in today's conditions I reckon that deflation is a more likely threat to stability than inflation. In *The Death of Inflation* I argued that the western world was just one recession away from deflation. In *Money for Nothing* I argued that the collapse of asset prices might well bring on that recession. Now we are in it. Falling consumer prices are upon us. In 2009, the consumer price index fell in the US, the eurozone, Japan, and China. In the UK this did not happen, mainly because of the inflationary effects of the weak pound. Nevertheless, the price level given by the index used in the old-fashioned measure of inflation, the RPI, did fall.

The proximate cause of falling consumer prices was the sharp drop in oil and commodity prices. Just as these commodities caused an upward shock to the price level in 2007/8, so they subsequently caused a downward shock when they fell. But once they have stabilized, that is the end of it. Unless something else changes, inflation will return to its underlying rate. The question is what that underlying rate will be.

As I argued at the beginning of this chapter, in today's conditions there is a good chance that the underlying rate of inflation will fall sharply – even into negative territory. For the collapse in the level of aggregate demand will put sharp downward pressure on inflation. As prices are cut in the face of weak demand, firms' profits will collapse and they will sharply reduce their payrolls. Unemployment will rise. In these circumstances, the rate of pay inflation will collapse. Indeed, there have already been some cases where the workforce has agreed to significant wage cuts in order to preserve their jobs. The last time such a major change in the climate governing pay happened in the UK was in the early 1990s. Pay inflation came down sharply from 8–10% to 3–4%, where it has remained ever since – until now.

To get into mild deflationary territory, pay does not have to fall; it merely needs to rise by less than the rate of productivity growth, with the result that unit labor costs fall. Once you reach that point you have the precondition for deflation, without any help from lower commodity prices or squeezed profit margins.

In most of the developed west, the underlying growth rate of productivity is about 2%. Accordingly, if the average rate of pay increase falls below 2%, the conditions will be in place for sustained deflation.

Because this did not happen quickly in response to the rises in unemployment that followed the Great Implosion, many people, ordinary and expert alike, have tended to believe that their initial fears of deflation were misplaced. They should beware. The time lags can be quite long. In the case of the Japanese "Lost Decade," although the economy went into recession in 1991, it was not until 1994 that price deflation set in and pay did not start to fall on a sustained basis until 1997.

In fact, I reckon we could be in a state of underlying deflation quite soon. Once we have reached this stage, expectations of deflation can start to build, and thereby become the cause of further deflation, mirroring what happened with inflation.

The consequences

Deflation is not necessarily a disaster. Indeed, in stable times a moderate rate of deflation could even be a good thing. But we are not in stable times. The danger now is that the expectation of falling prices will inhibit borrowing and spending and persuade people to sell assets in order to repay debt, thereby extending the depression through the process known as debt deflation, which the American economist Irving Fisher laid out, in theory, in the 1930s, and which the people of Japan experienced, in practice, in the 1990s.

Still, why worry? The textbooks show that deflation is dead easy to cure. So it is – in the textbooks. What is more, so is inflation. That should give pause for thought. The problem is that usually the textbooks are purged of all politics, all conflict between different interest groups, and all uncertainty. Central banks choose the inflation rate they want and that inflation rate duly emerges. If they don't like deflation then they can, and should, stop it. Just increase the money supply. Hey presto. "With one bound, he was free," and such like.

So why did the Bank of Japan find it so difficult to stop deflation in the 1990s? Because it did not apply a large enough dose of the monetary medicine? Yes, of course. But why not?

I have puzzled over this long and hard. I think the answer lies with the interaction between uncertainty and the different interests of various groups in society. In the textbooks there is no problem over the issue of how much monetary stimulus should be applied. If the central bankers don't know by how much to increase the money supply, they should just increase it by a dollop, and if that doesn't work, just apply more, and more, to the point of infinity.

Yet too large a dose might create inflation – just as the monetarists worry about today. Moreover, some people gain from deflation and others lose. The temptation is for the central banks to advance cautiously, applying small doses of the medicine and hoping it will be enough, then giving more, and then still more, if this proves not to be sufficient. The result is a natural tendency for the central banks to act too little, too late, and for deflation to ensue. What was true for Japan in the 1990s could easily apply to most of the rest of us in the decade ahead.

I discuss this issue in more depth in Chapter 8, where I tackle the measures needed to get us out of the mess we are in. Here I will confine myself to saying that although quantitative easing has already been deployed on an apparently massive scale, I suspect that this will not be enough, and central banks will be reluctant to push the policy to the extreme. The result could easily be a bout of deflation, which could rumble on for a few years.

Moreover, the economy could readily experience more than one burst of it. For the factors I discussed above that are pushing us toward deflation will not exert their full force simultaneously. It is quite possible that the end of the falls in commodity prices will cause measured headline inflation to pick up, just as the collapse of demand and rising unemployment are starting to bring falls in core inflation, accompanied by sharp downward pressure on pay. In that case, the initial bout of deflation would be followed by a low rate of inflation, followed by deflation, followed by – who knows what.

It is important for people not to be taken in by the end of the first bout of deflation and not to be persuaded that the deflation danger is over. The deflationary threat will be grumbling along for a good time yet.

The new policy regime

This will be all the more likely if the monetary policy regime changes in the way I expect. I am going to discuss the desirable and likely future policy regime in Chapter 9. But at the risk of letting the cat out of the bag, I must say something here. Straightforward targeting of the CPI with no special regard to asset prices looks to be merely a staging post on the way to a new policy regime. Having been through what we have experienced, the Greenspan doctrine (which I explained in Chapter 1) is dead. Bubbles are *so* last year.

If I am right about the coming policy regime, the result will be that when, at some point in the future, asset prices start to show signs of a boom, the monetary authorities will seek to suppress them again, even if this implies consumer price inflation turning negative. The implication would be greater instability of inflation in the short run – sometimes plus 1%, 2%, or 3%, and sometimes *minus* 1%, 2%, or 3%, in the interests of greater stability, more broadly defined, in the medium term. If I am right, moderate deflation will become part of our normal experience.

However, to emphasize the point with which I started, this does not mean that we can forget about inflation. Although *The Death of Inflation* was a good title it upset quite a few policymakers, several of whom reacted as though they thought the booksellers who had listed it under the fiction section had got it right after all. Surely, they said, inflation cannot be dead in the sense that it could never reappear? Of course not. There is a continuing danger of inflation; there always is.

Yet a resurgence of inflation doesn't look likely any time soon. Even if we experience a commodity-induced bout of high inflation in 2010 or 2011, and even though we will always need to keep the supplies of stakes and garlic at the ready, to my mind inflation looks like giving the appearance of being dead for many years to come. Wouldn't it be ironic if, just as the monetarist back-woodsmen were stirring up renewed anxiety about inflation, the world were to fall into its first experience of sustained price *deflation* since the 1930s?

It would be ironic, but it wouldn't be nice. It would heighten the chances of experiencing an extended economic downturn, reminiscent of the Great Depression. That is why, in Part III, I lay out an approach to boosting aggregate demand and forestalling deflation. However, before we go on to discuss the treatment, we need to establish just how sick the patient is. Sticking plasters are fine for superficial cuts and grazes, but they are absolutely useless in cases of severe internal bleeding. What has happened to the world economy is not minor and it is not accidental. The Great Implosion, and the possible deflationary, or inflationary, dangers yet to come, are the direct result of a profound weakness in our economic system – the trouble with markets.

Part II

The Trouble with Markets

4

Where Markets Work Well – and Where They Don't

What is the market? It is the law of the jungle, the law of nature. And what is civilization? It is the struggle against nature.

Edouard Balladur, Prime Minister of France, 1993[1]

Capitalism is the worst system of economic governance ever invented – apart from all the others.

With apologies to Winston Churchill[2]

As the financial system imploded in 2007/9, the people who always say that this is the end of capitalism as we know it said that this is the end of capitalism as we know it. And, for once, you could see why. With the world plunging into a serious recession, accompanied by financial collapse and perhaps by deflation, things were most definitely in a parlous state.

This doesn't *necessarily* bring a threat to capitalism itself, though. After all, at some stage the financial system will be fixed, demand will revive, the economy will recover, the deflation threat will fade, economic growth will resume, and unemployment will fall back. At some point, even property prices will rise. Indeed, by the time you read this, these things may already have happened. So what is all the fuss about?

I reckon that this time, finally, those people who always see an existential threat to capitalism are right. Sometimes the world goes through a step-shift. Just as the experiences of the 1930s and the Second World War ushered in a period of managed capitalism, which attempted to marry individualism and collectivism, and the fall of the Berlin Wall in 1989 signaled the collapse of communism and the complete ascendancy of libertarian thinking, so the world is at a major turning point now. Even an early economic recovery will not enable the forces for change to be withstood. One way or another, the boundaries between markets and the state are being redrawn.

The financial markets are the cutting edge of capitalism: competitive, innovative, influential – and hugely successful. If their success turns out to have been a fraud, what can this say about the rest of the market economy?

Yet we all have a huge stake in the survival of the market economy. It has been the fount of our prosperity – and it still is. It isn't perfect, but it never has been. Indeed, market economies suffer from several serious problems, which governments have dealt with by some form of intervention or control. What is more, these interventions and controls led to the market economy becoming, on the whole, more successful than ever.

So the conventional, classically inspired, textbook version of capitalism, free and uncontrolled, has all along been a fairytale. But finance capitalism has enacted the fairytale in real life – complete with witches, hobgoblins and wicked stepfathers – although without the fairy godmother. In what follows, I show the range of interventions and controls that is necessary to make the market economy work in practice, as distinct from in the simple textbook. I also highlight latent weaknesses in the market system that western societies still haven't adequately addressed.

Paying close regard to the model of human beings and human society used in these textbooks really matters because it has been, and still is, hugely influential in society.[3] Specifically:

- The discrepancies between the theory and the reality explain why the financial structure that led to the Great Implosion developed.
- Belief in the textbook version persuaded the authorities to allow the financial markets to do their own thing.
- Belief in the textbook version has persuaded many people that the apparent success of the financial markets offers a blueprint for how the rest of society should be structured.
- Belief in the textbook version stands in the way of the successful reform of the system.
- Belief in the textbook version as some pure form to which society should aspire stands in the way of developing a more humane form of capitalism better suited to humanity's true nature and to our needs in the twenty-first century.

In what follows, I describe the market system's great strengths, which make it so important that we save it from the threats it now faces. I also lay out its serious weaknesses, from which we need the state to rescue us. In the next chapter, I show how finance capitalism, the quintessence of the fairytale, has brought the reality close to disaster. In Part III, I show how the system can yet enjoy a happy ending. Both capitalism and the problems that it throws up are continually changing, so the place to start is with the history.

The evolution of capitalism

If you listened to the business school professoriat, you could readily be forgiven for believing that the system we call capitalism, otherwise known as the *market economy*, was not only the natural state of affairs for humankind but also the eternal one – here since the beginning of time and destined to govern our economic affairs until the crack of doom. Of course, we cannot be sure about the future, so perhaps the forward-looking aspect of this view will be proved right. Perhaps. But we can be sure about the past, and on that it is most definitely wrong.

Although there have been economic transactions since the beginning of society, the market economy as such did not develop in Europe until between the fifteenth and eighteenth centuries. Obviously there was money before this time, and there was wealth. And there was the usual panoply of motivations and emotions associated with these things, including ambition, greed, envy, and covetousness. There were even some people in precapitalist times who became rich through the pursuit of profit.

But this is not enough to make a market economy. That involves the dominance of market relations; that is, relations where economic activities and transactions are driven by the pursuit of gain. This was largely frowned on in the ancient world, as it was under feudalism in the postclassical, precapitalist world. As Robert Heilbroner put it: "The profit motive, we are constantly being told, is as old as man himself. But it is not. The profit motive as we know it is only as old as modern man."[4]

Merchant adventurers have also existed for thousands of years, but they were the exception rather than the rule. Indeed, in the Middle Ages the

Church's teaching was that no Christian should be a merchant. Although it has been argued that the advent of Protestantism was a prerequisite for the rise of capitalism, according to Heilbroner, the Pilgrim Fathers who set foot in America in 1620 would have regarded the idea that the pursuit of gain was a tolerable aim in life as "nothing short of the doctrine of the devil."

When the market economy did emerge, it did not sprout up fully grown but rather evolved gradually over time. After all, even in nineteenth-century Europe, agricultural production was dominated by propertied families who owned large tracts of land that had been inherited, and treated as a patrimony, rather than priced and dealt in as a factor of production. Meanwhile, large numbers of agricultural workers – although they were not serfs and might own some land themselves – were in practice tied to a locality. They lived a life in close association with their fellows and with their "betters," the lords and squires, who similarly felt ties of loyalty to land and people.[5]

For the economy to be fairly described as a market system, both the factors of production – land, labor, and capital – and the goods and services they produce have to be transacted in markets. It must have been well into the nineteenth century before this was true of most economic activity in Europe. Even in Britain, the location of what has been termed the "Great Transformation" and where the market extended furthest, there were large parts of society beyond its reach.[6]

Ownership changes

Moreover, the ownership structure of business was very different from today until late in the nineteenth century, even in Britain. The joint stock company, one of modern capitalism's vital components, began with the East India Company in 1600, but it wasn't until the 1880s that this became the dominant corporate organization in Britain, as an increasing number of established, family-owned companies converted to joint stock form. Guinness, which converted in 1886, is a famous example.

Yet there was another transformation of ownership that had to be passed through to reach today's position. For at first the new joint stock companies were owned by large numbers of individuals. The predominance of *institutional*, as opposed to individual, ownership of shares, another key characteristic of modern capitalism, did not really begin to be established until well after the Second World War. In all major countries at the end of the war, a majority of shares were still owned directly by individuals. In America, the percentage was over 90%. In the UK, the percentage was still 60% in 1957.

By contrast, individuals now own a pretty small proportion – about 28% in the US, 15% in the UK, and less than 20% in Japan. Pretty much everywhere, the counterpart to the falling percentage holdings by individuals has been increases for pension funds, insurance companies, mutual funds, business corporations, and foreigners – most of whom would have been these same categories of investor, only domiciled abroad.

The historical record

Even in the part of the world where its hold was strongest – principally the British Empire and the United States – the period when capitalism was both dominant and pretty much unfettered was extremely short: at most 100 years, and probably more like 50 years, from the mid to late nineteenth century to the outbreak of the First World War. I hesitate to call this the Golden Age of Capitalism, but it was at least the relatively pure age. Government interference in its mechanisms was minimal to nonexistent. Government expenditure itself was minimal: about 7% of GDP in America and 10% in Britain.[7] There was no use of fiscal policy to manage aggregate demand; indeed, no fiscal policy at all, other than the objective of reducing the interest burden of the national debt and balancing the budget.

Moreover, the blunting and distorting of incentives through taxation were at a minimum. During the second half of the nineteenth century in the UK, income tax was rarely above 3% and only applied to incomes well above the average. In the United States, income tax was introduced in 1862 – and abolished in 1872. There was no inheritance tax anywhere in the developed world.

Nor was there monetary policy as we know it. Most countries were on the Gold Standard, which meant that the objective of central banks was simply to maintain exchangeability into gold at a fixed exchange rate. America did not even have a central bank.

Virtually nowhere did the state own or direct industries. Outside the British Empire (which followed a policy of free trade), the state did actively interfere in international trade, but apart from this it did not interfere in the workings of markets. Antimonopoly legislation was not introduced in America until 1890 and, in a formal manner, in the UK not until 1948.[8]

The result of this capitalist nirvana was an average annual rate of growth of per capita GDP between 1850 and 1914 of 1.1% in France, 1.2% in Germany, 1.2% in Britain, and 1.5% in the US. By comparison with the pre-capitalist era, these growth rates were fantastic. As far as we can tell, from prehistoric times to 1500 the total growth in per capita incomes was about 50%, amounting to an average annual growth rate of next to nothing. Between 1500 and 1820 things were better: in western Europe the growth of per capita GDP may have reached the heady rate of about 0.2% a year.[9] So no wonder that the idea became widely established that capitalism was the bringer of prosperity, as Marx freely acknowledged. For him, capitalism was an undoubted advance on what had gone before, albeit just the forerunner of the perfection that was yet to come.

But the comparison between the capitalist nirvana and the period of managed capitalism after the Second World War is rather different. In the 25 years from 1950 to 1975, the average per capita growth rates were 3.7% for France, 4.6% in Germany, and 2.2% in Britain and the United States. Of course, you can attempt to dismiss the relevance of these postwar growth rates on the grounds that they reflected recovery from the devastation of the war – and they did. But as time rolled on, postwar reconstruction faded in importance, yet growth rates in the west, although lower than in the immediate postwar years, still exceeded those realized during the capitalist nirvana. Between 1975 and 2008 the average growth rate of per-capita GDP was 2% in the US, 2.1% in the UK, 1.6% in France, and 1.7% in Germany. These were well above nineteenth-century growth rates.

The ideological battle

Bearing in mind this record, how was it that in the 1980s the idea gained widespread acceptance that completely free markets and minimal government hold the key to prosperity? I think there are two reasons. First, this period saw the culmination of the Cold War. There was an ideological battle being fought between capitalism and communism. The result of this struggle was that a vital question was obscured: What *sort* of capitalism was best? In other words, recognizing that markets on the whole worked pretty well, which bits of a market system did not? And which bits required a helping – or restraining – hand from the state? In this regard it is significant that the novelist and philosopher Ayn Rand, who had such an influence on the young Alan Greenspan, was a Russian emigré, imbued with a hatred of the Soviet Union, whose fall she correctly foresaw.[10]

The second reason is that the system of managed capitalism had its serious crises, which suggested that in many cases state intervention had gone too far and the market mechanism had been enfeebled. There was evidence that high levels of welfare spending and heavy taxation had blunted the incentive to work in the UK and much of continental Europe. Germany, the home of the wonder economy of the postwar years, was now increasingly seen as the sick man of Europe. As regards the supply of labor and several other areas, what most western countries needed was not less of the market but more.

However, as so often in the world of ideas, things went further. The recognition that there had been excesses and failures during the era of managed capitalism led to the conclusion that the whole idea of managing it was wrong. Never mind "back to the future," "back to the past" was a more appropriate rallying call. And the past in question was the capitalist nirvana of the nineteenth century. Thus, an intellectual consensus was formed that dominated thinking among policymakers, analysts, journalists, central bankers, and thinkers of all sorts – and large parts of the general public. This new consensus threw the baby out with the bathwater.

The strengths of the market system

When it works well, the market system is a remarkable mechanism for utilizing scarce resources for productive ends – and for distributing the benefits far and wide across society. The essence of the market system is that free "agents" try to maximize their own "utility," or wellbeing, by comparing the market prices for goods and services with what they are worth to them. Buyers buy when their own expected utility is greater than the price; sellers sell when the price is greater than their costs. Provided that prices are free to move, they will adjust to the competing forces of supply and demand. When demand exceeds supply, prices will be forced up. When supply exceeds demand, they will be forced down.

And these price changes will send signals to producers to bring the amount of the different goods and services that are produced into line with what people want, and to consumers to bring what they want into line with what it is possible to produce, given the constraints imposed by limited resources and existing technology. In essence, this signaling mechanism enables the market system to wring the most out of any economic situation – not the best of all possible worlds, but the best possible result in the circumstances.

The mechanism has two drivers: self-interest and competition. Self-interest drives "economic agents" to try to gain the most they can from any situation, and competition works to constrain how much they actually get. The success of the market mechanism depends on a continual interplay between these forces. Firms try to use any new technological advance or economic change as a way of boosting their profits; the chance of doing this acts as a spur to seek improvements in efficiency and advances in technology. But as competition subsequently eats away any advantage they are temporarily able to acquire, the benefits are spread throughout society through lower prices.

Thus, although Marx saw capitalism as a system that would eventually lead to the impoverishment of the masses, in practice it has done exactly the reverse. Not only did the market system enable the enrichment of millions of ordinary people in the west in the nineteenth and twentieth centuries, but more recently it has enabled hundreds of millions of people to emerge from abject poverty in China and most of Southeast Asia.

The freedom connection

In addition, capitalist economies have on the whole been free, and more recently fully democratic, societies, whereas socialist ones have not. There are some exceptions and qualifications. China has managed to embrace most of the market mechanisms of classic capitalism, albeit in controlled form, but no one in their right mind could accuse it of being a democracy. But I cannot think of a single example of a centrally planned economy that has also sustained a real democracy.

This is not accidental. In a socially owned and centrally planned economy, every individual's livelihood is directly or indirectly dependent on the state. Even if a system like this could be a democracy in a narrow sense, it is difficult to see how it could preserve the basic institutions of freedom, including the rule of law and the independence of the judiciary. Accordingly, even if the system we call capitalism were not the most economically efficient and dynamic of arrangements for governing our economic affairs, there would be a strong argument for it on grounds of freedom and justice alone.

It would be an overstatement to say that, as an explanation for the advance of humankind and the triumph of the west over the last 200 years, the nexus between markets, democracy, and freedom was the truth, the whole truth, and nothing but the truth. But it would not be an overstatement to say that it was both mostly true and most of the truth.

Market weaknesses

Despite the overwhelming theoretical support and practical confirmation of the efficiency of markets in general, both economic theory and practical experience have established a long list of cases where markets, free and unfettered, bring inefficiency.

◆ Left to their own devices, markets develop anticompetitive structures and behavior. Adam Smith, the eighteenth-century economist and philosopher, who can justifiably be regarded as the father of Economics and is widely believed to have first convincingly argued the case for free markets, himself recognized as much. He wrote: "People of the same trade seldom meet together, even for merriment and diversion, but the conversation ends in a conspiracy against the public, or in some contrivance to raise prices."[11] It is all very well lauding the model of competitive markets, but the evidence overwhelmingly supports the conclusion that in modern conditions such a system cannot survive without state intervention to preserve it. So "free" markets can be the very opposite of competitive markets.

♦ Nowhere is this more true than in the labor market. There is a natural tendency on the part of labor to combine by forming trade unions, often across whole industries or even several, which thereby can acquire and exercise a dominating influence over individual firms. Only the state can preserve the semblance of a competitive labor market by restricting unions' activities through the power of the law.

♦ There are many activities that are natural monopolies, or near monopolies, such as water provision or rail travel. Where these exist, the only options are unrestricted private monopolies that charge high prices and thereby limit usage, wasteful duplication of infrastructure as firms try to compete, state ownership and control, or private ownership regulated by the state.

♦ There is a series of aspects of society where individual activity creates an effect on others that is not taken account of when the individual decides to undertake the action, make the purchase, or whatever. Such effects economists term "externalities," reflecting the idea that the effects are external to the person making the decision. Examples include all sorts of pollution,[12] and the various activities that are thought to contribute to global warming. Where such externalities exist, it is hopeless to expect the market, driven as it is by self-interest, to produce an efficient solution.

♦ There are some situations where self-interested individuals or firms interacting with others will produce an inferior outcome for all and where the only way to reach the optimum solution is to cooperate. (This is known in the economics literature as the "prisoner's dilemma.")

♦ There is a series of public goods where the market, unaided, cannot facilitate adequate provision (or in some cases any at all), because the goods in question need to be provided for everyone. The classic example is defense against foreign attack.

♦ Similarly, there are public bads, such as disease. Public health cannot adequately be protected by the market.[13]

♦ In some cases, notably where the far future is involved, or where rational decision making involves making a careful assessment of risks, or in the weighing up of immediate pleasure against subsequent pain, individuals often make decisions that are not in their own interest.

◆ Often buyers and sellers have asymmetric information, and this distorts transactions between them.

◆ Although it is presumed that in general adults are the best judges of their own interests, children are not in a position to make informed, rational decisions.

◆ Some activities, even though they are freely entered into by consenting adults, may be deemed immoral and may be made illegal. Indeed, more generally, where there is a moral aspect involved it may be appropriate to restrict markets, or to put an activity outside the market realm, either because the use of the market mechanism may corrupt or degrade, or because market incentives are actually less efficient than reliance on moral suasion.[14]

These defects in the market mechanism are serious, but they are also fairly tractable. The way in which capitalist societies have dealt with them has been to modify or restrict the market, either through regulation and price control, through the imposition of taxes and subsidies, or through the outright prohibition of "bads" and the public provision of "goods." The existence of these defects does not present some fatal challenge to the market system in practice, but it does represent a challenge to the pure market system in theory. The idea that we would all be better off if the market were left completely alone has no support from the evidence, simply because no modern society has ever tried this – and with very good reason. Yet many of these defects find expression in the financial markets and are a leading source of its failings, as I shall discuss in the next chapter.

Fairness and solidarity

There is another layer of intervention that occurs for different reasons. Efficiency does not necessarily gel with fairness, and the market system may readily produce a distribution of income that seems unfair or unjust.

Moreover, the conflict, bad feeling, and lack of solidarity to which such an income distribution gives rise may well mean that in the long run it is not only unjust, but inefficient as well. Accordingly, it is common practice in capitalist countries for the state to seek to flatten the distribution of income that would emerge if market forces were left completely untrammeled.

This has a clear connection to the current situation with regard to bankers' pay, which I will discuss in the next chapter.

The macro problem

But there is a potentially much more serious defect in the market system. This is the macro problem; that is, the Keynesian problem of how all these self-interested agents interact and how the economic system behaves *as a whole*. The classical economists didn't see that there was any such problem. They argued that if people decided to save more, this increased desire to provide for the future would be transmitted through the financial markets and emerge the other side as an increased preparedness to invest.

The composition of GDP would change, to be sure: more people employed on construction sites and building machines for factories and fewer dishing out bread and arranging circuses. But no matter. The overall system would be fine. So where's the problem?[15]

The problem, as Keynes so brilliantly exposed, is that in a money economy, people do not experience the increase in desired savings as an increased desire, or need, to invest. Admittedly, the act of saving results in an increased flow of money into financial balances. However, the act of nonspending (the same thing) results in an increased *need for* finance on the part of all those people who used to benefit from the spending that has now been cut back. So the increased *supply* of finance is met by an increased *demand* for finance. There is no downward pressure on interest rates and no direct incentive for people to invest more.

Indeed, quite the reverse. With consumer demand falling, many prospective investors will hold back, for fear that their projects will not meet with adequate final demand. Thus the downward impulse to demand is compounded.

The Keynesian challenge

This insight of Keynes was a bombshell. I think it is still not properly understood today.[16] The first part of the Keynesian message is disturbing enough: if
something should occur to depress aggregate demand, then men and machines
will lie idle "through no fault of their own." But the second part should be
more disturbing still to the defenders of the market system. Once aggregate
demand has fallen, men will not readily be able to get themselves back into
employment by virtue alone; that is, as the result of their own efforts.

The reason is that the real wage for which men were prepared to work
before – and, by assumption, still are – is now too high for their employers
to be able to employ them, for the simple reason that the employers cannot
sell their output. They cannot sell their output because everyone else is in the
same position. Every economic agent is caught in a trap that is not of their
own making. This is a macro problem *par excellence*.

When you think about it, this message is really subversive, because macro
problems require macro solutions and that implies the need for collective, as
opposed to individual, action. Moreover, if things go badly wrong on the
macro front, all the stuff that Adam Smith was banging on about – economies
of scale, competition, and the invisible hand – are simply overwhelmed in a
sea of unemployment.

The implication is that if full employment is to be restored after a fall in
aggregate demand, it may require deliberate action by the policy authorities
to reduce interest rates, expand the money supply, cut taxes, or increase government spending. No wonder that so many orthodox economists found
Keynesian economics so threatening, and no wonder that they spent so much
effort in trying to neutralize it.

This they did by bastardizing and emasculating it, with the result that the
readers of a standard macroeconomics textbook today can imagine that the
Keynesian message amounts only to a different view about the coefficients
in a few equations – something that the econometricians ought to be able to
sort out, given sufficient time to apply the instruments of torture to the data.
In fact, though, the full understanding of Keynes' discovery of the macro
problem drives a sword through the heart of the case for laisser-faire.

This is of clear relevance to today's crisis. As I shall explain in Chapter 6, at a global level there has been a huge increase in the overall desire to save, as reflected in the emergence of large trade surpluses in Asia and elsewhere. This has not caused an offsetting increase in desired investment in the west. Instead, it induced policymakers to cut interest rates, which stimulated consumption and led to the bubble. And the Great Implosion has itself landed us with the macro problem, with a vengeance. As I shall argue in the next chapter, the financial system's ability to create the macro problem of depressed demand, or to make a macro problem that originates elsewhere a great deal worse, means that it simply cannot be left to its own devices.

On the practical front, until recently anyway, defenders of classical purity were able to take refuge in the notion that whatever relevance Keynes' message had for the 1930s, it was now simply old hat. Yet, as both Japanese experience in the 1990s and experience now with the Great Implosion amply testify, this is simply not true. The macro problem is still very much with us and it always will be. Moreover, as I shall argue in Chapter 8, it requires a Keynesian solution.

Human nature

If Keynes brilliantly uncovered the latent macro problem within the market system, he left more or less undisturbed two deep problems within its micro structure; that is, with the two drivers of the market system, self-interest and competition.[17] In some ways, these problems are more troubling for the free market model. They have played a major part in the failings of financial markets, which contributed to the Great Implosion. And addressing them will form a major part of what needs to be done to reform the capitalist system, both to make it more robust and efficient and to make it more acceptable to modern man.

Economics is based on a very particular view of human nature, embodied in the idea of *homo economicus*, the individual who makes the self-interested, rational decisions on which the success of the system depends, acting in competition with other individuals who behave in the same way.

His motivations are plain and simple: he is a utility-maximizing machine, trying to increase pleasure and reduce pain, without limit, and without regard for anyone else. H*omo economicus* is a bloodless, artificial creature who is remarkable in at least one major respect. Although, to the best of my knowledge, he has never set foot on the earth, he has nevertheless left huge footprints all over society.

In fact, society is obviously not completely atomistic in the way that this crude, individualistic world view implies. For at the very bedrock of society is not the individual but the family. Many actions are undertaken that do not seem to be in the direct interest of the actively engaged "economic agent," but are rather in the interest of her family as a whole.

For the purveyors of the pure, rational, self-interested model, superficially at least, this seems to pose no problem. Whatever actions and motivations they wanted to ascribe to individuals they now simply ascribe to families or households, and the same inexorable logic applies. Or, at least, they think it does. However, the family is a mini-collective and the supposedly atomistic individual is now seen to make decisions in the interests of the collective. And, as we shall see in a moment, there is another collective right at the heart of the market economy.

There is no doubt that *homo economicus* is a simplifying assumption that yields results of analytical value and frequent applicability. But as an attempt at a total description of what drives human beings, there is also no doubt that it is profoundly misleading. There are two problems: the first concerns rationality and the second concerns motivation.

Homo economicus is both rational and far-sighted. However, real people are different. Economists and psychologists have proved that people are often inconsistent and are frequently befuddled and confused. Moreover, they fail to take account of future consequences. Often such behavior is not the result of not *seeing* the future consequences, but rather of choosing not to act on what is seen – people who want to lose weight but always want to start the diet tomorrow; or people who want to give up smoking but always need the next cigarette.

The apparent myopia individuals typically exhibit is not always irrational. The fact that people have limited life spans has major implications. It imparts to our lives, including our financial lives, a certain shape, rhythm, and sense of time, even a sense of urgency.

Self and social

The selfish nature of *homo economicus* immediately runs up against a key problem. Human beings are both individuals and social creatures. Being social, how can their motivations be purely individual?

Some of this social aspect is far from altruistic. Much of people's motivation for advancement is driven not by their desire for an absolute amount of something or other, but rather by their desire to have more than someone else in the group. Sometimes their motivation is to have broadly the *same*, and indeed to *be* broadly the same, as other members of the group, in order to gain acceptability. The evidence is overwhelming that relativity is the key to much human activity – and also to much human happiness.[18]

The social factor even applies to what people *think*. Believing the same thing as other people makes life easier. Holding unconventional views can be isolating. As I shall show in the next chapter, this is of major relevance to financial markets.

There is a host of other examples of group influences that *do* reflect altruistic motivations. Some people freely give their blood. Others risk their lives for no monetary reward, crewing lifeboats that set to sea to save drowning people. The only reason can be because they care about others and derive satisfaction and pride from putting that care into practical effect.[19]

Sometimes selfless acts are small, sometimes they are enormous. But even the small ones can make a big impact. I am reminded of the time my friends Walter and Doreen Newlyn, traveling in their motorized caravan, broke down in a remote part of Scotland with the mists swirling about and no telephone available to call for help. They were at the point of despair when out of the mist appeared Robbie, a crofter, who repaired their vehicle and eventually sent them on their way. Much though Walter and Doreen pleaded with Robbie to accept some payment for his considerable time and effort, he would have none of it. They had been strangers in need and he had merely done his duty and helped.[20] Evidently Robbie was not *homo economicus*.

At the other end of the spectrum, it is well known that parents will often make great sacrifices for their children – including, *in extremis*, laying down their lives. But let us not forget the phenomenon of huge numbers of people *volunteering* to fight in wars, and in the course of fighting often taking

enormous risks to save their comrades. This is exactly what my father, a ser-
geant in the Royal Fusiliers, did in the First World War, and the injury he sustained in the process plagued him for the rest of his life. What did he feel
about what had happened? Pride, perhaps. He wouldn't say. Certainly, he
never complained about what had happened to him. As for his superiors, the
young officers who led their men "over the top" to face a hail of bullets and
near-certain death in the battles of Ypres and the Somme, whose *utility* do
you suppose they were maximizing?

Money matters

For some people, making money and spending it on themselves is an overwhelming obsession and hardly anything else counts. This appears to be an
apt description of many an investment banker, for whom the condition often
seems to amount to a mental disorder. Nevertheless, the idea that everyone
is driven by an insatiable lust for money and material consumption is ludi-
crously crude. At the sharp end of the economy, for its real creators and drivers, the entrepreneurs and the inventors, money is seldom the driving force.
What drives them is the sheer pleasure of creation, the joy of envisaging
doing and developing something and then working to make it happen. Money
is usually no more than a way of keeping score.

Or consider the motivation of professionals, such as teachers, doctors,
lawyers, social workers, or soldiers. Are they interested in making money?
Of course they are. Are they *only* interested in making money? Usually not.
(Although I have my doubts about the lawyers!) This comes down to pride
and professionalism. Most people in these walks of life want to provide a
good service because they are proud of what they do.

In the case of the older, established professions, such attitudes and behavior are enshrined in professional codes of conduct. Failure to conduct yourself
appropriately risks not only loss of self-respect but also, additionally, loss of
reputation, or even loss of the right to practice. We don't normally think of
similar factors affecting manual workers – and there usually aren't the same
formal group structures to act as sources of approbation or disapproval.
Doubtless many unskilled workers performing their humdrum tasks are
scarcely conscious of how well or badly they are doing them, but in principle,

pride or shame can be experienced by every simple workman doing something that can be done well or badly.

The most telling encapsulation of these points about motivation and the role of self-seeking behavior comes from the ghastly events of September 11, 2001 in New York. The image that really sticks in my mind is of the blue-collared members of the New York City fire service, making their way up the smoke-filled staircases of the remaining twin tower, to try to save lives, as so many white-collared "masters of the universe" made their way down. Bonuses? Utility maximization? Not for the fire crew. They were simply doing their job. If they had feelings at the time beyond sheer fear, they were surely feelings of duty. And for those who came back, besides the feelings of relief – and grief – there were surely also feelings of pride.

Split personality

Believers in the pure textbook model have a way of reconciling their creature, *homo economicus*, with the characteristics of actual people who don't quite conform to it. They say that man behaves like *homo economicus* for part of the time, principally his working time, but outside those hours he is free to be more roundedly human – to be generous and caring and to be a responsible citizen. But when he steps back into the office or factory, or when he goes shopping, he puts these aspects of his nature to one side, rather as though he were changing clothes, and becomes *homo economicus* again.

This split personality is psychologically implausible. When human beings are obliged to behave this way they become depressed, or even mentally ill. The natural thing is to be more roundedly human all the time. Of course, this means a good deal of selfish, self-seeking behavior at work; how could it be otherwise? Humans have these tendencies hard-wired into their nature. But this does not mean that workers should be hostile or even indifferent to their colleagues; quite the opposite. The workplace is an important social center, perhaps the most important such center in most western societies.

Moreover, the people working in an enterprise, both foot soldiers and sen-ior management, do not have to see themselves in an adversarial relationship to their customers. On the contrary, in the best companies, both the employees and the individuals owning and running them derive feelings of satisfaction and pride from knowing that their customers feel happy with the good or service they have bought from them.

Furthermore, it is not that having feelings of this sort necessarily costs a person, or a business, money; often quite the opposite. The crude model of the market system has profit as the driver, but in practice, even if profit is the ultimate motivation, it is probably best not to aim for it directly. Rather like happiness, it is most likely to emerge as the by-product of pursuing something else for its own sake.

The creative and the distributive

If economic theory's essential idea of what human beings are really like is flawed, so also is its central idea about how they relate to each other, and how economic activity is best organized.

The whole of economic life is a mixture of *creative* and *distributive* activities. Some of what we consume is created out of nothing and adds to the total available for all to enjoy; but some of it merely takes what would otherwise be available to others and therefore comes at their expense.

At any given stage of economic development, successful societies maximize the creative and minimize the distributive. Societies where everyone can only achieve gains at the expense of others are by definition impoverished. They are also usually intensely violent.

Imagine a man living on his own in a subsistence economy. He collects berries and nuts, and he hunts and fishes. Everything he produces is his. There is no one else whose income he could redistribute to himself. Everything he does is *creative*. Once other people appear in the region, however, even if he has no direct economic interaction with them, the distributive issue rears its head. The berries and nuts he collects could be collected by someone else.

Things are more complicated if some of these hunter-gatherers combine their efforts. Once people start to work together, whether in hunter-gathering or in production from the land, the combined output should rise, because of the benefits of specialization described, and lauded, by Adam Smith.

If they compete to see who can work hardest and hence justify the highest reward, this could lead to them having even more for both to enjoy. But if they compete by arguing about who should get what share of their combined output, this will tend to reduce it. And if one is allowed to steal the other's, there is no incentive for either to do any work at all.

Competition in modern society

In a modern society, the scope for distributive gains is enormous. You go for an interview for a job; you get it; you celebrate. In reality, though, there is no direct gain for society as a whole. There is one job and umpteen candidates. You have succeeded and someone else has failed. Net, net – zero. And the same applies to firms competing for business.

So why do we encourage competition? Because we reason, and experience confirms, that such competitive behavior generally works to enhance overall performance and output. That is, after all, why capitalist societies have achieved higher levels of material success than socialist ones.

The more developed a society becomes, the more it stands to gain from harnessing competition to foster behavior that increases total output. But also, the more at risk it is of behavior that merely redistributes rather than creates. When taken to extremes, such behavior can reduce the total amount of output. In some cases, the really clever thing for a society is to get individuals and families competing over the extent to which they contribute to the public weal. This was brilliantly achieved in Renaissance Venice. The leading families regarded how many and how powerful were the galleys they financed for the defense of the republic as a matter of pride and prestige (which might lead to subsequent advantage).[21]

The creative/distributive spectrum

Let's think about the spectrum of jobs available in today's society. Consider the doctor tending to a patient or the midwife helping to deliver a baby. Everything they do is creative rather than distributive. Interestingly, the same is not true of teachers. They are further along the spectrum toward distributive gains. Some, perhaps most, of what they do is devoted to enhancing the objective capacities of their charges, the pupils. But much of it is about advancing the interests and life chances of their charges against those of other teachers.

Or consider the marketing executive for a washing powder manufacturer. Her job is pretty much purely distributive. It is to do her best to ensure that her company sells more washing powder than its rivals. If she succeeds, the rewards will be greater for her and her company. But her success will be mirrored by other companies doing badly. Her contribution is purely distributive. Nevertheless, her work can create value for society at large if it ensures that the best company "wins," or at least if it ensures that no one company can dominate the market and thereby behave against the public interest.

Most jobs are a mixture of these two extremes. There are some people who may derive active delight from the knowledge that their working life is devoted to making sure that someone else loses, but most people do not function that way. They like to have a sense of worth, and that sense usually comes from the belief that they are contributing to society. This is why people with jobs with a higher creative content will often be happier than those who have jobs with a lower creative content, even though the latter may earn much more money.

You could say, I suppose, that this is why traders need and "deserve" so much more: their job is so mind-numbingly boring that only the money justifies it, and they need bucketloads of the stuff to dull the pain. Perhaps this explains why so many banks euphemistically refer to the pay of their employees as "compensation" – and why they give them so much of it. There is much that they need to be compensated for.

The nature of the firm

So, rather than allowing or encouraging a competitive free-for-all, finding the right balance between competitive and noncompetitive elements is central to the success of society. Moreover, this balance is at the heart of the institution that is ubiquitous in the market economy and central to its success: namely, the firm.

Why do firms exist? Why isn't the economy characterized by a vast array of competing *individuals*, or at least families?[22] Adam Smith's famous pin factory appears to be organized as a single firm. The several processes involved in making pins, which are split between different people in order to benefit from the division of labor, are held together in a *collective* enterprise. Although it is possible to imagine each worker being self-employed and negotiating prices with the other workers in the factory, this would be a practical nightmare that would introduce countless inefficiencies and lead to lower output. This is true across the economy as a whole.

At the other extreme, it would be possible to imagine the whole economy being run as one giant firm – but it wouldn't work very well. In many ways this is exactly what the communist system was all about, and it *didn't* work very well.

So the great paradox, whose profound importance is not fully appreciated by so many supporters of the competitive ideal, is that the market economy is not a sea of atomistic individuals, avidly competing with each other, but rather a mixture of *competition* between firms, and *cooperation*, or even *command and control*, within them. Moreover, this structure exists because it is efficient. As the economist Ronald Coase explained, the firm ends where, at the margin, cooperative or command-and-control systems become less efficient than arm's-length, competitive market relations.

Motivation and togetherness

The advantages of this collective at the very heart of the market economy are not merely a matter of the engineering aspects of economic processes. They are intimately bound up with the softer, touchy-feely stuff to do with group identity and individual motivation.

It is very striking that firms often strive to inculcate "team spirit" in their staff, and try to foster a distinctive corporate culture and identity. This is sometimes taken to extremes by Japanese companies, with their company songs and corporate exercise sessions, but in a lesser way most western companies try to do something similar. The reason is clear: they want their employees to be working cooperatively rather than competitively. They know that workers who have a strong bond with their colleagues tend to be happier, and happier employees make better workers.

One of the clear signs of a dysfunctional company is where the constituent parts are effectively fighting against each other. In essence, what is happening is that people are behaving to others inside the company as though they were outside it; if you like, behaving as though they were not "family." Where this happens, it may be because the effective boundary between competition and cooperation has changed and needs to be redrawn. Or it may simply be because this particular firm is badly run, so that the bonds that may bind people together are not fostered and maintained.

The theoretician can try to neutralize the significance of the existence of firms by assuming that the firm behaves just like an individual – effectively collapsing its collective identity into a single profit-maximizing whole – but this really won't wash. Companies are social constructs. How people employed in them behave is a social phenomenon. And how companies do and should behave in relation to the rest of society is also a social question. Companies are part of the institutional structure of society. Institutions matter. About this, the desiccated, inhuman, utility-maximizing machine that is *homo economicus* has nothing to say. I have a good deal to say about it in a moment.

Instability and insecurity

I have argued that there are serious problems with economic theory's version of what makes people tick and the role of competition. There is another problem arising from the interaction of the two. It is paradoxical that the basic models of perfect markets are completely static, yet the very essence of the market economy in practice is change. The economic growth the market system produces creates change – and the market system is good at adapting to change that occurs from this or other sources. However, there is a limit to the amount of change that human beings can reasonably take – and a lower limit to the amount of change that they actually *like*.

There are countless examples of people spending umpteen years acquiring skills that the progress of technology or competition from outside sources renders either obsolete or sharply reduced in value. In the pure market system such people are left to make their way as best they can – or not. The knowledge that such a fate can befall you will act as a spur to acquire the "right" skills, or even to acquire several rather than just one. But it is difficult for anyone of conscience and sensitivity to argue that as a matter of justice, in a rich, developed society, people whose livelihood is lost or destroyed as a result of unforeseen change should simply have to put up with the consequences without any form of support.

Of course, some change is desirable, sometimes even longed for, to stave off boredom. But there are limits. Humans' dislike of change goes deeper than mere fear of material loss. We appear to have an innate attachment to people, places, and activities, and we wish to measure the progress through our life against fixed points described by such things. So it is that people form lifelong attachments to colleges, regiments, villages, or sports teams.

Because of their role as generators of status, position, pride, and social activity, as well as simple providers of money, *businesses* can also inspire such feelings in people. Karl Marx talked about the alienation of workers from their activities because, under capitalism, they were treated as mere cannon fodder in the productive process. In much of the capitalist system, at least until recently, workers, both white collar and manual, have in fact come to feel rather the reverse; that is, positive *identification* with their working activities and place of work. After all, that is why, above and beyond mere loss of material wellbeing, unemployment often brings such misery and loss of self-esteem.

So the unpredictable dynamic of capitalism, the creative destruction that is the source of much material prosperity, is also at the root of so much human unhappiness. This is surely one of the reasons why globalization gives rise to such feelings of fear and loathing in many people. It is not just the threat to their material livelihoods that worries people, but the sense of all-consuming, never-stopping, uncaring change, which brings instability of structures and unquietness of mind.

How pay is not determined

Firms are the intermediating mechanism through which labor is supplied to the economy. I say "supplied," but this is an area where the market doesn't work the way it is supposed to. The reason is that it is very difficult to get effective markets in labor. Human beings and their social structures keep getting in the way.

Economists' supply curves, which relate the quantity of a good that will be supplied to the price at which it will be supplied, give the impression that they are precise and mechanical. That may be true when you are dealing with the supply of a *thing*: how much wheat can be produced from a given amount of land, for instance. But when it comes to people, there is nothing mechanical about it at all. It is completely up in the air and it will depend critically on the feelings of the people involved. As with so many other things, these feelings will chiefly concern one's position relative to others, and associated concepts of "fairness."

The determination of pay is a fuzzy area at all levels, but the higher you go up the ladder the more serious the fuzziness becomes. There may be another individual out there somewhere in "the market" who could do a particular executive's job as well, or better, for less. But can you, the company's senior manager, take that risk?

In practice, although senior managers and chief executives are sometimes defenestrated, this is almost always because of some supposed mistake, policy disagreement, or "personality clash" – almost never over the issue of pay. The CEO of a major company rarely leaves to join another in order to increase his or her remuneration package.

When you think of the absolute centrality of price in the way the market mechanism is supposed to work, this is astonishing. Contrast this situation with the ordinary market world. Those self-same companies who never fire a senior manager because he or she is too expensive relative to what is available in the market all the time make purchasing and sourcing decisions on exactly this criterion. All of us do this when we go shopping.

I address the question of how pay is determined in practice, and the implications this has for bankers' pay, in the next chapter.

The agency problem

Nevertheless, in a normally functioning economy, even if the market did not naturally set pay at a competitive level, you would surely expect the owners of corporations to exert their influence to this end, thereby increasing the profits of the firms they own and increasing the capital value of their investment.

In practice, such influence is usually not exerted. This is an example of the difficulties caused by what economists know as the "agency problem." In a modern market economy, most large firms are not run by their owners but by a professional management team that is nominally employed by the owners. The management supposedly acts in the interests of the owners. But in practice, with the managers in day-to-day control of the company and the owners typically diffuse and disorganized, as well as subject to their own problem of ownership at a distance, the managers are in a position of great power. This can amount to what the British minister Lord Myners has referred to as "the ownerless corporation."

The issue for the theory of how a capitalist economy is supposed to work is that, unless pressures are brought to bear on managers, they may run companies for their own benefit, or indeed for no one's, rather than for the benefit of shareholders. In this way the interaction of self-interest and competition will fail to deliver the goods for society as a whole.

Supposedly, the way to avert this danger is to rely on scrutiny by the shareholders who, after all, "employ" the managers, and to try to align the interests of managers and shareholders by granting the managers shares, share options, and various incentive schemes, in the hope that they will behave more like owners.

On the whole the "carrot" has not worked very well, because it has encouraged excessive attention to the short-term performance of the share price rather than the long-term health of the business. The "stick" has not worked very well either. There has been a significant problem with the shareholders who are supposed to wield it. In today's world, as I pointed out earlier, they are predominantly institutional funds of some sort – pension funds, insurance companies, and fund managers – acting on behalf of still more distant owners – the already, or soon-to-be, retired and the mythical Belgian dentist. These institutional funds are themselves run by management teams, who are in the same relationship to the ultimate owners as the managers of the companies they own are to them. We are back to the agency problem at one remove. Who guards the guards?

Moreover, institutional shareholders suffer from "liquidity fetishism," as Keynes called it; that is, an overemphasis on the ability to access invested capital at short notice. Yet resources invested in buildings and factories cannot be turned into holidays and haircuts. Real assets have long lives and cannot be liquidated without loss. And real businesses need to have long time horizons to be able to manage real assets well. So the creation of liquidity for individual investors, although it is a clever product of the financial system, shouldn't be taken too far.

Yet we have a financial structure where most institutional investors' holdings in companies are regarded as short-term trading chips, to be cashed in at will. Given this, why should we expect investing institutions to behave like owners, with a long-term interest in the management of the business? In general, they don't.

The fact that corporations are run in the interests of their managers, or in response to institutional shareholders' pressure for short-term share performance, affects not only the setting of executive pay but all aspects of major corporate decision taking, including those decisions that govern the level of real investment in plant, machinery, buildings, software, training, and skill acquisition. As I shall argue in the Conclusion, the result is too low a level of real investment.

Success despite failings

Accepting that the market system is better than any alternative, I have produced quite a list of failings. That the market system is not perfect should not come as a surprise. After all, the market is a human construct, and humanity is flawed. Even so, the extent of the market system's shortcomings compared to the theoretical ideal raises the question of why it has nevertheless been so successful, and so widely accepted, for so long.

My answer is fundamentally subversive. (If you are in the wrong company you must keep this thought to yourself, or whisper it quietly only to your friends.) In most western democracies, the market system has been so successful because it has been controlled.

This is the institutional and structural context in which finance capitalism has risen to dominance over the last 30 years. Its rise has been the quintessence of the free market ideal and free market thinking. Nevertheless, as I have shown, the free market ideal is a far cry from how the market economy has worked in practice.

The modifications and restrictions imposed on the market system by the state have been its vital supports. But, as I will show in the next chapter, the rise of finance capitalism has undermined these vital supports. If we are not careful, its fall could bring the whole superstructure crashing down on our heads.

5

Why Financial Markets Fail

I believe that banking institutions are more dangerous to our liberties than standing armies.

Thomas Jefferson, 1802

I have never adhered to the view that Wall Street is uniquely evil, just as I have never found it possible to accept with complete confidence the alternative view, rather more palatable in sound financial circles, that it is uniquely wise.

John Kenneth Galbraith, 1954[1]

I made a mistake in presuming that the self-interest of organizations, specifically banks and others, were such that they were best capable of protecting their own shareholders and their equity in the firms.

Alan Greenspan, 2008

Finance is extremely important – but it is also extremely fragile. And financial markets are prone to behavior that has implications against the public interest. Although they seem to embody the essence of individualistic competition, they are uniquely given to bouts of herd behavior. In the language of the last chapter, financial events can have enormous externalities, and the preservation of financial stability is a public good.

In short, far from representing some pure form of capitalism that we should seek to spread to other parts of the economic system, the financial markets exhibit a remarkable combination of its failings, including some hardly seen elsewhere, from the consequences of which we require state intervention to protect us.

It has taken a disaster to show us conclusively what we should have known all along. Not all markets are the same. The market for oranges is not the same as the market for labor, intellectual capital, or financial assets. In practice we learned this before, in the 1930s, but we have forgotten the lessons and continued to believe in a fairytale theory – and to persist in the infantile idea that financial markets represent some sort of blueprint for the rest of society. Lord Stern has described global warming as the greatest market failure in the history of humankind. He *may* be right about the science of global warming, but he is surely right about the structure of the economics surrounding the issue; that is, about the presence of an externality. As regards the magnitude of the possible market failure, however, I think there is a worthy competitor: the financial markets.

The importance of finance

Financial development enables people and firms with ideas, ability, and opportunity, but no money, to invest profitably, using the money of others who don't have the ideas, the ability, or the opportunities. It allows people to redistribute consumption through their lifetimes, including providing for a comfortable retirement. It enables them to live in a house that they own before they can afford to buy it outright. It enables risks and uncertainties to be offloaded, pooled, or minimized, with the result that better and bolder decisions can be made, and yet people, both private individuals and corporate executives, can sleep easier in their beds.

In short, without the development of finance over the last few hundred years, economic growth would have been lower, and people would have been less wealthy – and probably more troubled and insecure.

Moreover, once an economic system has become financially developed, it is enormously dependent on the financial sector's continued health. Without the continued flow of finance to those with deficits, spending and production would plunge. A collapse of the financial system is the equivalent of switching off the electricity supply.

In the language of the previous chapter, a failure in the financial system can readily set in train a sharp fall in demand; the Keynesian macro problem. And if a shock should occur outside the financial sector, the degree to which the economy suffers the macro problem will depend critically on how robust the financial structure proves to be.

And if individual banks or financial institutions should fail, because of the concentration of financial assets in particular institutions, people can be ruined by a financial collapse in a way that has few real economy counterparts. Typically, a person has a pension with one pension provider, or at most a few. Savings may be spread around several banks, but seldom around hundreds. Often people have the bulk of their savings with one institution.[2] So financial failures have the capacity to bring both individual and systemic catastrophe.

What makes finance special?

The financial world is extremely dangerous because of four characteristics that the real economy does not share:

- Financial structures are quintessentially fragile.
- Financial wealth can appear from nowhere – and disappear into nowhere.
- Financial changes can happen with enormous speed.
- Debt ("leverage") allows people to "gear up" the effects of changes in asset values.

The financial system is inherently fragile because it depends on trust. A debt involves a *promise* to repay. A deposit is made at a bank in the depositor's belief that if she needs it, she can get her money back.

In fact, the liquidity that each of us prizes in our own financial affairs is impossible to secure if we all seek to realize our savings immediately. At the financial system's very root, therefore, is a precarious relationship between the individual and the collective.

The psychological nature of wealth

If this fragility of the system is troubling, the nebulousness of wealth is doubly so. Whereas machines, bridges, or factories are real and unchanging, the value we place on them, the amount of *wealth*, is a human construct, and is subject to all the vicissitudes of human nature and human behavior.

I am not here referring to what people often describe as "paper" wealth – the various financial instruments, including stocks and shares – as distinct from so-called real wealth. These paper instruments ultimately come down to a claim on certain real assets. Moreover, and more disturbingly, these real assets are themselves only worth what human beings think they are worth. Wealth is a concept that connects present and future. It is the value of something now that will produce income, or at least will, we hope, still be there in the future. This has uncertainty and variability written into its very nature. We do not know the future, least of all our own. There is no determinate value for "real wealth": it is always up in the air. How wealthy society is depends on our feelings and expectations. So far from being *real*, real wealth is in fact thoroughly *psychological*.

When there are major changes in the value of shares – so many trillion dollars "wiped off" the stock market, etc. – I am often asked where the wealth has gone. "It must have gone somewhere!" people say. After all, an individual who sells their shares will have put the money in a bank, or in some other parking place, somewhere.

However, this does not happen at the collective level. If you sell shares in Yahoo and put your money in the bank, you have preserved your wealth, but someone is still holding the shares, and as the price drops their wealth will fall. The wealth has gone nowhere; it has simply disappeared into thin air, whence it came. Our wealth is simply what we collectively think it is. As such, it can go up and down with our whims and emotions – and it does.

The speed of finance

Precisely because of their lack of rootedness and their intimate connections with human nature, financial values can move dramatically in the space of moments, and on the basis of very little. This means that it is far easier and quicker to make fortunes – and to lose them – in financial markets than in almost any other activity. It is not unknown for stock markets to double in a year or two. Annual rates of increase of stock prices of 20% or even 30% are commonplace; property prices likewise. Plenty of people in western societies have been enriched by surging property prices. As a result, professional investors, and many a man or woman in the street, are always looking for the next 20 or 30%.

By contrast, the accumulation of productive real assets such as buildings, bridges, or machines proceeds slowly. Countries get rich through hard work and saving, made more exciting only by the power of compound interest. Rapidly developing countries may be able to grow by 10% per annum. Advanced countries, however, have to scrape by with 2 or 3%. At this rate, enrichment is painfully slow. But hold on. If the economy is only growing by 2 or 3% real, which if you add on an inflation rate of 2–3% means an increase of 4–6%, how can large numbers of people get rich though property or stock exchange gains of several times these percentages? They cannot, of course. All can get rich through an illusion, while it lasts; or some can get rich through redistribution from others. But all cannot genuinely enrich themselves at stupendous speed.

The power of debt

The effects of the elasticity of wealth – and the precariousness of our financial structures – are compounded by debt. Its magical qualities mark the fourth sharp divide between the financial and the real. If you are trying to make money by selling your labor, how much you can make is dictated by the rate for the job. This is as true for a bus driver as it is for a doctor. If you are selling your labor, the only way you can "gear up" your returns is by employing people. But not everyone can do that. We cannot *all* employ each other and thereby gear up our incomes in relation to the effort we put in!

However, with capital it is different, as every mortgage holder knows. If the return on an investment is 10% and you put in 100 of capital, then your return is 10. If you do the same but also borrow 900 at 5%, your return will be 55; that is, 100 gross minus the 45 you have to pay as interest on the 900. Leverage transforms a return of 10% into one of 55%.

The ordinary punter is not actually able to borrow money to buy securities in the same way as to buy residential property. That is one of the reasons why residential property is so popular as an investment vehicle for private individuals, and why bubbles involving large numbers of people usually have residential property at the bottom of them.

But the financial professionals also regularly depend on debt for their returns. Banks are in the lending business, taking in deposits and lending the money out, way in excess of their capital. Other parts of the system are highly leveraged too. Hedge funds operate with enormous leverage. That is one of the ways in which they have been able to generate such spectacular returns. Private equity firms act in a similar way.

Yet leverage works both ways its wonders to perform. When assets fall in value, leverage destroys capital at a faster rate than the rate of decline in prices. That is why so many hedge funds have been wiped out by the events of 2007/9.

These characteristics play a vital role in what I identify as six key failings of financial markets:

- They are prone to bubbles that, when they burst, can endanger the stability of the whole financial system.
- They engage in much activity that is purely distributive.
- They push up the pay of financial professionals to levels out of all proportion to the value their work contributes to society.
- Consequently, they have a natural tendency to take up too many resources.
- They are naturally prone to generate significant amounts of fraud.
- Their values poison the values of society and thereby threaten its stability.

I discuss each of these failings below.

Being wrong in good company

It is scarce wonder that, until recently at least, most orthodox economists did not believe in bubbles, or if they did, they thought they were a feature of the economic history books alone. The reason is that they believed in *homo economicus* – and he doesn't do excess.

By contrast, in the world beyond the textbook and the ivory tower, bubbles are endemic. In the conditions of profound uncertainty that dominate life they arise naturally from man's real nature, in particular from the interaction between the combination of myopia, optimism, greed, and "group think."

"Group think" is a natural consequence of man's social nature and his social circumstances, as I discussed in the last chapter. Because no one knows the future, and yet the future is of overwhelming relevance to the present, human beings have to develop a strategy for dealing with fundamental uncertainty. Financial markets find that the best way to deal with this is by adopting *conventional* views.

As long as you hold a conventional view – that is, the same sort of view that other people hold – then you can do business. If you hold an utterly different view, it is difficult to function at all: difficult to hold your job if you are a financial executive; difficult to retain respect if you are a forecaster, analyst, or commentator; sometimes difficult to maintain *self*-respect when you compare your investments/prognostications with the current behavior of markets. Conventional views are like currency. If you have unconventional views it is rather like being in China and holding only Indian rupees.

It is a commonplace that economists always disagree. Supposedly, if you put two economists in a room together you will get 10 opinions. In fact, when it comes to forecasting the future, the striking thing is how *little* their opinions differ. Their forecasts tend to huddle round the consensus like tramps around a fire.

The result of this behavioral trait is that in both the financial markets and economic forecasting, the way to achieve short-term economic success and to protect peace of mind is to forecast what other people will think.

In a much quoted passage in his *General Theory*, Keynes brilliantly encapsulated the behavior that results from the overwhelming urge to adopt conventional thinking:

Professional investment may be likened to those newspaper competitions in which the competitors have to pick out the six prettiest faces from a hundred photographs, the prize being awarded to the competitor whose choice most nearly corresponds to the average preferences of the competitors as a whole; so that each competitor has to pick, not those faces which he himself finds prettiest, but those which he thinks likeliest to catch the fancy of the other competitors, all of whom are looking at the problem from the same point of view. It is not a case of choosing those which, to the best of one's judgment, are really the prettiest, nor even those which average opinion genuinely thinks the prettiest. We have reached the third degree, where we devote our intelligences to anticipating what average opinion expects the average opinion to be. And there are some, I believe, who practise the fourth, fifth, and higher degrees.[3]

When the power of conventional thinking drives prices up, there is a powerful factor working to keep them there or drive them still higher: everyone is apparently better off. The world seems wealthier and for no extra effort. It is "money for nothing." And when no one can categorically say whether a surge in asset prices is a bubble or not, and all are apparently benefiting from it, there is a natural forward momentum. Who wants to upset the applecart?

Life cycles

All this interacts with humans' innately limited timespans. In most organizations ten years would be a long time for an executive to be doing the same job. In many cases he or she would move on after two or three years. In the economy at large, however, other rhythms are at work. It is possible for people to have successful careers while following what turns out to be entirely the wrong strategy, simply by being lucky in their timing.

As we now know, while the property and credit booms were building, the chances of a bust were rising. However, it was easy for the executives concerned not to see this, or to choose not to acknowledge it. Even if they did see it, the chances were that the change would not happen on their watch. They would have moved on to pastures new, perhaps even to the ultimate of rich pastures, a banker's retirement. Why rock the boat?

This has a corporate dimension, which explains why so many banks were caught up in the housing market bubble. With the benefit of hindsight, it would have been better for individual banks to have stood aside, tightened lending criteria while other banks were loosening theirs, and let their exposure to the housing market fall back. Nevertheless, hardly any banks did.

And with good reason. In practice, if the chief executive of a major banking group had stood out from the crowd and said, "It's a bubble and when it bursts it will be a disaster," he would not have lasted long before being ousted from his job. For there was apparently money to be made. No one wanted to be losing out while the market was going up. Accordingly, any banking chief executive who had his doubts was better advised, in the words of Citigroup's erstwhile chief executive Chuck Prince, to "keep dancing."

Gambling and the human connection

If the economics of the real economy can be thought of as a mixture of engineering (i.e., production conditions) and social organization (the nature and motivation of firms), then the economics of finance can be thought of as a mixture of applied mathematics and human nature. The characteristics of finance that I described above make clear the essential human aspect, and emphasize the potential for shifts of emotion to reverberate around the system and produce huge shocks. Unfortunately, finance theory has developed the mathematics *ad absurdum* and forgotten about the human nature. This is why the banks' risk models proved to be so useless when faced with the events of the Great Implosion, whereas a student of financial history would have found them both understandable and immediately recognizable.

A good deal of finance theory was developed using examples from the world of gambling, but especially from the sort that involves precisely specifiable probabilities: roulette, for example. This led the theorists up the garden path, because the events to which banks and other parts of the system are exposed are governed by pure uncertainty rather than precisely quantifiable probabilities, and because, unlike in roulette, the chances of an event occurring are affected by those playing the game. (I make more of these points in Chapter 9.) In short, if you want to look to the world of gambling for inspiration and enlightenment as to what might happen in the financial world, then you need to direct attention not to the casino, but to the racecourse. And the horse race that might best prepare you for the unpredictabilities of finance is the Grand National.

Interestingly, although many economists were initially very "sniffy" about the development of modern finance theory, regarding it as essentially applied mathematics with little or no economics in it, in fact its failings exactly mirrored the fundamental weaknesses of economic theory – the absence of the human factor, an underweighting of the complexity of historical processes, the conflation of uncertainty and risk, and the failure to understand how people behave in groups.

Moreover, as the decades wore on and financial theory became more respectable, its senior practitioners became exalted members of the established community of economic theorists. Meanwhile, some of the key tenets of the new subject of finance theory, such as the efficient markets hypothesis, became established as part of the core of many an economics course, thereby bolstering the case for free markets.

Zero-sum games

In the last chapter I explained the contrast between creative and distributive gains and emphasized the way in which ensuring the right balance between the resources devoted to the pursuit of each is vital to a society's success. Part of the answer to why there is so much financial activity in relation to the gains this produces for society is that much financial activity produces purely distributive gains; that is, gains that are of no net benefit overall. Such activity is what economists refer to as "zero-sum games."

Think about the vast effort investment banks pour into getting information quickly so as to be able to trade on it profitably. Sometimes fortunes ride on whether bank A or bank B gets the information first. But does it actually matter overall whether the information appears at 12 o'clock, 12.01, or even the next day? It does not matter a bean. Yet a good deal of the money that investment banks (and hedge funds) make comes as a result of being there first, sometimes nano-seconds in front of the runner-up.

This is a case where the value to the individual or the individual firm is greater than the value to society as a whole. It is a case of a reverse externality (an internality?). Moreover, in the end this becomes a negative-sum game, because all firms feel that they have to invest resources to be there with the information as soon as possible.

On the face of it, financial *investment* as opposed to trading is not like this because asset prices can, and usually do, rise over time. There is an overall gain to be shared out for everyone. But this will happen whether or not particular investors make money by being invested in the right mix of assets. Someone making super returns does so at the expense of someone else, and all those professionals devoted to investing well are trying to get advantage for themselves or their clients at the expense of someone else. So this, too, is distributive activity.

What about the hedge funds, whose ability to go short – unlike traditional institutions such as the pension funds, which are "long only" – enables them to make money in a bear market? Aren't they making creative gains? To the extent that they make money in such conditions, then some other investors must be registering extra large losses. It is impossible for us all to "go short" on the assets and enterprises that produce our livelihoods. The world is long only. Investment managers and hedge fund operatives may amass untold millions, but this money "earned" does not correspond to gains for society as a whole. They are distributive gains, won at the expense of others.

You could say that in the process of hedge funds or other investors trying to buy cheap today in order to sell dear tomorrow, the market is being made more efficient. These activities are helping both to establish the "right" price and to stabilize the market. But are these gains worth much to society? Not a lot. Admittedly, if some investors could stand out against the crowd and thereby help to prevent bubbles, they would be performing a public service of considerable worth. In practice, though, for the reasons I gave above, this is extremely difficult to do.

Similarly, the huge amount of trading activity that goes on between banks, hedge funds, other investors, and industrial and commercial companies is in essence distributive. What is gained by one player must be lost by someone else.

Nevertheless, this idea of zero-sum gains needs to be treated carefully. Just because an activity is zero sum in a narrow, financial sense does not necessarily make it zero sum in an overall sense. Person A who sells a share to Person B may not be doing so because she thinks the share is going down, but simply because she needs the money. In that case, there is a positive sum to the transaction, namely her being able to do whatever she wants with the money. Equally, the motive might be to adjust the risk of the portfolio. Indeed, it is perfectly possible for both parties in a transaction to be doing this, such that the transaction makes both better off, even if there is no change whatsoever in the price of the asset.

Even where this is not the case, there is a justification for so much apparently zero-sum activity in financial markets. That is that it confers gains for society because it increases "liquidity" – that is, it enables each of us, both individuals and businesses, to transact quickly and cheaply, or to get our money back, at short notice and without loss.

For instance, it is good that firms should be able to raise money by issuing securities. They will be able to raise money more easily and cheaply if such securities are tradable. Similarly, currencies have to be exchanged to facilitate trade and cross-border investment. Such markets will be more efficient if there are people undertaking trades in currencies for purely financial reasons.

The cost of liquidity

However, in a number of instruments the markets have taken the provision of liquidity well beyond the point of usefulness and to a stage where at the margin it brings no net benefit and even creates a net loss. The ability to trade means more trading. More trading implies more volatility. More volatility increases the incentive to trade, for both hedging and speculative purposes. So the emergence of markets naturally tends to generate market activity – much of it activity that wouldn't have been missed if it hadn't been possible.

More than this, the existence of financial markets fosters short-termism. When there are market prices against which fund managers can be assessed on a short-term basis, they will be so assessed, usually quarterly, even though the underlying activity undertaken by the firms whose shares are being traded may take years, or even decades, to come to fruition. The quarterly assessment of fund managers against some benchmark judged by market value encourages herd behavior by the fund managers.

Similarly, the development of a market in bank loans over the last 20 years has probably had a marked effect on the behavior of the banks originating the loans. Before securitization, a bank would have to reckon on holding a loan on its books until maturity. With securitization, it may reckon on being able to offload it onto others whenever market conditions are suitable. Yet although an individual bank may dispose of an asset in this way, the overall banking system cannot do so. It is stuck with the asset until maturity.

Why is there so much distributive activity?

Given the above, the question remains as to why the financial system sustains so much purely distributive – that is, zero-sum – activity. There are five main reasons. First, the gains to the winners are very large indeed. These gains act as a massive draw, even when the overall sums on offer for all are zero or even negative. In other words, there are similarities with the world of gaming and betting. People on average believe that they will be winners, even though, on average, they assuredly cannot be.

This belief is aided by the second factor. In finance, because of the dominance of genuine uncertainty about the future, it is particularly easy for everyone to believe that they will be winners. Person A buys a share from Person B thinking that the share price is likely to go up. Person B thinks the opposite. They cannot both be right, but at the time of the transaction, both can readily *believe* themselves to be so.

Third, the returns may not *appear* to sum to zero because of the way they are accounted for. In many financial businesses, foreign exchange for instance, the creative gains from providing a service, exchanging money, are intertwined with the distributive gains from selling/buying at the right price. Lots of banks think that they are gaining from the latter; some are, but collectively the system cannot be.

Fourth, gains and losses are often distributed unevenly over time, with a succession of up years, followed by one or two very large down years. When this happens it is possible for the players involved, both traders and their employers, to persuade themselves that the first extended phase is the product of skill, and the second, if and when it comes, is the result of outrageous fortune. Bankers took extraordinary risks in lending so heavily to what seem now to have been poor credit risks. While the economic boom continued and the low interest rate policy of the Greenspan era persisted, they would get a good return. The problem would come only if there were a financial crisis. In fact, much of banks' activity in the boom years amounted to "picking up nickels in front of a steamroller."

Fifth, the losses to offset the financial professionals' gains land up in places with special characteristics. After all, who is buying the various financial products that the banks are selling? For the banking sector as a whole, the answer is usually companies of all sorts, industrial and commercial as well as financial. And who is making the decisions to engage in this activity? Why, the senior corporate executives, of course.

Now, as I argued above, one of the justifications for apparently zero-sum trading, hedging and the rest, is that the risk is pooled, offset, shifted around the system, or reduced, such that real businesses can be run better, with a productive gain for society. But are the risks that corporate executives worry about the risks that should really matter to their companies? After all, what they are all too often concerned about is promoting their own interests and saving their own skin.

The situation is similar with "financial engineering." What does it do to increase the real productivity of companies and the underlying assets? You would be hard put to come up with a plausible positive answer. In that case, you have to ask why so much of it goes on. The answer is to enhance the short-run performance of the shares, and therefore the rewards of senior executives. Or consider mergers and acquisitions (M&A) activity. Countless academic studies have shown that on average, in the long run, such activity destroys wealth.

So elevated levels of financial activity – and the huge fees that companies are prepared to pay for this – are partly another manifestation of the agency problem discussed in the last chapter. In essence, when a senior corporate executive makes an agreement with an investment bank, or some other financial services professional, he is paying money to promote his interests or cover his backside. Yet there is a marked asymmetry – it isn't his money that he is forking out, but it is his backside that he is covering.

Similar points apply to financial investment. Why do pension funds, insurance companies, and fund managers do so much churning of portfolios? The answer is not because, overall, such activity is profitable. We know that it is a zero-sum game. On the whole, it is not even as though much of this shifting of assets can be justified on the grounds of risk minimization. Usually, it is just the result of "a change of view." The reason is a misguided belief on the part of the fund manager that he can "beat the market" – and a realization that if he does nothing but leave his clients' funds invested in the assets he originally chose, it will be difficult to justify his exorbitant salary and bonus.

Why don't the ultimate investors, the owners of the shares or the beneficiaries of the insurance or pension policies, penalize such behavior by voting with their feet? The answer is because these retail investment services are another part of the financial world where the market mechanism doesn't work very well. Ordinary investors find finance both boring and baffling; charges are usually opaque; once you have entered into an arrangement with one provider it is usually difficult or expensive to switch; and there is a widespread view, probably correct, that one provider is about as bad as another.

Why do bankers earn so much money?

That so much useless activity takes place in the financial markets is one thing, but why do bankers and other financial professionals earn so much money for doing it? We can quickly eliminate one possible answer to the question, mainly the idea that their pay mirrors the input of effort and talent. This suggestion is so outrageous as to be risible.

On the whole, bankers and other financial professionals are able and clever people who work hard. Still, I have never understood why they should earn umpteen times what a top professional would earn in the law, accountancy, or brain surgery.

If, by and large, financial professionals do earn hugely more, it must be because the market mechanism that determines their pay doesn't work very well. Indeed, it doesn't. The reasons are different at different levels and for different sorts of financial activity, but the common theme is market failure, namely the interaction between markets with profoundly different characteristics: the market for financial services, the market for people, and the market for corporate control. The result is a level of pay in financial services for senior people, junior people, people of high talent, low talent – and no talent at all – out of all proportion to their contribution to society.

Senior executives
At the top of a large corporation, it is usually difficult to determine what someone's true contribution is. What their pay turns out to be is therefore the result of all sorts of social factors and political pressures within the organization. This is true not only in banks but throughout the corporate system.

It is otiose to describe how senior executives' pay is determined as a market process. There are remuneration committees that supposedly review pay in accordance with market principles, but their members belong to the same corporate club.

One of my favorite examples of remuneration committees at work is the one that approved the compensation package of Dick Grasso, the chairman and CEO of the New York Stock Exchange (NYSE) from 1995 to 2003. He was asked to resign in 2003 after uproar over a $139.5 million lump sum that he proposed to withdraw immediately from his pension fund and an additional $48 million bonus. The payment was approved by the NYSE Compensation Committee, which included several of the great figures of Wall Street.[4] One committee member is reported to have thought that Grasso's proposed payment was a typing mistake.[5] Mind you, Grasso had the last laugh because he won a court case over the $139.5 million and was allowed to keep the lot. He never received the $48 million.

Although sometimes remuneration committees seek advice from firms of remuneration consultants, these firms seldom cause a stir. Why would they want to? They know that most of the executives commissioning their services are benefiting from the self-same remuneration practices – and this means, of course, that so are they.

In any case, what are they supposed to do? If other firms in the sector are paying more, and as pay rates in the sector are drifting up, that is what they must report. When client A, in response to this news, increases its pay rates, the remuneration consultant can report upward pay pressures to its clients B–Z. Nice work if you can get it.

Because of the natural tendency for executive pay to levitate, the multiple of an ordinary worker's pay that a chief executive receives is now many times larger than it was 50 years ago, without any convincing evidence that this reflects superior performance. According to research published by Cornell University, in the US in 1965 the ratio of average *total* CEO *compensation* to that of the average worker was 24:1.[6] Forty years later, it stood at 262:1.[7]

Moreover, this multiple differs considerably from country to country. Why American chief executives need be paid so much more to perform their roles than their counterparts in Japan or Germany, let alone the Nordic countries, defeats me.

Lesser mortals

What chief executives are paid also affects what executives on the next tier down are paid, in banking as in the rest of the corporate sector. However, although the "compensation" of senior executives is often spectacular, there are relatively few of these people. Consequently, the role of their pay in affecting the overall distribution of income, the size of the financial sector, and even the incentivization of excessive risk taking is limited. The more important issues surround the remuneration of more ordinary executives and traders.

On the whole, run-of-the-mill people in financial services are readily identifiable with a stream of revenue and their contribution to it can usually be measured in some way. Nevertheless, for such people the market also doesn't work the way it is supposed to, but for different reasons.

First, the distribution of gains and losses over time, which I argued above explains why so much financial activity takes place, also explains why many financial professionals get paid so much. Banking appears to be vastly profitable in the good years and disastrous in the bad ones, even necessitating huge public support.

It is often alleged that over the long term, the airline industry has never made any money. It looks as though something similar could be true for the banking industry, at least in the US and the UK, although, in the good times at least, investment banks make very large profits indeed. The evidence suggests that bankers' pay fully reflects the profits in the good times, but not the losses in the bad times. The recent report by Andrew Cuomo, Attorney General of the State of New York, put it pithily: "Thus, when the banks did well, their employees were paid well. When the banks did poorly, their employees were paid well. When the banks did very poorly, they were bailed out by taxpayers and their employees were still paid well."[8] The report points out that two firms, Citigroup and Merrill Lynch, suffered massive losses of more than $27 billion at each firm. Nevertheless, Citigroup paid out $5.33 billion in bonuses and Merrill paid out $3.6 billion. What is more, these two firms were in receipt of TARP (i.e., publicly funded) bailouts totaling $55 billion. To put that Merrill figure into context, it was nearly equal to the US government's entire aid budget for sub-Saharan Africa.

The report goes on to note: "For three other firms – Goldman Sachs, Morgan Stanley, and J.P. Morgan Chase – 2008 bonus payments were substantially greater than the banks' net income. Goldman earned $2.3 billion, paid out $4.8 billion in bonuses, and received $10 billion in funding. Morgan Stanley earned $1.7 billion, paid $4.475 billion in bonuses, and received $10 billion in TARP funding. J.P. Morgan Chase earned $5.6 billion, paid $8.69 in bonuses, and received $25 billion in TARP funding."

Just to put those figures into perspective, the Goldman's bonus pool amounted to an average of $160,420 per Goldman employee, getting on for three times the average American employee's total compensation for a year. And that was in a bad year for the financial system!

The second characteristic of the financial sector that promotes high pay is that even when a certain sort of financial activity is zero sum at a particular time, the returns to the winning parties are so enormous that the professionals who appear to be responsible for securing these gains are highly sought after and highly rewarded. Meanwhile, the professionals who are "responsible" for the corresponding losses do not suffer commensurately. The worst they can suffer is not to be paid at all, which would scarcely offset the winners' rewards. In practice, even the losers usually get a fair bit more than nothing.

The ratchet effect

Third, for most financial professionals, rather than there being a *rate* of pay for the job, in practice there is an acceptable *range*, which may be quite wide. What determines where pay will be in that range comes down to perceptions, bargaining power, corporate politics, culture, and policy – and the brass neck of the individuals concerned.

The fact that there is a range is extremely important. For if an executive, or any other employee for that matter, pushes up his or her pay to a higher point within the range, this will bring about no countervailing market mechanism whatsoever. Supply and demand won't get a look in; the opposite will happen. Within the firm, as other people come to learn of A's success, they will want to match it. In an industry characterized by strong information flows across firms, even people in other firms will learn of A's success and will want a similar increase. In this way, the pay levels of a whole firm, or even a whole industry, or a whole class of employees across several industries, may levitate above what you might expect from the skills, abilities, knowledge, or workload of the individuals concerned.

Lack of competition

Fourth, in many cases where banks and other financial service providers make lots of money, even when properly measured over time, they do so because the markets in which they operate are not very competitive. In effect, the provision of many financial services is heavily concentrated. Of all 56 banks cited on the S&P 500, FTSE 100, and DJ Euro Stoxx, the top 3 accounted for about 25% of the capitalization of the whole sector, the top 8 for over 50%, the top 16 for 75%, and the top 25 for about 90%.

These statistics do not do justice to how concentrated individual financial activities are. According to one study, the top 10 banks globally accounted for 76% of international IPOs (initial public offerings or flotations) and 87% of US market IPOs.[9] According to another, the top 5 US banks were responsible for 56% of US M&A advisory work and 50% of US syndicated loans.[10] The best way to think of the competitive structure of investment banking is as an oligopoly.[11] Ironically, the Great Implosion has led to even greater concentration at the top, as investment banks Lehman Brothers and Bear Stearns have disappeared and some others have been humbled, leaving the competitive position of those that remain even stronger – as evidenced by Goldman Sachs' 2009 results.

Moreover, the profitability of investment banking is increased by other features that mark it out as a less than normal, competitive market. In particular, there are marked asymmetries of information between the banks and their clients, all the more so because the banks' activities stretch across many different areas, where conflicts of interest are intense.

Even so, you would expect the usual forces of competition to come to bear. In theory, if investment banking is so profitable this should encourage new firms to enter the market, paying their employees less and undercutting the fees and charges of better-established firms. In practice, this hardly ever

happens. Insiders are virtually never challenged by outsiders. Because reputation is so important, it is very difficult for a new financial firm to get going
without having seasoned professionals – and to employ them it will have to
pay at least the established market rate, if not more. Furthermore, on the
whole, the consumers of many financial services are not very price sensitive.
If you are taking M&A advice, for instance, the second best is often not worth
having, even at half the price.

Ironically, the very tendency for pay in financial services to settle well
above the "competitive" level, and for employees to take a large proportion
of the profits when things go well, acts as a barrier to entry for new firms
and hence an explanation as to why high profitability can persist.

At the retail end of financial services, despite the appearance of competition given by the large numbers of providers, because of asymmetries of
information and opacity in the charging structure, most services are provided
in a noncompetitive way, again with the result that the interests of the ultimate customer – the retail client – are not properly reflected through the system. Across much of the financial sector there is a tendency to regard retail
customers as helpless victims, there to be exploited, rather than as business
partners from the satisfaction of whose needs derives the justification for
profit. More milchcow than market.[12]

Mind you, just because an activity is hugely profitable does not mean that
the profits *have* to accrue to the employees rather than the shareholders. That
this often happens in financial services is due to other peculiarities of the
market analyzed in the previous chapter; that is, the inadequate exercise of
power and responsibility by the owners of businesses, namely large institutional shareholders. Most institutional shareholders are themselves weak and
supine institutions whose senior executives are on the same gravy train, and
hence have little incentive to cause a derailment by questioning levels of pay.

Why is the financial sector so big?

There has been a dramatic change in the weight of financial services in the
economy. The sector accounted for less than 3% of the US economy in 1950,
3½% in 1960, and still only 4% in 1970. But in 2007, on the eve of the Great

Implosion, the sector's share had risen to about 8%.[13] In the 1970s, the share of the financial sector in US domestic corporate profits was about 20%. In 2002, it exceeded 40%.[14]

Doubtless some of this is perfectly normal and healthy, as people have a tendency to demand more financial services as they get richer. However, the above analysis has provided two other explanations for the current size of the financial services sector in our economy, and these are neither natural nor healthy. First, much of this activity is producing only distributive gains. Moreover, a great deal of this activity, consuming enormous resources of effort and talent, takes place because of the inefficiencies and market failings of other parts of the economic system – both industrial and commercial companies and the retail financial industry.

Second, as I have discussed, the people employed in financial services are, by and large, paid far too much. They are paid too much because the market in people does not work very well at the best of times. Pay levitates well above the level that would emerge in a fully competitive market.

In the previous chapter I referred to the way in which capitalism tends to disperse the benefits of technological advances across society as a whole, even though individual agents, both people and firms, are engaged in a constant attempt to bag the benefits. In the world of finance, by contrast, there is a marked tendency for the practitioners to be successful in snaffling a huge proportion of the gains for themselves – with very little, or even sometimes a net negative, left for everyone else.[15]

Consequences of overexpansion

Naturally, this has a huge impact on the distribution of income, with bankers and other financial services professionals able to live the life of old Riley compared to other professionals of similar ability. Houses, holidays, home helps, and school places all gravitate their way with consummate ease.

But the consequences of a bloated and distorted financial system are not only distributional. The prevailing structure of pay in the markets, quite apart from the level, incentivizes risk taking, with the result that the whole financial and economic system is endangered.

We must be careful, though, about what precisely is wrong about the structure of financial professionals' pay. In some quarters, *bonus* is now a dirty word. It shouldn't be. There is nothing wrong with the principle of variable pay. Indeed, the fact that in financial businesses pay can in principle just as easily go down as well as up can add much to firms' robustness in the face of business downturns, and can serve to enhance management's ability to manage.

It is the way in which bonuses are structured and paid that can be lethal. In particular, the banks' habit of paying out large amounts in cash in response to short-term performance, and without the possibility of clawback, is what incentivizes risk taking and increases short-termism. When a bonus is regarded as an entitlement, and when the absence of one makes people think they have not been paid for doing a job, then the bonus culture has gone mad.

There are also real economic costs from the financial sector's overexpansion. The most important aspect is the excessive use of talent in activities that are not of great value to society. Some of the people in financial markets are very talented indeed. This may seem surprising; you might think that clever people would be drawn to more "creative" activities. Admittedly, when engaging in creative activities, clever people will in general be more successful than their less clever equivalents. In the old days, grand British families would not consider finance a worthy occupation for their most able sons. It was the least able who were encouraged into the church, the army, or the City.

But cleverer people are also likely to be better at distributive activities. If the gains they can accrue for themselves are greater in the distributive sphere than in the creative, many will be attracted to those activities. The result could be that the cleverest people in society are devoted to activities that yield no societal benefit at all – or even destroy wealth.

Interestingly, this is clearly recognized by many bankers and financial analysts of an older vintage. Albert Wojnilower, a veteran economic and financial commentator who is still a legend on Wall Street, puts it pithily:

The economic growth of the US depends on a system that rewards long-term risk-taking, hard work and perseverance. Such a system cannot survive the competition for talent and capital that comes from an industry addicted to high-stakes short-term betting on the price of the lottery tickets we call securities.[16]

Moreover, we need to consider the identity of the investors who are making a lower return to make it possible for hedge funds and other sophisticated investors to make a higher return. They are the investors in slow-moving and restricted institutions such as pension funds and insurance companies, or central banks whose market activities are dictated by some objective of public policy, rather than private gain.

Yet there are reasons why we should want such institutions to be this way. Pensioners do not want their pension funds to be run like hedge funds – and with good reason – or their insurance companies, or their central banks. So we have allowed, and even encouraged, a system to develop in which clever people make huge amounts of money out of institutions that, for reasons of public policy, we constrain to behave in a way that allows scope for such profits to be made. Is that clever or what?

Perhaps the greatest problems are caused by the interaction between financial markets and the real economy. There, time horizons are longer, price adjustments are more sluggish, and motivations less single-mindedly selfish. And so much the better – for them and for us. But how are they able to withstand the onrush of supercharged greed that floods out at them from the financial markets? If we think that it is right and proper – and economically advantageous – that some parts of the economic system should *not* be organized like Goldman Sachs, then we should make sure that they are protected from those parts of the system that *are* organized like Goldman Sachs.

The wealth creators?

I recently read an article by a leading British journalist decrying the widespread condemnation of bankers' and hedge fund executives' high remuneration on the grounds that these people, it said, were "the wealth creators." It argued that we should be praising, and even aping, such people rather than criticizing them, and thereby concentrating on the distribution rather than the creation of wealth.

This completely misses the point. We shouldn't be mesmerized by the umpteen million dollars squirreled into some private corner or other. The question is, what has the process that generated this money contributed to the common weal? For the world as a whole the answer is usually perfectly plain: nothing. (But for countries such as the UK that happen to have been rather good at financial services and therefore end up providing them also for clients based in other countries, the answer is rather a lot. The City is a massive source of net income for the UK.)

In the last chapter, I showed how, in any society, there is a spectrum of activities whose contribution runs from the purely creative to the purely distributive. In our society, at one end you could put midwives, among others. At the other end are the winners of the lottery. Beyond this and into negative territory are the criminals, who subtract value. In between there is a mishmash of occupations and activities with a wide spread of creative and distributive components.

Much of what goes on in financial markets belongs right at the purely distributive end. The gains to one party reflect the losses to another, and the vast fees and charges racked up in the process end up being paid by Joe Public, since even if he is not directly involved in the deals, he is indirectly. Higher financial charges both increase the costs of industrial and commercial companies, which raises the price of goods and services, and reduce the returns earned by the organizations that invest money on clients' behalf.

Even what the great investors do belongs at the distributive end of the spectrum. The sums earned by the most successful suggest achievement of startling magnitude. Here the managers of the top hedge funds, for instance, leave even the investment bankers standing. In 2008, John Paulson, the founder of Paulson & Co, was paid $1.9 billion. Meanwhile, James Simmons, the founder of Renaissance Technologies, managed to get by on $2.8 billion, which would be just about enough to pay 60,000 people the average American wage for a year.[17] Hedge funds and other investors *do* provide some service to society in improving the efficiency of the market. And some of the great investors have been decidedly activist in the management of the companies in which they have invested their money, thereby helping to counteract the passivity of the investment institutions. But a huge wedge of investor activity is purely speculative in nature. And the size of the rewards does not correlate with the contribution of their activities to society. Such investors belong somewhere close to the lottery winners. Meanwhile, there is surely a legitimate question about quite how many lotteries a society should have – and indeed how large the prizes should be.

By this I don't mean to suggest that investment success is always down to luck; rather that the activity does not add a great deal to society's overall welfare but redistributes it from others to the successful investor. The genius of the great speculative investors is to see what others do not, or to see it earlier. That's all. This is a skill; of that I have no doubt. But so also is the ability to stand on tip-toe, balancing on one leg, while holding a pot of Earl Grey tea above your head, and successfully pouring the contents into a cup that is seven feet below you on the ground, without spilling a drop. I am not convinced, though, of the social worth of such a skill, still less of the wisdom of encouraging the brightest and the best of our society to try to perfect it.

Yet that is what we have done with financial markets. It is commonplace for successful business people to look on the activities of those in the public sector with disdain since what the latter do, they think, is merely redistributing wealth, rather than creating it, thereby imposing a burden on those who do create wealth. This view is not without some justification. However, the irony is that some of the activity that takes place in the public sector is genuinely creative, while a large part of what goes on in financial businesses, owned and managed by the private sector, is completely about distributing wealth – with large parts of the loot going to the practitioners.

The fraud connection

All of the above has concerned activities that, although they may be distorted, are nevertheless honest and take place within the law. However, financial markets are also uniquely prone to dishonest activities. Fraud is especially prevalent in financial markets because of the intangibility of what is traded, the opaqueness of financial structures, genuine uncertainty about the future, and the huge sums that are apparently on offer for doing very little. Although fraudsters always abound in financial markets, they are more plentiful and their frauds more spectacular in bull markets – probably because it is easier to generate apparent gains and because surveillance standards are laxer. Similarly, financial busts have a way of exposing fraud.

The property bubble that led to the Great Implosion was accompanied by many a fraud that is only now being uncovered. Most of the problems have centered around buy-to-let and self-certified mortgages – known in the US as "liar loans." These frauds usually involve the fraudsters colluding with solicitors and other professional intermediaries to inflate the value of properties.

In April 2009, five fraudsters were jailed at the UK's Newcastle Crown Court after admitting that their company had been involved in an £80 million buy-to-let fraud, selling dilapidated homes to 1,750 investors. According to the Serious Fraud Office, the fraudsters funded lavish lifestyles and went on "a staggering spending spree – buying racehorses, splashing out £200,000 on designer clothes and £500,000 on a fleet of luxury cars."[18]

The biggest fraud to have emerged from the Great Implosion was Bernard Madoff's nice little earner. This appeared to be a remarkably successful $17 billion hedge fund, but turned out to be a remarkably successful $50 billion Ponzi scheme. It is impossible to imagine anything remotely on this scale outside the financial markets. Moreover, the Madoff affair is notable not only for its scale but also for what it revealed about the financial system. For Madoff did not only dupe unsophisticated individual investors but large banks like Santander and HSBC, and sophisticated, professional investors, such as the fund manager Bramdean, run by Britain's investment "superwoman" Nicola Horlick, who were charging their clients large fees for their investment expertise.

This is a prime example of the efficient markets theory in action. Even sophisticated investors were insufficiently careful about where they put their clients' money, because someone else in the system could be presumed to be doing the due diligence that they themselves were not prepared or able to do. If other, savvy investors were putting their money with Madoff, then it must be OK, mustn't it? Anyway, if Madoff were at all dodgy, then the regulators would have rumbled him, wouldn't they?

In fact this case also laid bare the complete inadequacy of the regulators. Harry Markopolos, a former fund manager and long-time critic of Madoff, tried for nine years to expose the fraud. He blamed staff incompetence at the US Securities and Exchange Commission for Madoff not being discovered earlier. Markopolos told a Congressional Committee:

> *I gift-wrapped and delivered the largest ponzi scheme in history to them. Most officials did not understand… the 29 red flags that I handed them.*

Professional pride and ethics

Perhaps the suspicion of fraud is one of the reasons why, at the retail level, people learn to treat financial "professionals" with considerable suspicion. What a contrast this makes with other parts of the economic system. In some parts of society we trust the providers of something we need not only, or in some cases not even principally, because we rely on their sense of self-interest, or because of concern for reputation or fear of the regulators, but because of a presumption of integrity on the part of the provider.

This is surely true, for example, of our visits to the pharmacist. We expect pharmacists to operate according to an ethical code and to take a professional pride in what they do. What is more, while there are occasional rogues in this profession, as in all the others, most of the time we are right to expect this.

A similar thing is also true of the best-run businesses. Although there are plenty of fly-by-night firms, and some big, well-established firms selling things that may be deemed harmful, on the whole we do not expect good, well-established businesses intentionally to sell things that are defective, dodgy, unethically produced, or unequivocally harmful, no matter how profitable such sales might be. The justification for our expectation is that it would not be in the businesses' long-run interests to do this. For the best businesses, however, the real reason is that the executives and the employees would not want to do this because it would be wrong.

When it comes to matters financial, however, in general we do not expect the providers of financial services to behave in this way. We think that they are in it for what they can get and, if we are not careful, they will get more by ensuring that we get less. What is more, much of the time, regrettably, we are right.

This must be extremely galling for the many financial professionals who genuinely do see looking after their clients' interests as both the motivation and the justification for what they do.

In wholesale financial markets, motivational and ethical questions rise to a higher pitch. Although there are many fine people who work in financial markets, some of whom I am honored to have worked with myself, I do not believe that the way in which financial markets have operated over the last 30 years encourages a healthy attitude to wealth, or to fellow human beings. The individuals who rise through the markets to become leaders of banks or other financial institutions are often notable chiefly for their greed.

It is sometimes argued that whatever other merits or demerits they have, at least financial market professionals work extremely hard. Many do, but I am not sure that they work any harder than many other professionals, or indeed even some ordinary workers like milkmen or bus drivers, who also get up early or work late, and often work very long hours to achieve an adequate income. Nor is it true that everyone in senior positions in finance works extremely hard.

The case of James "Jimmy" Cayne, former chairman of Bear Stearns, is striking. *Fortune* said that in July 2007, when two of Bear's largest hedge funds were collapsing, Mr. Cayne – who, according to the *Wall Street Journal*, had earned $34 million the previous year – spent 10 of 21 working days out of the office playing golf and bridge at a tournament in Tennessee. The *Wall Street Journal* said that in March 2008, when Bear collapsed, he was playing in a bridge tournament in Detroit, without a mobile phone or email device. It added that in summer weeks, he typically left the office on Thursday afternoon and spent Friday at his New Jersey golf club, out of touch for stretches. Even when he was in the office, he tended to leave at 5 pm.[19]

It has been common in recent years to speak of senior executives as "corporate leaders," as though they run their companies by being a source of inspiration and example "to the troops," whose best interests, of course, they have at heart. Of course. I suppose the idea is that they could be compared to military leaders, even the sort who lead their men into battle. Unfortunately, for many of our "corporate leaders" in the financial world the comparison could not be more misplaced. Far from following *them* into battle, it wouldn't even be rational to follow them into a bus queue.

Culture and values

In the furore that followed the Great Implosion there was widespread public outrage at what bankers had got up to. It seemed as though the public was baying for a hanging or two of the individual bankers who were deemed responsible for major disasters, and/or were thought to have paid themselves "too much." At one point, the house of Sir Fred Goodwin, the former Chief Executive of RBS, was attacked, and his own personal safety was in jeopardy.

This public mood of hatred toward bankers and the personalization of responsibility for what had gone wrong went much too far. Although some individuals were culpable for both their greed and their incompetence, all bankers were operating in a culture of poisoned values. Before the Great Implosion, society smiled on their success. The real fault lay with the prevailing culture, and with the system that allowed and encouraged their behavior.

I once knew a very successful trader, turned senior investment banker, who divulged to me how he had made all his money. "I robbed a bank," he blithely admitted. What he didn't quite say, although he might have implied it, is that what made this alright was that the bank was robbing everyone else.

Plenty of people would think it was more than alright. In 1989 Michael Lewis published a book called *Liar's Poker*, in which he exposed the rampant greed and hubris of Wall Street. In 2008 he revealed that after the book's publication, he found himself "knee-deep in letters from students at Ohio State who wanted to know if I had any other secrets to share... They'd read my book as a how-to-manual."[20]

Moreover, these values spread out beyond the financial sector. It is surely the success of the financial markets and the huge rewards enjoyed by their leading practitioners that have been responsible for the increasing greed and narrow self-interestedness, reflected in increasingly gargantuan pay levels for senior executives, in much of the nonfinancial world. What goes on in the City of London and on Wall Street has, if you like, infected executive attitudes to jobs and remuneration throughout the economy.

The sums are extraordinary. In 2008, Hugh Grant – not the actor, the CEO of Monsanto, an agricultural company – was paid $65 million, or more than 1,300 times the pay of the average US worker, and 163 times the pay of the

US President. He was by no means top of the league. In the same year, Lawrence Ellison, the CEO of IT company Oracle, was paid $556 million.

There is the argument that such pay is needed to motivate top managers. Yet it is very difficult to see how this can work, except possibly in a relative sense; that is, relative to other overpaid executives. At least the outgoing Chief Executive of Shell, Jeroen van der Veer, who in 2008 received a 58% pay rise to 10.3 million euros, had the decency to admit as much. He said: "You have to realize: if I had been paid 50% more, I would not have done it better. If I had been paid 50% less, then I would not have done it worse."[21]

There are also examples of enormous payoffs to executives when they leave. In 2007, Chuck Prince, CEO of Citigroup, was paid $68 million to go. Stanley O'Neal, CEO of Merrill Lynch, was paid $161 million.[22] What is the theory behind enormous executive payoffs? Can it be the idea that if executives did not know they would receive such sums if they failed, they wouldn't be prepared to put in their best efforts to ensure they would succeed?

The bonus culture has even spread to the public sector. The head teacher of a school in Wembley, north London, received £130,000 in bonuses over two years.[23] It has surely also infected the attitudes of UK Members of Parliament, who appear to think that considerations of duty and public service are old hat, and that their job, like everyone else's, is to maximize their own material rewards.

Motivation and remuneration are further examples of economic behavior that is subject to externalities, one of the areas of market failure I identified in the last chapter. If large parts of the economy consist of operations where executives take pride in what they do, are motivated by their contribution to society and the status that flows from this, and are remunerated decently but modestly, it is correspondingly easier and more appropriate for you to feel and behave this way. If, by contrast, wherever you look, businesses are run by cowboys on the make, who are excessively rewarded – and even honored – for what they do, then you will feel both naive and stupid if you see your own role in any other way. Bad pay practices drive out good.

It turns out that, in our society, the easiest way to make an awful lot of money is to take it, legally, from someone else. Not only do we allow and encourage sky-high returns to be available for distributive activity, but society also accords high status to the people who enjoy these sky-high returns. It makes no distinction between the man who makes his money through an invention and the man who makes it through a bet. But do we have to admire such activity? Do we have to give someone an award or an honor for doing it? By behaving in this way, it is as though society is giving a slap in the face to all of its members who just get on with doing a decent job, never mind those who are actually motivated by the idea of public service.

In the previous chapter, I argued that in contrast to the assumption of self-ish, maximizing behavior at the heart of free market theory, in reality in much of the market system people are motivated by a desire to contribute or achieve something for the common good. What is more, on the whole it is a good thing that they should feel this way – good economically, good for their own happiness, and good for the cohesion of society. However, in the financial world, the pressures are all in favor of the behavior that the red-raw free market theory assumes: self, self, self – and to hell with anyone else.

The values of modern financial markets, dominated by a devil-may-care worship of greed, are deeply corrosive of the values that hold society together. They are also deeply corrosive of the values that underpin successful business.

The triumph of finance capitalism

The triumph of finance capitalism and the increasing dominance of its values in the 1980s and 1990s coincided with a period of considerable prosperity. At the root of this development were the fall of oil and commodity prices, the associated sharp fall in inflation, the rapid growth of international trade, the emergence of China as a major supplier of cheap goods, and the remarkable advances of technology.

What did free *financial* markets contribute to this surge of prosperity? In my view, not a lot. Admittedly, it is possible that even the frothy aspects of the financial markets have been vital components of their ability to provide cheap finance and to allocate capital efficiently. And it is true that recent financial development lowered the cost of finance for many an expanding company or ambitious entrepreneur. In this way, it should have contributed to higher investment and a better allocation of resources. However, in the west, real investment was not in fact particularly high, and much financial activity involved the trading of financial instruments or the financing of mergers and acquisitions, which, the evidence suggests, on average destroy value rather than create it.

Certainly, the availability of cheap money helped to finance a consumer boom in the Anglo-Saxon countries. But that is no miracle; more of a mirage. Consumer spending can increase without a rampant financial sector.

 Meanwhile, the economic development of Asia was not dependent on rapid financial development at all. Nearly all of Asia's growth, particularly after 1997, was internally financed, and it was driven by net exports. The financial sector remained, by and large, undeveloped and unsophisticated. Indeed, the Asian miracle financed the excessive growth of consumption in western societies.

In the west, financial development provided the froth – and the personal fortunes – but not the substance. Then it brought on the collapse. The Anglo-Saxon countries, increasingly aped around the world, had allowed and even encouraged a monster to develop at the heart of the economic system.

Ironically, not only did the United States fail to see the damage that an out-of-control financial sector was doing to its economy, but it tried to foist this model onto other countries, including the emerging economies of Asia, which were inherently suspicious of it. To their credit, their suspicions have been vindicated.

And now they are openly critical. Speaking at the 2009 World Economic Forum, China's premier Wen Jiabao attacked western banks for their "blind pursuit of profit and lack of discipline." Kishore Mahbubani, dean of Singapore's Lee Kuan Yew School of Public Policy, said that the lessons Asians would learn from the crisis were: "Do not liberalize the financial sector too quickly, borrow in moderation, save in earnest, take care of the real economy, invest in productivity, focus on education."

Vindication is usually cheap, but in this case it has been inordinately expensive. In the process of rejecting the Anglo-Saxon model, Asian countries have contributed another twist to the tangled web of financial relations and created another source of financial instability – from which both they and the countries of the west are suffering. For in the age of globalization, the trouble with markets is not only domestic but international – in both origin and effect.

6

The Chinese Connection

It is confusing right and wrong when countries that have been overspending blame those that lend them money.

Wen Jiabao, Chinese premier, 2009[1]

The international dimension provides a broader canvas on which the failings of financial markets discussed in the previous chapter leave their mark. It also supplies a fundamental cause of the financial instability that found expression in the Great Implosion – namely, the huge imbalances in trade. These threaten to cause further currency instability, and even to lead to the closing down of the open international trading system.

Indeed, it is impossible to understand the factors that led to the financial bubble that in turn resulted in the credit crunch without grasping the essential international contribution. And, as I shall argue in Chapter 9, it is impossible to see a way out of our current plight that does not radically remake the current international financial regime.

The trouble with international financial markets is that they are now operating within the shell of a fractured international system at a time when the world is moving to a completely new order. The old global money, the dollar, is in danger of suffering from a profound loss of confidence. Meanwhile, the dominance of its issuer, the once hegemonic power, the United States, is rapidly fading. Most importantly, the system is struggling to accommodate the rapid rise of a new global power, China, which is an altogether different creature from most advanced western countries: it confronts different problems; it thinks about the world differently; and it acts outside the cosy club of established relations between countries. Although the twin problem of global imbalances and the fragility of the international monetary system is multifaceted, China is at the center of both components.

Getting the measure of global imbalances

We need to put some scale on these trade imbalances. Over the 1990s, among G-20 countries the average current account imbalance was 2.3% of GDP. Over the three years 2006–8 it had risen to 5.4%. In 2007, the year that the Great Implosion began, America ran an external deficit – that is, an excess of imports over exports – of 5% of GDP. This was not a new phenomenon; it had been in deficit for 16 years.

America's current account deficit has recently shrunk to just under 3% of GDP. However, this is not altogether surprising – and it is not a bit reassuring. America has benefited from lower oil prices and suffered a major contraction in her economy. It is perfectly normal for the latter to lead to an improved trade balance as companies and individuals scale back their purchases. But what would happen if the recession were to end? Or oil prices were to soar again? On all known form, without a major increase in domestic demand in the rest of the world and/or a major fall of the dollar, the deficit would resurge and we would be back to the problem as it existed before the Great Implosion. So the figures for 2007 remain highly relevant.

In 2007, America's deficit amounted to some $730 billion, a sum that, if things continued as they were, the US had to attract each year in investments or loans to pay for the excess of its imports over its exports. This amounted to almost $3,000 each year for every man, woman, and child in the United States.

Some other countries also ran large deficits. The UK's was 4% of GDP, Australia's 6%, and Spain's 10%. However, the much smaller size of these other economies meant that in terms of billions of dollars, America's deficit was far and away the largest.

Corresponding to these deficits, and indeed financing them, were some large surpluses. The main ones in terms of shares of GDP are shown in Chart 1. (There is no mention here of the eurozone because its aggregate balance is close to zero. However, there are some very significant differences between member countries, which I discuss later.)

What should strike you from the chart is that all the world's major surplus countries are either Asian, oil producers, or Swiss. As the last category is necessarily restricted to a membership of one, it need not detain us for very long.

Chart 1: Major External Surpluses and Deficits (Current Account), % of GDP, 2007

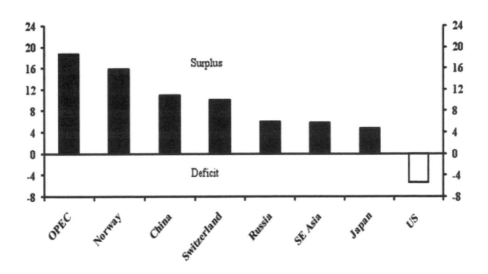

Chart 2: Major External Surpluses and Deficits (Current Account), US$bn, 2007

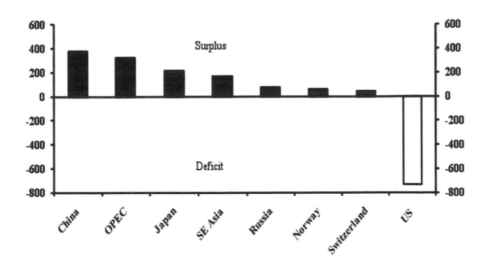

(I will, though, say a little about Switzerland later.) Indeed, when you look at the surpluses in $ billion, as shown in Chart 2, Switzerland fades in significance and it becomes clear that all of the major surplus countries were either Asian or oil producers.

The consequences of the surpluses were the same, but their origins and the ultimate significance for the world economy are completely different. Accordingly, I will deal with them separately. Before we get to this point, though, we need to establish why this set-up of large deficits and surpluses is so pernicious.

Accounting for debt

If the countries of Southeast Asia, the oil producers, the Swiss – or anyone else for that matter – choose to run large current account surpluses, so what? What has this got to do with the bubble in real estate and credit that led to the Great Implosion?

Everything. The essential truth that holds the key to unlocking this question is an apparently innocuous piece of accounting. For every deficit there must be a surplus – and for every surplus there must be a deficit. The accounting may be simple, but the implications are profound. The deficits of consumers in the west are the flipside of the surpluses of savers in the east.

As I explained in Chapter 1, in running a surplus the super-saving countries have spent less than their income, thereby, in the absence of offsetting measures or events, causing world GDP to be lower and unemployment higher. This is the exact equivalent of what happens when there is a spontaneous increase in the desire to save in a domestic economy.

Won't the extra savings by the super-saving countries of the world automatically keep the west from depression? After all, they cannot put the money under the bed. And they don't. On the contrary, they invest it in western financial markets.

You might readily believe that by lending the money out or investing it, the super-savers are putting back what they took out. But they aren't. This is exactly analogous to the argument about saving in a domestic context that I explained in Chapter 4. Financial flows are not the same as demand for output. Suppose that western consumers decide to save more. This increases the amount of money they put through savings channels. But it also increases the demand for finance from those whose goods and services now go unbought. The increased flow of finance corresponds to the increased need for finance. In the process, though, the demand for goods and services has been reduced.

It is the same at the international level. The super-saving of certain countries, reflected in enormous trade surpluses, has the capacity to unleash the Keynesian macro problem that I identified in Chapter 4, and to do so on a massive scale.

The savings glut

One way of putting this is that the world is suffering from a savings glut.[2] This idea has given rise to considerable controversy. Critics argue that if you tot up savings across the world they do not come out to be unusually, let alone "dangerously," high. High saving in Asia is offset by low saving, or even dissaving, in the west.

As a matter of fact, this may well be right; as a matter of argument, it completely misses the point. The argument is that high *desired* (*ex ante* in economists' parlance) saving has threatened a potential recession. At first, this was forestalled by western monetary authorities through the policy of stimulating increased spending (i.e., reduced saving) on the part of western households. Then came the Great Implosion and the recession. In typical Keynesian fashion, the recession reduced both the amount of spending and the amount of saving. But dissaving by governments (i.e., increased government deficits), both passive and discretionary, gradually replaced dissaving (borrowing) by the private sector.

By its very nature you cannot assess the validity of the "savings glut" view by totting up the total amount of saving. What you measure will have no bearing on the issue at hand. It is like trying to assess the demand for Microsoft shares by adding up the number of Microsoft shares held. In this case, it is the share price that brings demand into line with the fixed supply. In the case of the macro economy, it is the level of income that brings desired savings into line with desired investment.

A second critique of the savings glut idea is that it isn't so much a glut of savings that is the problem as a dearth of investment. I have considerable sympathy with this view. As I argued in Chapter 4, there is a constitutional weakness in the nexus that connects savings with real investment. It would have been a legitimate response to a surge in global saving for the west to have stepped up its investment in real plant, machinery, and buildings. In the event, this didn't happen, so the problem has an investment dimension as well as a savings one. (I will discuss the roots of this investment dimension in the Conclusion.) Yet the international imbalances did not begin with a collapse of desired investment, but rather with an increase in desired savings. This is the sense in which I think it is more appropriate to regard the issue as one of savings glut rather than investment dearth.

A different sort of critique points to the role of the policy of very low interest rates chosen by the western monetary authorities. This, critics say, is the real culprit in stimulating excessive western spending and borrowing. Supposedly there is a dichotomy between the "savings glut" and the "monetary policy" explanations for what happened.

I believe that this dichotomy is a false one. These things are two sides of the same coin. The policy of low interest rates was a response to the very low inflation and weak demand in the west – and these were largely a response to the super-saving of Asian countries (plus the oil producers, the Swiss, etc.).

Direct connections

Some people argue that trade imbalances are enough on their own to explain bubbles in financial markets, because the surplus countries poured capital into western financial markets and this raised asset prices. In its starkest form I don't accept this view, because it forgets about the offsetting western deficits that required finance. Nevertheless, there is something here after all, because of different asset and liability preferences in different parts of the economic system. The proceeds of huge trade surpluses have typically wound up in the hands of central banks as increases in their reserve holdings, and central banks have a marked preference for holding government bonds.

By contrast, western consumers would typically tend to finance themselves with bank borrowing. If the imbalances had not existed then the extra assets in the hands of western consumers and companies would probably have been held mainly in bank deposits. Accordingly, you could argue that the effect of the trade imbalances was a net increase in the demand for securities (and therefore a rise in their price), with a particular effect on the price of government bonds.[3] But this effect is surely minor compared to the effects of sharply lower interest rates imposed by central banks to offset the impact of the surplus countries' saving. The monetary policy stimulus (or, if you like, the monetary policy mistake) was, in fact, the consequence of the savings glut.[4]

The Governor of the People's Bank of China, the Chinese central bank, Zhou Xiaochuan, has gone so far as to argue that the reserve currency status of the dollar is one of the leading causes of the bubble, and hence of the subsequent crisis, because Asian countries have had little alternative but to pour money into dollar markets.[5] I don't share this view. Asian countries would not have faced a question about where to put their massive reserves if they had not been running huge current account surpluses on the back of currencies artificially held down by intervention on the exchanges.

Admittedly, given that they were building up reserves in this way, they had to invest them somewhere. If they had more effective options over which currency to put them in then the dollar would have been lower and other currencies higher, which would have transferred economic activity from the rest of the world to America. Perhaps also there would have been less of a bubble in the US and more of a bubble elsewhere, but that is about it.

Nevertheless, Mr. Zhou has made some interesting and powerful points about the design of the international monetary order that have much to commend them. Indeed, I shall argue in Chapter 9 that although the role of the dollar has *not* been one of the major causes of the current crisis, it may yet be one of its casualties.

Active and passive

Having said that world trade imbalances were at the root of what went wrong, it takes two to tango. So why should we pin responsibility for the unbalanced state of global trade on the surplus countries? Why aren't the deficit countries equally responsible?

In an accounting sense they are. But that is about the only sense in which they are. Countries rarely, if ever, set out to run deficits. At most, they may embark on policies that have deficits as their consequence. If so, they often try to minimize them, consistent with maintaining the benefits of the policies that give rise to them.

By contrast, countries often do set out to run surpluses as an act of policy. The reason is that surpluses amass assets; deficits amass debts. Assets confer power; debts confer weakness. Assets lead to future advantage; debts to future disadvantage. Assets put time on your side; debts put time against you.

For all these reasons, when there is a severe imbalance in trade, pressure is felt more strongly on deficit countries to correct the imbalance. Yet if a deficit is to be corrected, someone else's surplus needs to be reduced as well. At first sight, it may not matter which countries feel the pressure most strongly as long as the imbalance is corrected. And if all you cared about was the imbalance that would be fine. However, hardly anyone, or at least hardly anyone sane, cares about the trade imbalance for its own sake. What matters is what the imbalance – and the correction of the imbalance – does to aggregate demand, and hence to prosperity.

If deficit countries take action to reduce their deficit by *reducing* aggregate demand, this will cause lower output and higher unemployment. If surplus countries take action to reduce their surplus by *expanding* aggregate demand, this will bring about higher output and lower unemployment. In both cases, these effects will be felt not only in the countries taking the action but also by their trading partners.

Furthermore, as a matter of history, how the recent imbalances came about was through a change in the Asian surplus countries. They underwent an economic transformation that dramatically increased their prosperity. They embarked on policies designed to increase their exports, intervening massively in the foreign exchange markets to hold down their currencies and build up huge reserve holdings. In all this, the countries of the west were largely passive. Their role was confined to keeping their markets open and their consumers spending.

Why not just lie back and enjoy it?

Even so, isn't how much other countries wish to save up to them, and shouldn't the west simply let them get on with it? Isn't the saving of the east a boon for the west? Plenty of people think this way – including a good many economists. Yet it seems to me that this is an unreasonable proposition, as I argue below.

It is important to get straight at the outset, though, that my argument here is not an invective against trade with the emerging markets in general, or China in particular. It is not growing trade links with Asia that pose these problems, nor it is high Asian savings *per se*. If Asian countries wish to run a very high level of savings and investment, that is up to them. The matter only involves the west when one exceeds the other. And then it *must* involve the west because national savings exceeding national investment means running a current account surplus. And a surplus for Asia implies a deficit for the rest of the world.

At the risk of oversimplifying the issue, let us call the surplus country China and the deficit country America. So what, some economists say, if Chinese surpluses oblige America to run deficits. Global imbalances are an example of so-called intertemporal trade; that is, China is a net exporter of goods and services to the world now, but when, at some point in the future, it decides to spend the money it has accumulated, it will become a net importer. This is just like ordinary trade where one country exports the goods and services in which it has a comparative advantage and imports those in which others have a comparative advantage.[6]

The only difference here is that the two sides of the exchange are separated in time. However, this separation itself has benefits. It enables China to acquire security and to diversify its investments, which is particularly valuable at a time when its domestic financial system is undeveloped and it would otherwise be prone to making bad investments at home. On the other side of the exchange, by running a deficit with China, America is not only able to benefit from cheap Chinese goods and thereby enjoy higher present consumption, but it is also thereby able to offset domestic inflationary pressure.

This is merely another example of the gains from trade and, just as in the ordinary case, both parties profit by it.[7] They should be left to get on with it, for all the usual reasons. Free markets work best, and all that stuff. Far from worrying about the Chinese surpluses, America should simply lie back and enjoy them. If the Chinese want to offer America all these cheap goods and cheap money to buy them, how is America worse off?

This is a nice story – and it comes straight out of the economists' book of the best fairytales. It would work out fine if America were able safely and profitably to generate domestic demand to offset the demand sucked out by the Chinese or, to put the matter the other way round, to absorb the savings generated by the Chinese. But, as we have seen, it is not. The corporate sector proved unwilling or unable to absorb them, with the result that the money went to consumers – with the consequences that we see all around us.

An offer or an order?

Perhaps the issue will seem clearer if I put it in more homespun terms. If a bank or financial institution approaches you through the post, or over the internet, offering to lend you money, invest in one of your enterprises, or buy part of your house, this is indeed a free gift – apart from the inconvenience and hassle of getting them to go away! You can say yes if you want to, or say no and carry on with the rest of your life without any change.

Things are not quite the same, though, at the macro level. For the rest of the world to offer its savings to you, in net terms, it must be running a surplus. For it to be running a surplus you must be running a deficit. In other words, the offer of finance is rather more complicated than the equivalent offer from a bank to you as an individual. It is a package – rather like the offer of a new car from a car manufacturer, along with the finance to pay for it. Still, you might think this is not so bad. Again, you can say no and be no worse off. Who knows, you might find the offer so attractive that you take it up.

Except that this still does not quite capture the essence of the "Chinese offer." It is, rather, a three-part package: you lose your job, get provided with the goods and services you would have spent the money on anyway, and provided with the finance to buy them.

Now you may not see this offer as so attractive. After all, although not working may seem OK for a while, there are some things about work you might quite like. Anyway, the result of taking up this offer is that you are in debt, and the debt is growing year by year. Some time you will have to go back to work with a vengeance to pay the money back. So maybe the offer is not so appealing and you decide to turn it down.

Then you find out that it is not an offer, it's an order. You are told that you have lost your job, but you can still enjoy your old standard of living, if you like, and not pay for it – yet.

What you might now do is to get another job, if you can. If you manage to do this, and if it pays as much as the old job, then the net effect is positive – that is, the offer of all the stuff you used to buy without paying for it now. You face a choice: if you accept the job, you could enjoy a much higher standard of living now, spending the income you earn from your job and receiving the goods and services provided by the Chinese, at the expense of having to pay back the same amount they lend you, plus interest, later. Or you could have the same standard of living as before, using the goods sent by the Chinese, but using the money from the new job to invest in some asset or other. If this investment is profitable, over and above the interest rate you have to pay, you will make a profit and be better off. If not, then you won't.

In practice, the west has, by and large, chosen the first of these options – keep working and spending. The result is a higher immediate standard of living than would have been possible without the "Chinese offer" but at the expense of a lower standard of living later, corresponding to the need to pay back the debt to the Chinese!

Is it right to blame this on the west? To say, in effect, that it should either have turned the Chinese offer down or deployed the money more effectively? The way to "turn the offer down" while maintaining full employment would be for the Chinese to end their surplus, which, if the Chinese don't take action to increase aggregate demand and won't allow their exchange rate to rise, means the west restricting imports from China.

As for the west making better use of Chinese money, this is not so easy to achieve. The whole point is that the west didn't choose to be in this position in the first place. As China became more successful at trading with the west, if the west wished to maintain full employment it had to find ways of spending the Chinese money. If there had been plenty of profitable projects beforehand, presumably companies in the west would have undertaken them anyway. (I will review some of the reasons why western corporations did not step up their investment in the Conclusion.)

The bubble connection

Nevertheless, the connection between the eastern surpluses and the western bubbles is not cast iron. It would have been possible to have had a credit binge and a bubble in western societies without an external contribution. This would simply require that those people, institutions, or sectors that were running deficits were offset (and financed) by other people, institutions, or sectors within the domestic economy that were running surpluses.

Yet such binges and bubbles are unlikely to be on the same scale as what we witnessed in the run-up to 2007/9. For a real macro-bubble to get going, all sectors of society need to be taken in. They are all likely to require finance, rather than some providing finance to others. Such finance can only be provided from the outside, by another country.

Moreover, bubbles are all about illusions. A macro-bubble rests on an illusion of overall prosperity – something that promises "money for nothing." What better way of fostering this illusion than by receiving a flow of goods and services from abroad without having to pay for them? That is what running a huge current account deficit, financed by someone else's surplus, does.

Furthermore, a macro-bubble needs the connivance of the monetary authorities. They will not always be taken in. In the run-up to the current crisis, however, the super-saving of the eastern countries provided the stimulus for the policy of low interest rates that was the fuel for the bubble. In fact, its contribution was three-sided: the flood of cheap imports from Asia beat western inflation rates down; the resulting loss of demand in the west threatened to cause a recession; and the flow of Asian capital provided the finance to keep western consumers spending.

Motives and explanations

So why would a country want to run a huge current account surplus? To people obsessed with financial balances this may seem obvious, but once you look behind the platitudes it is anything but obvious. The end of economic activity is consumption. Investment is not good in itself; it is just a means to this end. And *bad* investment is just like consumption – only without the enjoyment.

If a country runs a surplus, what it is doing is giving away goods and services, which could be consumed domestically, in exchange for pieces of paper (i.e., claims on other countries, whether equities, bonds, property, or bank deposits). While this might make sense as a temporary measure, as a plan for the indefinite future it is madness.

By contrast, the widely derided position of running a deficit makes perfect sense – as long as you can get away with it. You receive a supply of goods and services and you give them pieces of paper in return. What limits the attractions of this strategy is that, in the end, you cannot get away with it; although many countries have managed it for quite a time.

I think that the right way to think of this is that exports are simply the price you pay for imports. Why pay more than you have to? The upshot is that although trade doesn't have to be balanced all the time, in general, for countries at a similar stage of development, a rough balance over a run of years makes sense.

The factors that explain why today's surplus countries choose to *pay more than they have to for their imports* – and the arguments as to whether their behavior is justified – are different for the three different country groups I identified at the beginning of this chapter, so it is best to treat them separately. I will start with the group of countries whose behavior is most readily explicable: the oil producers.

The producers of liquid gold

In 2007, the oil aspect of global balances was at least as important as the Chinese aspect. A large part of the shock that hit the industrial world in 2007/9 was the result of the huge increase in oil prices. Indeed, you could reasonably say that the world has suffered not one shock but two: the credit crunch and the sharp rise in energy and commodity prices.

The oil producers can be divided into three: Russia, Norway, and the countries of the Middle East. The positions of these three are different and need separate analysis. Russia is on a see-saw. Between 2004 and 2008 it ran a huge current account surplus, averaging 9% of GDP, and a fiscal surplus averaging 6% of GDP. Since the marginal rate of tax on oil is around 85%, soaring oil prices swelled the state's coffers.

From a long-term perspective, huge Russian surpluses do not appear to make a great deal of sense. After all, in terms of per capita incomes, Russia is a relatively poor country and it has a huge need for spending on infrastructure. What held the government back from spending the oil revenues was a lack of confidence that oil prices would stay strong, combined with a worry about future political and economic instability, based on the country's recent history. In any case, with the oil price now well down, Russia looks likely to experience a few years of both current account and fiscal *deficits*, so there does not seem to be scope for major stimulatory action by the Russian government.

Norway is in a completely different position to Russia. She is an extremely rich, small country, thanks largely to oil. It is not unreasonable that she should save a high proportion of her income against the day when the oil runs out. However, the scale of her surpluses is staggering. This decade, surging oil prices led the Norwegian current account surplus to rocket from an average of around 2.5% of GDP in the 1990s to 16.4%, or around $60 billion, in 2007. Even with oil at $40–50 per barrel, Norway still records a surplus. In 2009, this looks likely to be about 17.5% of GDP.

Of the oil producers, the ones in the Middle East seem to offer the best hope of a contribution to increased global aggregate demand. Dubai, which does not produce much oil, has embarked on a massive construction boom and has become heavily indebted. By contrast, the overall picture among the oil-producing sheikhdoms remains one of relative restraint and huge current account surpluses. In 2007, the aggregate current account balances of Middle Eastern oil exporters (Bahrain, Iran, Kuwait, Libya, Oman, Qatar, Saudi Arabia, Syria, UAE, and Yemen) was equivalent to 21% of their combined GDP.[8]

Why should these countries run such surpluses? For some, the justification is that the oil will soon run out. Mind you, that is a double-edged sword. Faced with that prospect, it may be true that a country should not blow its immediate oil revenues on a massive consumption splurge, but this does not mean that it should not spend heavily on investment to provide for its future, post-oil. That is exactly what Dubai has done.

For the large oil surplus countries, though, fear of oil running out is not the predominant reason for caution. That is a sense of insecurity stemming from the region's experiences in the 1970s. Then, many countries built up huge current account and fiscal surpluses and it was widely believed that it would be impossible for their governments to spend them. However, the combination of lower oil prices and a spending spree on everything from armaments to hospitals saw the surpluses turn into deficits within a few years.

Saudi Arabia is a classic case. As oil prices rose from $4 to $11 per barrel, its current account surplus rose from $2.5 billion in 1973 to $23 billion in 1974. Initially, the government was slow to increase expenditure, fearing that the rise in oil prices would not last. But the government increased spending enormously in 1975, (mistakenly) thinking that high oil prices would persist. When oil prices dropped back, Saudi Arabia's massive current account surplus fell precipitously and eventually turned to a *deficit* of $2 billion in 1978.

A few years later, after the second oil shock, Saudi Arabia's current account surplus reached 26% of GDP in 1980 – only to turn into a deficit of 13% in 1983 as oil prices fell back again sharply. A similar pattern can be seen in neighboring countries.

From where things stand today, what happens to the oil price, and how the oil producers behave, is critical to the outlook for aggregate demand in the world. Nevertheless, although it was important in the story of what caused the events of 2007/9, there are two reasons the oil producers deserve less attention in what follows than China and the other surplus countries of East Asia. First, the oil price has already fallen back sharply to the point where some of the oil surpluses have been significantly reduced, or even turned into deficits. Second, for several of the large surpluses that remain, there are legitimate reasons why there is limited scope for the beneficiaries to reduce them substantially by sharply increasing their spending.

The burghers of Mitteleuropa

On the face of it, the eurozone does not figure large in the litany of global imbalances. Its current account balance with the rest of the world is just about zero, which is why it didn't feature in Charts 1 and 2. However, this disguises some dramatic imbalances between its members. In 2007, while Spain's *deficit* was 10%, Italy's 2.5%, and Greece's 14%, Germany's *surplus* ran at 7.7% of GDP (over $250 billion).

If the rapidly growing countries of Asia and the oil producers insist on running large surpluses, you would think that the eurozone, along with the US and the UK, would be running large deficits. But it isn't. Why not? The answer is Germany.

The bulk of the reason for Germany's surplus relates to the behavior of its consumers; or rather nonconsumers. Germany's growth rate has for years been constrained by their conservatism. Indeed, the level of German consumer spending has barely budged in ten years. This is partly explained by the very slow growth of consumer incomes. Indeed, the share of labor in national income has fallen considerably. But in addition, the household saving rate is around 11%, much higher than in the US and the UK. The widely espoused apologia for high German savings is that these reflect the fact that the population is aging very quickly and the public pension system will be unable to cope. Quite possibly. But over and above this, the German people remain ultra-cautious to an extent that cannot be fully explained by this factor alone. The prevailing culture is the very opposite of the Anglo-Saxon spend now, pay later ethos. Meanwhile, high German savings are not fully utilized by German business to finance investment.

Why don't the German authorities take action to discourage or offset such excessive net saving? A German monetary policy response to this situation is impossible, because interest rates are set for the eurozone as a whole by the European Central Bank. A German *fiscal* response, however, is possible, and the German government showed this by announcing in 2008/9 a series of measures that amounted to a fiscal package worth 3.5% of GDP. Nevertheless, it could do much more. (I take this subject up in more detail in Chapter 8.)

The problem is largely in the mind. A really large German fiscal stimulus is inhibited by an inherent Teutonic caution about such matters. Moreover, the Germans do not see their current account surplus as a problem, or indeed anybody else's problem. Their attitude seems to be that if only the rest of the world, mainly in this instance the Anglo-Saxons, would be more like them, there wouldn't be a global economic crisis.

This is outrageous. It is impossible for everyone to run surpluses. Just as for China, there is nothing wrong with a high personal savings rate in Germany; quite the opposite, if that's what people want to do. The problem only comes when these savings are not absorbed by domestic investment. This is the position in Germany, hence the huge current account surplus. If Germany insists on running surpluses, it is implicitly insisting that someone else must run deficits. Given the way the world is, that someone will have to be the Anglo-Saxon countries (led by America). As and when a global strategy is hammered out to deal with the deficiency of global demand, which I discuss in Chapter 8, a German expansion plan will have to be part of it.

Similar reasoning applies to Switzerland. As a proportion of GDP, Switzerland's surplus is even larger than Germany's – 13% in 2007. Admittedly, it fell to about 8% in 2008, but this is still very large. Naturally, as a much smaller economy the absolute size is much smaller – $70 billion in 2007 – but this is still a significant number.

The demographic situation in Switzerland is similar to Germany. But why don't the Swiss authorities take action to increase domestic demand? After all, the Swiss fiscal position is sound. In 2009 the government deficit was about zero and net government debt was not much more than 10% of GDP. The answer, I suppose, is that the authorities do not see high national savings and a current account surplus as a problem. But Switzerland is suffering from the Great Implosion like everybody else. Although it is a small country, Switzerland will also need to make a contribution to achieving a global solution.

Asian surpluses

Now we come to the main course: Asia. Straightaway, though, it needs to be broken down into its constituent parts, starting with Japan. If the world is to regain economic and financial balance, which I discuss in Chapter 8, an expansion of Japanese domestic demand and a higher exchange rate for the yen would make a valuable contribution to the overall solution.

But I wouldn't hold your breath. Japan's surplus is nothing new; she has been a persistent surplus country since 1980. Nor was there a policy change over the last decade. Moreover, even more than the countries of Mitteleuropa, Japan has the excuse that its population is aging rapidly. At some point, the rising proportion of its population that is retired will cause a sharp drop in the savings rate, with the result that the Japanese surplus should fall. With interest rates effectively at zero, and Japanese government debt still very high, there is not a lot of scope for the authorities to take stimulatory action.

Moving swiftly on to another of Asia's giants, although India is a hugely important country with a big future, she does not figure much in the present debate about trade imbalances, simply because she is running both a significant fiscal deficit and a current account deficit, and she has for a few years.

Therefore focus needs to be directed toward China and the group of smaller Asian countries usually referred to as the Asian "tigers": Korea, Taiwan, Hong Kong, Singapore, Malaysia, Thailand, Indonesia, and the Philippines. China's significance for world trade is huge and she is running a surplus of about 10% of GDP. While each of the tiger economies is small, as a group they are large. They account for 5% of world GDP and 13% of world exports. In 2007, the combined current account surpluses of emerging Asia, excluding India and China, came to $168 billion, or around 6% of its combined GDP.

So why are the countries of emerging Asia, including China, running such huge surpluses? One idea can be quickly dismissed, namely the notion that such high surpluses are natural for countries in their position. In fact, you would think that the natural order of things would be for the older, richer, less rapidly growing countries to invest money in the younger, poorer, rapidly growing ones. In other words, you would expect China and the Asian tigers to be in deficit and America to be in surplus, so that China and the tigers were net importers of capital and America a net exporter.

Nineteenth-century Britain is the classic example of a country in the position of world economic dominance that America now occupies. For most of the century, however, she ran a large current account surplus, which gave her capital to invest in emerging markets around the world. The outward flow of funds from Britain financed the development – and the current account deficits – of umpteen countries, including the United States, Australia, India, South Africa, and much of Latin America.

Nor is it true that China has always run a huge current account surplus. Until 2002, her surpluses were small. Admittedly, this was a far cry from the substantial deficit that emerging countries could be expected to run, but at least it wasn't a massive surplus. From 2000 to 2008, China's surplus rose from $1\frac{1}{2}$% of GDP to 10%. Similarly, from the 1970s to the late 1990s, the Asian tigers, along with the rest of the developing world, nearly all ran small current account deficits.[9]

The crisis of 1997

The seminal event that changed the Asian current account position, and in the process set off the chain of events that led to the Great Implosion, was the Asian financial crisis of 1997. There had previously been a huge boom in the region, which attracted massive inflows of foreign capital. Then in 1997, boom turned to bust as investors pulled out of the region. Asian currencies plunged in value, domestic investment spending dried up, and unemployment soared, leading to sharp falls in consumption. As domestic demand was hit, the current account deficits of the worst-affected countries rapidly turned into surpluses. Korea, an economy the size of Canada on the eve of the crisis, moved from having a deficit of 4% of GDP in 1996 to a surplus of 12% two years later. For the economies of emerging Asia combined (again, excluding India and China), a deficit of 2% of GDP in 1996 turned into a surplus of 8% in 1998.

These surpluses were the natural result of a collapse of domestic demand and a fall in imports. Nevertheless, the initial shock in 1997 that depressed domestic demand and slashed imports does not explain why large surpluses remained a decade later when growth and prosperity were restored. The explanation for this lies in the response of Asian policymakers to the crisis. Having seen the damage inflicted by runs on their currencies, they decided to ensure that this could never happen again. In short, they decided to run their economies so as to produce current account surpluses. China's surplus did not take off until 2002, several years after the crisis of 1997, but the influence of this episode on the thinking of the Chinese authorities, and on the policies employed, was similar.

Hoards of reserves

There was another dimension to this change. If a country switched from deficit into surplus, this meant that it would not be reliant on inflows of foreign capital from the rest of the world. However, this would not by itself give its monetary authorities ammunition to protect its economy and currency from whatever buffets arose in the international monetary system. For this it needed *reserves*; that is, holdings of foreign currency assets in the hands of the government or central bank.

Accordingly, after the events of 1997, the countries of East Asia, including China, set about building up their holdings of foreign exchange reserves, principally dollars. The way of doing this was for the central banks to intervene in the foreign exchange markets, selling their own currency in exchange for foreign currency.

This the central banks of Asia did with a vengeance. The result is a reserve hoard now grown to gargantuan proportions. At the end of 2008, China's reserve holdings amounted to $2,000 billion, or just short of $2,000 for each of its citizens. Given that at this point the average Chinese worker was earning about $2,200 per annum, this is a truly remarkable sum. In the rest of Asia reserves totaled just over $2,500 billion, giving an overall Asian total approaching $5,000 billion, up from a mere $560 billion in 1997.

The Chinese wall

So I come to the explanation for this phenomenon. Most of what I say is going to refer to China, although much of the argument is also applicable to the Asian tigers. The big difference is probably the greater role of the 1997/8 Asian crisis in motivating the policy of the tigers.

Given that its people are still so poor, why does China export so much capital? One answer, which is superficially appealing and is sometimes advanced by the Chinese authorities and their apologists in the west, is that it doesn't "do it." The surpluses simply emerge as a result of China's phenomenal advance and extreme cost competitiveness.

This really won't wash. As I pointed out earlier, the Chinese (and other East Asian) monetary authorities have intervened massively to hold their currencies down, which has had the effect of boosting the current account surpluses. Moreover, even if the authorities were fully passive, in the sense of letting the exchange rate reach its own level and not undertaking any measures to boost exports or reduce imports, there would still be a question to answer. The current account position of a country does not just emerge "naturally"; it is the result of the interaction between the actions and proclivities of the private sector on the one hand and economic and monetary policy on the other.

So, if China is running a huge current account surplus, it is open to the Chinese authorities to operate policies that would eradicate the surplus, just as countries that are running a deficit often choose, or are forced, to operate policies that eradicate the deficit. That the Chinese authorities do not do so indicates that in some sense that they have chosen this state of affairs. The puzzle is why.

Straight from the textbook

The textbook solution to China's position would be a major increase in the exchange rate, coupled with a looser stance of fiscal and monetary policy. One without the other would be unsatisfactory. A higher exchange rate would tend to reduce exports and hence reduce GDP and employment. Looser fiscal and monetary policy would increase domestic demand and threaten to cause overheating, leading to inflation. The result of a judicious combination of a higher exchange rate and easier fiscal and monetary policy, however, would be slower growth of net exports, offset by faster growth of domestic demand, resulting in a reduced trade surplus or, in the extreme, no surplus at all, and no change in the overall level of demand and employment.

So why don't the Chinese authorities follow such a strategy, instead of running substantial surpluses? One explanation is that they really don't look at export surpluses the way a western economist would. Indeed, they may take a *mercantilist* view of the world; that is, they believe, in contrast to the view I expressed above, that their country's economic interests *are* best served by boosting exports, since the size and success of export industries are crucial to economic growth.

You can readily see why they might believe this. After all, the history of Asian development has been a history of export success. This was the story with Japan, Taiwan, Korea, and all of the Asian tigers. Success in world export markets meant technological excellence, which then fed through to the domestic economy. If this is the well-worn Asian path, why should China choose any other?

In fact, this argument is not sufficient to justify China's trade policy, because the same level of export success can be achieved with a wide variety of levels of imports. A given degree of export success is therefore compatible with a wide variety of outcomes for the current account surplus. The telling question for China is therefore not why she wants to achieve such a high level of exports, but rather why she wants to sustain such a high current account surplus.

Perhaps the Chinese authorities are extreme mercantilists and believe that not just exports but *surpluses* are a good thing. Yet if they are a good thing for all countries, there is a conflict, because one country's surplus must entail another country's deficit. Why should the countries of the west passively allow the rapidly growing countries of the east to run surpluses and thereby snatch advantage for themselves and disadvantage for the west?

While the authorities may believe that a major export surplus is needed in order to generate sufficient jobs, this is a canard. A higher surplus does indeed imply a bigger boost to jobs, other things being equal. If that were all there were to be said, however, the world would be in a pretty sorry state as every country sought to generate jobs by effectively stealing them from others through running a large trade surplus! Fortunately, there are other ways of creating jobs. Countries that don't trade at all can have full employment, as can countries that run balanced trade or even current account deficits.

The allure of reserves

Perhaps the Chinese authorities are mercantilist in a financial way; that is, it is the reserves they want, rather than the surpluses. After the experience of 1997, wanting some increase in reserves in order to provide security is understandable enough. The authorities may also see political advantages for China in amassing such reserves. These certainly give the country more clout in the world, and they potentially allow it to build up substantial stakes in many western enterprises.

It is not obvious, though, that in this regard the perceived interests of the Chinese government necessarily coincide with the actual interests of the Chinese people. The Chinese government surely cannot believe that such a strategy offers the best hope of a decent return on investment. After all, China, not the west, is the rapidly growing economic area. Moreover, whatever the Chinese authorities decide to do about the exchange rate in the next few years, on a medium-term view the chances are that the renminbi will have to rise by a considerable amount, implying capital losses on assets held in foreign currencies. This puts China in a real bind, which I will discuss in a moment.

Either way, you would think that at some point the stock of reserves would be big enough, and the Chinese authorities would therefore desist from the policies that are causing the stock to rise. As yet there is no sign of this.

Policy impotence?

Perhaps the authorities believe that although they can readily see what a higher exchange rate could do to reduce Chinese exports, they do not have the means to bring about the offsetting increase in domestic demand. That too seems implausible.

The authorities could reduce interest rates (although that might inhibit the attempt to get the renminbi established at a higher level). More importantly, the Chinese government could give instructions to state-owned banks to shovel more money out to enterprises, as it did in response to the sharp fallback in economic growth in 2008. However, given the dodgy nature of many of the Chinese banking system's assets, it may not be such a good idea to try to engineer expansion by increasing the size of banks' balance sheets any faster. That has rather unpleasant echoes of what happened recently in the west, with consequences that we are now living through.

Most importantly, the government has ample scope to relax fiscal policy. It announced a large fiscal package as the global economic crisis worsened in 2008. It has scope to go much further. In 2008, the government ran a deficit of only 0.5% of GDP and the stock of debt is low. Official figures put gross Chinese government debt at 20% of GDP, although that is almost certainly an underestimate. Gross debt is probably about 65% of GDP, and net debt probably only half that level at most. Given the country's extraordinary economic growth rates, these are low levels. A sustained fiscal expansion of 5% of GDP is perfectly plausible. In Chapter 8, I give examples of some of the concrete measures the government could take.

The focus of demand-boosting measures should not be investment, since in China this is already running at over 40% of GDP. The long-run objective of the authorities ought to be to increase the share of the economy accounted for by consumption. There is plenty of scope for this since, on average, the Chinese people remain poor, and household consumption accounts for just 35% of GDP, compared with between 60 and 70% in most western countries.

Mind you, Chinese real household spending has been increasing at 9–10% for the past couple of years. It is plausible that the authorities believe that it would be impossible, or dangerous, to increase this rate of expansion still further. I must say, though, that I cannot see why. Political problems frequently arise when governments, often driven by the IMF, seek to *reduce* the growth of consumer spending in order to release more resources to go into exports. However, it is most unusual for political problems to be created by measures designed to shift resources *into* consumption.

In many of the Asian tigers, the situation is rather different; it is not consumption that looks particularly low but investment. In Taiwan and Malaysia, for instance, the share of investment in GDP is not much different from the G-7 average. This does not undermine the logic of the tiger economies needing to expand domestic demand, but simply implies that they may need to look to different policies to achieve this objective.

Dislocation and distribution

There is another, eminently plausible explanation for the Chinese authorities' inaction. They may be very wary of the dislocation that would be caused by a policy of shifting resources out of exports and into consumption. Added to that, they may fear the distributional aspect, because there would undoubtedly be losers as well as winners, namely the workers in export-oriented businesses, some of whom would lose their jobs. Linked to this, they may fear that although the policy might work well in theory, getting the right balance in practice may be difficult, since the size of the two sets of measures needed to be exactly offsetting will not be known in advance.

Yet this hardly seems compelling. It should be possible to move along this path gradually, trying things out and learning by doing. Moreover, for anything except a sudden upward lurch of the exchange rate, continued growth in the output of export industries should not be immediately at risk. Rather, it should be a matter of output for export not rising as fast as it has been, while output for domestic consumption rises faster.

The attractions of doing nothing

My suspicion is that different parts of the Chinese establishment believe in different mixtures of these views, and even that who believes in what particular mixture might change over time. Moreover, although they are perfectly well aware of the argument for a shift of strategy, the authorities feel wary about trying to resolve the different interests that would be in conflict. Bearing in mind the perceived dangers attached to change, the default position is to stick with the strategy that has brought such striking success.

After all, the Chinese authorities have much to be proud of in what has been achieved for the Chinese people through the policies they have pursued, usually against western norms and often in the face of western criticism. In particular, they can argue that they have been right to resist western pressure to open up their capital markets, and that in doing this they have contributed to global financial stability.

However, China is sitting on a time bomb. As I argued above, choosing to run a huge surplus means that other countries have to run a huge deficit. This may not be what they would like to do and it may have considerable costs. For most of the last ten years, while China has been developing fast and amassing its huge export surpluses, those costs have not been obvious in the west. There was an apparently painless way of boosting domestic demand to offset the west's huge trade deficits, namely low interest rates and easy credit. In any case, the effect of China's competitiveness in keeping western inflation down was judged to be helpful.

We are no longer in such a world. The limits to the strategy of boosting western domestic demand are now obvious. Unless China acts to boost its consumption and reduce its reliance on a large trade surplus, the west will achieve the latter for China, by imposing protectionist measures, and the Chinese will be left trying to achieve the former in an atmosphere of deep economic and political crisis.

The dollar trap

It is in China's interest to boost domestic demand not only because this would both increase domestic living standards and fend off the protectionist threat, but also because it would help to release the country from a financial trap that is largely of her own making. It is all very well saying that China should allow her currency to rise, but if this were to happen, she would register a huge loss on her huge dollar reserve holdings. Yet the more she persists with the current policy, the more the reserve hoard grows, and the more vulnerable China becomes.

If America is forced to continue down the current path of running huge government deficits to prop up the American economy – funded, ultimately, by the Chinese surpluses – the more likely some sort of default becomes. The danger is that either America will openly renege on her obligations, or she will covertly renege by inflating and thereby depreciating the dollar. Either way, the Chinese government would register an enormous loss. China cannot both sustain her surpluses and make her reserve holding safe. She must make a choice. I analyze what China should do, and what America should do to help her make the right decision, in Chapters 8 and 9.

The Asian connection

So the Asian story is deeply connected with the financial failures that I analyzed in the last chapter and with the downturn of the global economy that
is the subject of the book. The Asian crisis of 1997/8 was a prime example of
the trouble with markets: a classic case of bubble and burst, one of the several
that have afflicted the capitalist system over the last 30 years. Huge amounts
of footloose western funds, marshaled and directed by western investment
banks, poured into economies with relatively primitive financial systems, in
search of a fast return – and then washed out again like a retreating tsunami,
leaving devastation in its wake.

When Asian economies collapsed in the wake of the financial crisis, these
same banks, western commentators, and the American policy establishment
were scathing about the Asian model of "crony capitalism." They argued that
Asian countries should open up their financial markets and normalize – that
is, westernize – them. How is the biter bit! At the time, to many Asian
observers, this advice looked like so much self-serving nonsense. Now, to
observers in both east and west alike, it looks plain naive.

Moreover, without this episode and the lessons learned from it, the behavior of the Asian tigers, and more specifically China, may well have been very
different, thereby lessening the downward impact on global demand and
reducing the impulses toward much lower interest rates in the west, which
were the leading proximate cause of the bubble that ended with the Great
Implosion.

As I shall show, although there is much that the west must do to put its
house in order, including learning quite a few lessons from Asia, it is difficult
to see how the world can escape from its current plight, let alone secure a
prosperous and stable future for itself, without a significant increase in Asian
domestic demand. For that to happen, the Chinese government will have to
take courage and change course. I have a good deal of hope that eventually
this is exactly what is going to happen. If it does, then the shape of the economy will be transformed – and with it the ability of individuals, firms, and
monetary authorities to forge a path away from depression toward recovery.

Part III

From Implosion to Recovery

How You Can Survive the Downturn
– and Prosper in the Recovery

The market can stay irrational for longer than you can stay solvent.

John Maynard Keynes[1]

It is difficult to get a man to understand something when his salary depends upon his not understanding it.

Upton Sinclair[2]

The tidal wave that smashed into the global financial system in 2007/9 not only wrought havoc among investment banks and wholesale financial institutions, but it also devastated the finances of many private individuals. Equity prices fell, property prices fell, commodity prices fell, interest rates fell. Eventually, even gold prices fell. Only government bonds delivered gains for their holders.

Falling asset prices quickly meant failing financial institutions. Banks failed across the board, but were propped up by governments; umpteen hedge funds failed and were allowed to go under; not many insurance companies failed, but virtually all of them suffered devastating losses and quite a few wobbled. Meanwhile, the value of pension funds' assets plunged, thereby intensifying the gloom that many people felt about their financial prospects in retirement.

What a far cry this was from the days, not that long ago, when it was widely believed that successful investment was a doddle and that, in particular, you were *bound* to make money in equities. We are now in a situation where many private investors are sick to death of all financial investments – and of all the financial professionals and institutions that sell them and manage them. For personal investors, the Great Implosion has given birth to the Age of Disillusion.

Yet people have got to do something with their money. As always, we want both to keep it safe and to earn a decent return on it. In the Age of Disillusion, what on earth should we do with it?

In Chapters 8 and 9, I will address the question of what governments and central banks can, should, and will do to get us out of the mess that we are in – and prevent another one like it. But individual investors cannot – and should not – merely wait on macro events. They need to put their own finances in order. That is the issue to which this chapter is addressed.

An economist's limitations

On the question of what to do with our money, unsurprisingly, I will give you an economist's answer. You can make of that what you will, but I am conscious that successful investment requires much more than mere economic wisdom. In particular, it depends on knowing the price at which to buy and the price at which to sell – and having the self-discipline to act on your assessment. That is something with which an economist, particularly one operating at a distance through the medium of a book, cannot help you.

What an economist can do, though, is to lay out the principal features of an economic scenario that will determine the returns on an investment, and to analyze the fundamental factors that will make some assets a good investment and some a bad one. That is what I am trying to do here. But I do it in a spirit of overwhelming modesty, and with keen awareness of the fundamental uncertainty that envelops us. I do hope that readers of what follows will regard this not as a substitute for good analysis and sound judgment, but rather as no more than a starting point for thinking about future investments, and as a friendly guide, which may help them to negotiate the choppy waters that lie ahead. For brevity's sake, I concentrate my attention on asset markets in the developed countries of the west.

I am conscious that we must beware of thinking of "the future" as a single period. The financial crisis of 2007/9 changed the world into a desperate, abnormal state. Phase 1 of the future will see the playing out of the powerful forces driving us down. Then, at some point, there will be a recovery. Indeed, recovery may already have started. This is what I call Phase 2. I even think it worth hazarding a few guesses now about the new normality that will descend on us once recovery is complete. This is what I call Phase 3. I will try to say something about how the various asset categories will fare in these three phases.

Doubtless you will want to know when these various phases will start and finish. Don't we all! There is not much I can add on this over and above what I said in Chapter 2, and that was precious little. The future remains unknowable. Nevertheless, even if we cannot know the timing of the transition through the phases, knowing that the future may well take this shape should help investors to avoid many a pitfall.

Safe as houses?

Given that houses are a large part of what got us here in the first place, they are, I think, the appropriate place to start. The most important point to grasp about the housing boom that preceded the current financial crisis is that it was global. By now, even the regulars down the Dog and Duck think they know where the crisis started: with American subprime mortgages. However, the really striking thing is that America was very far from having the most overblown of the world's housing markets.

If measured by the increase in prices from the first quarter of 1997 to the peak, that prize goes to Ireland, at almost 300%, compared to about 130% in the US. After Ireland comes the UK, with a cumulative rise of about 225%. There are seven other countries with cumulative increases greater than the United States. In decreasing order, after Ireland and the UK, they are Spain, Australia, Norway, Sweden, France, Denmark, and the Netherlands. After the US, but still showing high increases, come Italy, China, Canada, and Korea.

Some developed countries bucked the trend, but not many. In Switzerland, prices barely rose at all, in Germany they were about flat, and in Japan they actually fell.

Just because a market has risen a lot does not mean that it is overvalued. A large rise may be justified by an increase in the number of people willing, and able to afford, to buy houses. Or by a large rise in average earnings, whether real or nominal. Or perhaps the market was undervalued to start with.

In order to get a first stab at whether a housing market is overvalued or not, I look at the ratio of average house prices to average earnings. I regard this as better than so-called *affordability* – that is, the burden of mortgage payments as a share of income, taking account of changes in mortgage inter-est rates – because mortgage rates may go up and down by quite large amounts. Historical calculations of value based on affordability are also heav-ily distorted by the decline in the inflation rate during the 1980s and 1990s. This decline altered the level of the real interest rate implied by a given nom-inal rate.

Wherever you look, the house price-to-earnings ratio rose to absurd levels. In the UK it reached 6.3, compared to a long-run average of 3.7, and a previous peak of 4.7. My first presumption is that this ratio will head back to some-thing like its long-term average. This is what I regard as fair value.[3]

Catching a falling knife

Since house prices soared above fair value in the upswing, why can't they go well below fair value in the downswing? I think this is highly plausible. After all, the next few years will be characterized by high rates of unemployment and a shortage of mortgage finance. Confidence, as well as finance, is likely to be at a low ebb.

Accordingly, in making a stab at the possible size of the housing market correction, I assume that prices will drop 15% below fair value, in line with the weight of evidence from past house price corrections across Europe. I also assume that house prices take three years from their peak to reach their low point. These assumptions, combined with my forecasts for average earn-ings growth, allow me to derive the likely floor for house prices and, thus, the peak to trough fall.

What this approach shows is that, while the US and UK might see prices drop by 35% and 40% respectively, Ireland, Spain, the Netherlands, and Australia could all witness prices fall by rather more, with Ireland and Spain looking most vulnerable. France could experience falls of 30–35%, while Italy, Denmark, and Norway could all see prices drop by between 20% and 25%.

This does not mean that these are the percentages by which I expect house prices to fall in these countries by the time you read this. How could I know that? I do not know when you are reading it, nor by how much house prices have fallen in the interim. For all I know, even if both my reasoning and my estimates are proved right, you may be reading this when prices in your market have already fallen by 40%. In which case, pretty much regardless of where you are, they are unlikely to fall much further. And it is quite possible that even if my reasoning is correct, some other major event – for good or ill – may have interposed itself between the acts of writing and reading.

Moreover, the more slowly the price correction proceeds, the more likely it is that the size of the necessary price fall will be lower. This is because average earnings normally rise over time. Indeed, because of this, it would be possible for housing markets to get back to equilibrium – that is, fair value – without any falls in prices at all. If prices stood still, the upward march of earnings would eventually float the housing market off. Mind you, in the economic conditions that are likely to prevail in the next couple of years, that seems a pretty unlikely prospect.

If houses do indeed dip below fair value, this implies that they will again be a good-value investment. Hence Phase 2 could be characterized by a recovery period when house prices again increase by more than the increase in average incomes.

Back to normal?
Even while they are in the doldrums, but especially once a recovery has begun, some people may be of the view that house prices will quickly bounce back to where they were at the peak. That is the conclusion you would readily come to if you believed that what has happened in housing markets is simply the result of the marked collapse of mortgage availability caused by the financial crisis of 2007/9.

This view, precisely because it is so seductive, is potentially extremely dangerous. The credit crunch is not the fundamental cause of the sharp fall in house prices. The fundamental cause is the fact that prices were driven up to ludicrous levels in the bubble. The credit crunch was the trigger, but not the underlying cause of the collapse.

Accordingly, I suspect that it will be many years before house prices regain their old peaks, never mind scale new ones. I reckon that in America, the UK, France, Spain, and Ireland, a return to the previous peak in nominal terms will not be achieved before 2020. In the Netherlands it may not come until 2030. In real terms, previous peaks will not be regained before about 2040 – and more like 2050 in the Netherlands.

What is the endgame? What is the equilibrium rate of house price increase in Phase 3? This will differ considerably from country to country, in response to the local pressures of supply and demand. For most countries, though, a good starting point would be the presumption that house prices will rise at the same rate as average earnings. On past form, this might be about 4% in the UK and the US, but 10%, or even 15%, in some emerging markets.

Overall inflation conditions could make a big difference here. With unemployment set to soar in most countries, and price inflation set to be very low and in many countries negative, in the immediate future there will be powerful downward pressure on the rate of increase of pay. In many countries, the average rate of increase may well fall to zero, or below. Moreover, when the economy recovers, pay inflation will not necessarily return to the old markers. It wouldn't be surprising if pay inflation in the US and the UK ended up more like 2% than 4%.

Where there is a natural shortage of property, and the structural fundamentals are right, as in the UK, it might be right to expect house prices to rise by a little more than the rate of increase of pay, say 5 or 6% if pay is increasing by 4%, or 3 or 4% if pay is increasing by 2%. Nevertheless, this is by no means guaranteed. Moreover, it is a far cry from the 20% increases of 2002/3 – and a far cry from most people's expectations of what houses will naturally deliver. Most people are in for a shock.

I must give a further word of warning. The apparently dire outlook I describe above is predicated on what may readily turn out to have been an overly optimistic assumption, namely that the economy does not fall into sustained deflation. In order to reach equilibrium and form a base for recovery, house prices have to fall in relation to earnings. The above calculations assume that the price level is stable to rising gently and average earnings growth is no worse than zero. But what if deflation sets in and pay starts to fall? Then house prices would have to fall further just to stay in the same place in relation to pay.

Moreover, as I will show in a moment, conditions of deflation may readily result in high real rates of interest. If this happened, the equilibrium level of house prices would be still lower. In short, if you are hoping for a limited fall in house prices, pray that deflation is avoided.

Commercial property

Similar considerations apply to commercial property. This asset class doesn't usually figure prominently in either the portfolios or the attentions of individual investors. Interestingly, though, toward the end of the property bubble, many private investors *did* pile into commercial property – with predictably dire consequences.

They may have got their timing wrong, but they were right to give commercial property real attention. It is a hugely significant asset category. In the US, the stock of commercial property is valued at almost $2,000 billion, or about a quarter of the size of the government bond market, and it is of a similar relative size elsewhere.

Moreover, it looks to me as though the bubble in commercial property in the US and the UK, if not in the eurozone, was of about the same order of magnitude as the bubble in residential property. In the UK at one point, property yields were 0.8% *lower* than government bond yields. For an asset with uncertain returns, open-ended costs, and poor liquidity to command a lower yield than perfectly safe government bonds was pretty demanding, to say the least.

Accordingly, from peak to trough, commercial property prices may fall by about as much as residential prices; that is, about 40%. Given that they are also likely to overshoot on the downside, it is certainly possible that in Phase 2 there will be some pretty good returns available again, perhaps running at well above 10% p.a. But don't be fooled. The sustainable gains in Phase 3 will be lower. In the developed economies of the west, on a long-run basis, you might reasonably expect total returns on commercial property to average around 7–9% per year – an income yield of 7%, plus capital gains of 0–2% (underpinned by rental value growth roughly equal to the rate of inflation).

Interest on the wane

If the housing and commercial property markets are in freefall, the economy is soft for years, and inflation is rapidly turning into deflation, what is the outlook for interest rates? The answer is down and out. But there is a difference between short and long, between public and private sectors, and between what you get as a depositor and what you are charged as a borrower.

The place to begin is with official short-term interest rates, the rates that are set by central banks. The logic of the economic situation I described in Chapters 2 and 3 is that those rates should fall virtually to zero. In most countries of the developed west, and in Japan, this has already happened. Official interest rates are now effectively zero, or very close to it, pretty much throughout the developed world.

Many people find the idea of near-zero interest rates extraordinary – but we live in extraordinary times. Nor are near-zero rates unprecedented. The Bank of Japan maintained a policy of near-zero interest rates between 1999 and 2006. And in the Great Depression, US Treasury Bill rates were 0.01% in 1938 and 1939. There are a few isolated examples of rates being negative, briefly and slightly, but each has been a technical quirk and these cases need not detain us here. For all practical purposes we may assume that official interest rates cannot be negative, so they are now about as low as they can go.[4]

The zero era

Yet there is even more radicalism to come. Now that interest rates are just about down to absolute zero, they are going to stay there for a considerable time. The economic and financial crisis is going to be with us for several years. As I argued in Chapter 2, this is not a normal recession; it is more like a depression. As depressionary conditions linger on, so will the need to keep rates low. Indeed, if it is believed that interest rates will soon head back up again, this will undermine the effectiveness of the period of low rates. For this would cause longer-term interest rates to stay high, including the yields on government bonds, to which I will turn my attention in a moment.

High bond yields would further undermine the value of all assets, including equities and commercial property. They would also increase the cost of servicing government debt, the volume of which is now sharply increased pretty much everywhere as a result of the combination of recession, bank bailouts and fiscal expansion.

The second reason for believing that the period of low interest rates will be long is the likely course of fiscal policy. Across the western world, governments are becoming increasingly alarmed at the size of the borrowing they have to do in order to stave off financial and economic collapse. As soon as the economy looks like recovering, they will want to put fiscal stabilization at the top of the agenda. Tax rates will rise and/or spending will be cut. However, these measures, desirable or necessary as they may be, will be deflationary of aggregate demand. At best, they will tend to extend the period of economic weakness and slow the rate of recovery. At worst, they will take the economy back into the doldrums. In these conditions, the last thing that the world's central banks should do is to jack up interest rates prematurely. The economy will need all the help it can get from monetary policy.

We have the example of Japan to go on. During Japan's "Lost Decade" in the 1990s, the Japanese authorities did tighten fiscal policy when they thought the economy could stand it. Between 1998 and 2001, the cyclically adjusted budget deficit was reduced from 11% of GDP to less than 6%. In 2000, the Bank of Japan tightened monetary policy by raising interest rates from zero to 0.25%. Both of these measures are now widely regarded as mistakes.[5]

Bonds are the thing?

If official interest rates are indeed going to be zero, or near zero, for some time, then assets that carry a fixed rate of interest should deliver a good return. Naturally, the reliability of the issuer of the instrument is fundamental. Some bank-issued financial instruments do, and will continue to, carry fixed rates of interest well above current and likely future, official interest rate levels. But, of course, they will continue to carry bank risk. Moreover, it is very unusual for banks to issue savings products with a guaranteed fixed return over a period longer than two or three years.

Corporations often issue long-term fixed interest debt – corporate bonds – and these offer an interesting avenue for investment. The yields on these instruments can be decomposed into the equivalent of the yield on government bonds, about which I have much to say in a moment, and a spread paid to corporate investors for the risk implied by holding corporate as opposed to government debt.

This spread can be substantial. At one point when investors were particularly anxious, the yield spread for AAA-rated corporate bonds over UK government bonds (gilts) was as high as 3%, although it subsequently fell back considerably. This spread may allow the investor to gain a pretty good return from bonds even when the prevailing level of interest rates and government bond yields is low.

However, I have two words of warning. First, the economic conditions that are likely to prevail in the next few years will be very unfriendly to corporate bonds. Many companies will find it difficult to meet their interest obligations and many will default.

Second, the conditions of deflation, which I analyzed in Chapter 3, would be particularly unfriendly. Companies would find their selling prices falling but their interest obligations remaining constant, thereby intensifying the real burden of the debt and making default more likely. These points aside, the fate of corporate bonds will be closely related to the fate of government bonds. Accordingly, in what follows, although I am generally referring to government bonds, the message can usually be extended to corporate bonds also.

The long and the short

Even government bonds constitute a widely differing group of assets. The very shortest of government bonds are just like money market investments, except that they carry a government guarantee. All bond prices go up and down as market interest rates of the same period go down and up, respectively. But the shorter the bond, the closer the relationship is with current short-term interest rates, and the less scope there is for returns to vary. Accordingly, a government bond with, say, one year left to run to maturity will not make you much of a return, if at all, above near-zero official short-term interest rates, and no hope of making a sizeable capital gain on your investment.

At the other end of the spectrum there are bonds with maturity dates 30, or even 50, years into the future. In the UK, there are even bonds with no maturity date at all. With these long bonds, the immediate level of short-term interest rates, taken on its own, is of minimal relevance. What matters is primarily the prospective rates of inflation over the life of the bond.

If you are holding a bond that yields 4% and the inflation rate is going to be more than 4% on average, then you will get a negative real return. Prospective holders of this bond will fight shy of it and its market price will fall – to the point where the market is again prepared to take it on, believing that it will deliver a reasonable return, over and above the prospective rate of inflation. This might be a yield of 7%, 8%, 10%, or whatever, depending on how high the market thinks inflation might be, and on how high a level of real return it requires.

However, any of these rates would impose a thumping great loss on a bond you had bought on a 4% yield. Conversely, if the market thinks that inflation will be very low, or even negative, over the life of the bond, the market rate could easily fall below 4%, implying higher bond prices, and therefore capital gains for existing holders.

So bond markets vary across a spectrum. At the very short maturities yields are closely tied to current official policy rates; at the long end they are free to vary with the market's own views. I like to think of the curve that shows the yield on the whole spread of bonds, from the very short out to the very long, as a piece of string with one end nailed to a post but the other end floating about in the wind. The only fixed point is the nailed end; the rest of the string gets blown about and may be higher, lower, or level with the bit that is nailed to the post.

Bond market prospects

Could yields fall any further? In the 1930s, long yields dipped below 3% in the UK. In America, they dipped below 2% in 1940 and 1941. In Japan, during the 1990s, 10-year yields briefly touched 0.6%. If indeed we are entering an extended period of short-term interest rates at 0–1%, I could readily see 10-year yields at between 2% and 3% – perhaps even lower – which would confer capital gains on all those who had bought bonds earlier at higher yields.

The fall of bond yields so far has been greater than it would otherwise have been in the US and the UK because the central banks there have engaged in so-called "quantitative easing"; that is, making outright purchases of bonds from the market. (I analyze this policy in Chapter 8.)

As central banks struggle to stimulate demand in the economy at a time when interest rates are already at the zero bound, they may well massively extend their bond purchases, which could drive bond prices higher (and yields lower). The flipside of this, though, is that when the central banks stop this policy and then put it into reverse by selling bonds from their holdings, the price of these bonds could drop considerably.

Moreover, even without the policy of quantitative easing, the markets would be worried about an eventual surge of inflation. With such a policy, many market operators are terrified of it. And all this at a time when bond yields are very low. At some point, therefore, there is likely to be a sharp sell-off by investors. If this coincided with the central banks offloading large amounts of bonds onto the market, there could be a bond bloodbath.

Even if a bloodbath is avoided, at some point bond yields will surely have to return to a more normal level. In Phase 3, a normal level of yields could easily be 5–6%. If China and other surplus countries boosted their consumption to a very large degree, and if this coincided with a revival of domestic demand in the west, a period of higher real interest rates could be required to restrain inflation. This could easily imply nominal bond yields significantly above 6%.

There is a further word of caution that applies to indexed bonds. The evidence is that real yields can get very low indeed. At one point, the real yield on the British government's 50-year indexed bond was 0.5%.

Under conditions of deflation, you might readily expect real yields to get this low, or even lower. However, the zero bound to short-term interest rates implies a startling and unsettling result. As an economy flips over into deflation, real interest rates will rise – at just the time that the lack of demand for finance from attractive, creditworthy borrowers and the need to generate aggregate demand might ordinarily incline you to believe that they would fall.

With real short rates higher, investors will want higher real yields all the way down the yield curve. Indeed, since investors may be reluctant to push nominal bond yields all the way down to zero, this point may apply at bond yields a fair bit above zero.

These points about real yields apply to both index-linked bonds and conventionals; that is, those with a fixed coupon. (The yield on conventionals can be thought of as a compendium of the real yield, the expected rate of inflation, plus an allowance for uncertainty, liquidity, differences in tax treatment, and other factors.) So if real yields are forced higher by deflation, they will be forced higher for both the explicit real yields on indexed bonds and the implied real yields on conventionals. For conventionals this can occur without any change in the price of the bond, as a given level of coupon payments implies a higher real value, as consumer prices fall. With indexed bonds, however, it is different. Their coupon payments are tied to an index of consumer prices. Accordingly, if investors require a higher real return, the market price of indexed bonds will have to fall, thereby conferring losses on their holders.

This quirk complicates an overall assessment of indexed bonds. They are designed to give their holders a guaranteed real return if they are held to maturity. And they do – in conditions of both inflation and deflation. But many people also expect them to be safe and predictable instruments throughout their life, and not only if held to maturity. This they are not – particularly if the economy flips over from inflation into deflation.

Equities in an unstable world

During the financial crisis of 2007/9, some of the most acute pain felt by investors was over their investments in the equity market. From October 2007 to March 2009, equity prices fell by over 50% in the US, Germany, and France, and by only slightly less than this in the UK.[6] In the spring of 2009 the equity markets in America, France, and the UK were roughly where they had been six years earlier. But the Great Implosion came only a few years after another investment debacle, the dot-com boom and bust. The upshot is that in the spring of 2009 most equity markets were at the same level they had stood at in 1997/8. So investors had held stocks for more than a decade without making any capital gain – even in nominal terms. In real terms, of course, the picture was worse.

Even so, this was relatively mild by the standards of previous crashes. The Great Crash of 1929 was essentially a collapse of the equity market. Over a period of 33 months, American shares fell by 85%.[7] More recently, the peak of the Japanese stock market was reached in December 1989, when the Nikkei stock market index stood at almost 39,000. It then fell progressively to stand at less than 8,000 in April 2003, a fall of about 80%. Over the next three years it more than doubled – only to fall back again with the Great Implosion, to pretty much the previous trough. So at this point Japanese equities were only worth a fifth of what they had been nearly 20 years earlier. In the spring of 2009, Japanese stock prices stood at the same level as in 1983, more than a quarter of a century before.[8]

Equities did not participate in the bubble that preceded the Great Implosion, which was largely about the property and credit markets. It is not that equities have become immune to bubbles; quite the opposite. Rather, equities had *their* bubble earlier: the dot-com boom. However, as I pointed out above, they did suffer during the Great Implosion. The result was that, having gone into the crisis of 2007/9 not overvalued (except possibly in the US), equities came out of it undervalued, which then set up the conditions for substantial rises in 2009.

The return of the equity?

How are equities going to perform? The economic conditions of the next few years are going to be ghastly. Lower output always drives profits down. To make matters worse, in conditions of deflation it will be extremely difficult to push wages and salaries down commensurately with the weakness of selling prices. This will intensify the squeeze on profit margins.

Nevertheless, there are two positives in almost all western countries and a third in some. First, lower interest rates and bond yields will lend support to equity valuations; although most assuredly not if real rates and real bond yields are driven higher in conditions of deflation, as discussed above.

Second, valuations that are on the low side imply that once corporate earnings stabilize there is room for the market to advance. The one exception here is the US where, although not in bubble territory, equities came into the events of 2007/9 with a high price/earnings (P/E) ratio, in relation to a level of corporate earnings that was itself high as a share of GDP. Accordingly, the American market may struggle, even once the economy starts to recover.

The third advantage some countries' equity markets will enjoy is a lower exchange rate. The principal gainer here appears to be the UK. By March 2009, sterling had fallen by 27% since July 2007, serving not only to make the UK's exports more competitive, but also raising the sterling value of overseas earnings.[9] Naturally, exchange rate advantage cannot be enjoyed by all countries – at least not simultaneously – and what some countries gain, other countries lose.

The prime determinant of equity performance will be how soon the economy recovers and how rapidly the recovery proceeds. It would not surprise me if what I have called Phase 2 of the future produced rapid growth in corporate earnings, combined with a reduction in risk aversion toward equities, thus justifying a higher P/E ratio, resulting in a surge of the equity market, which would create a period of high equity returns.

However, it is important that investors are not seduced by this into creating yet another bubble once equities have returned to "fair value," whatever that is. In Phase 3, their performance on average could be pedestrian by the standards of the late 1980s – and by comparison to most investors' current expectations. Suppose that in the older-established economies of the west inflation runs at 2%. If you assume that companies pay out all of their earnings as dividends, once corporate profits have reached a sustainable fraction of GDP, this is the rate at which you should expect equities, on average, to rise.[10] On top of that you would receive the earnings return, which in the US and UK has historically averaged about 6%. If companies paid all of this out you would receive this amounts as dividends. If they retained it, you should receive it as capital gains generated by a higher share price. The more corporate earnings are retained, the greater the share of the overall return to investors that is accounted for by capital gains rather than income. So an average annual return of about 8% or 6% real seems to be a reasonable expectation. In practice, though, that will probably be a ceiling, since it does not take full account of insolvencies. Over the long run, equities seem to have delivered real returns of less than 6%. And even that may overstate the true return.

Commodities the savior?

Does investment in commodities represent an escape from the difficult environment confronting most conventional investment vehicles in the years ahead? There is a powerful argument for commodities. Important ones are in fixed supply whereas demand for them is increasing, especially because of the continued rise of China and other Asian countries.

Yet I don't accept this argument. It is true that many of the commodities we need, such as oil and minerals, are in limited supply. Admittedly, at some point in the future we will run out of these things; nevertheless, history suggests that this will be a long way off. We are continually adding to our estimates of the stock as exploitable reserves rise, partly in relation to accidental discovery but more in response to deliberate exploration and improvement in extraction techniques.

Ultimately, our demand for oil must fall, to accommodate itself to the limited supply. It is a race between consumers using up the stock and the development of other fuels. It is possible that such development will proceed only slowly, so that at some stage there will be a crunch point. It *could* come soon. However, I wouldn't want to draw that conclusion from the fact that in 2008 oil briefly touched $150 per barrel. After the second oil shock in 1979/80, plenty of commentators and oil experts were predicting oil Armageddon. In fact, from $40 a barrel in 1980, the oil price fell to $30 in 1982 and below $10 in 1986. From the prediction of absolute shortage to the reality of being awash with the stuff took just six years. It would not surprise me if something like this happened again.

The situation is more striking with regard to agricultural, soft commodities. These are producible materials and respond to all the usual economic forces. It is true that the production of them requires one particular input, namely land, whose supply cannot expand, but this limitation can be readily overcome through technological progress in the production process. Recently high prices are a great incentive to engage in the research and investment necessary to bring about these improvements.

The China factor

More fundamentally, I do not believe in the "China is different" thesis. In the 1950s and 1960s, the world economy actually expanded faster than in the pre-Great Implosion phase of strong global growth, as what we now call the eurozone recovered from the war and Japan recovered and developed. During most of this long period of rapid economic growth, the real price of commodities fell.

Moreover, it is not true that there will be a huge increase in the demand for food as China and India continue to advance. The popular version of this story centers on China and India changing to a level of meat consumption per capita that is similar to the Americans or Europeans. Since meat production requires a very heavy input of grains, this implies a bigger increase in the demand for grains than would follow from increases in real per capita GDP alone.

In fact, China is already at just about western levels of meat consumption per capita! Admittedly, the Chinese do not consume much beef, but they do eat huge amounts of pork. Meanwhile in India overall meat consumption is not high, but this is largely for cultural reasons. Given the preponderance of vegetarianism, India is never going to be a heavy consumer of meat products.

Nor does the popular conception about China's supposedly insatiable demand for metals stand up to close scrutiny. A large part of the demand after its entry to the WTO in 2001 was due to the huge increase in investment. Between 2004 and 2008, it was running at over 40% of GDP. Building roads, factories, power plants, and airports uses up massive amounts of materials, particularly of the metals that are in limited supply. By contrast, consumer spending is less resource intensive, and the resources that are consumed are more heavily weighted to producible resources such as food. As the Chinese economy rebalances toward consumption, the rate of increase of Chinese demand for commodities should ease back substantially.

Moreover, even in developing countries such as China and India, consumers and producers respond to incentives and to changing levels of sophistication and incomes. In these countries the resource intensity of GDP is set to fall fast, just as it did in the west, particularly once the relative importance of services starts to rise rapidly.

But even if I were persuaded of the argument for commodities in the long term, this still would not provide much hope for the immediate future. With the world looking likely to be weak for a number of years, even though commodity prices rebounded from the lows they reached during the financial crisis, it is difficult to believe that they are set to zoom ahead. Moreover, the overall price environment is unhelpful to their prospects. Commodities are real, and accordingly their price should be dragged down by all the same forces that are affecting the prices of ordinary goods and services.

Furthermore, after the commodities boom of 2007/8 in which, it seems to me, speculative investment played a large part, there may well be a revulsion against the use of commodities as a vehicle for investment. Indeed, I would not be surprised to see tight regulatory restrictions in this area.

Investment strategy

The picture I have painted gives a nuanced answer to the perennial investment question of "Where do I put my money?". The appropriate answer depends on the time horizon you are looking over and your taste for risk. In the immediate short term, from where things stand in the late summer of 2009, it seems to me that government bonds offer a relatively safe haven, with prospects of a reasonable return from further capital gains as market yields fall. By contrast, especially after the sharp rebound in prices in the middle of 2009, the immediate prospects for equities look distinctly unappealing.

In the medium term, the reverse is true. At some point, as and when conditions start to return to normal, interest rates will rise and investors will find the running returns available on bonds paltry. Mixing my metaphors, investors will have to be very fleet of foot to avoid holding the baby when the bond bubble bursts. Moreover, at that point, as the economic recovery starts to take hold and confidence returns, equities might start to perform – even though they did so in the middle of 2009, in anticipation of good corporate performance to come.

It is tempting to seek a way out from the apparently unappealing choices afforded by the usual asset categories by investing in hedge funds. This route is not available to ordinary investors, but many investing institutions that are the repositories of ordinary people's savings have taken it. Some have regarded hedge funds as an alternative asset category, thereby affording the opportunity for greater diversification when combined with conventional asset classes.

I am cautious about what hedge funds can offer. They make their money – when they do – by investing in the conventional asset classes. True, they can go short, and may therefore do well when conventional funds are doing badly. But hedge funds can only outperform to the extent that other investors underperform. The more money that is invested in hedge funds, the less scope there is for this to happen. If all investment funds were put into hedge funds, the average hedge fund return would be identical to the average return on all investible assets.

Meanwhile, the charges imposed by hedge funds are enormous. Indeed, the economist John Kay has shown how significant these charges can be and, by extension, how important it is to the return on any investment that they be minimized. If Warren Buffett had charged the investors in Berkshire Hathaway the customary hedge fund fee of 2% annually plus 20% of the gains in the fund, then of the $62 billion he has made for investors over 42 years the fees would have eaten up $57 billion, leaving only $5 billion net profit for investors. The moral is that minimizing charges on all investments is not some marginal extra but the *sine qua non* of successful investing.[11]

Avoiding the pitfalls

So far I have opined only about different asset types and how they might fare in the years ahead. However, there are also matters of investment style, which apply to investment in all asset types.

Successful investment requires patience and long time horizons. Unless you are blessed with substantial knowledge of the market from frequent exposure to dealing information, and good information at that, trading – that is, buying and selling the same financial instrument over short periods – is a form of gambling. Sometimes you win and sometimes you lose. To succeed overall, you need nerves of steel. By definition not everyone can succeed, because for each winner there must be a loser. Worse than that, again like gambling, administering and facilitating the activity actually require real resources and carry costs. Accordingly, it is not even a zero-sum game. Collectively it must generate net losses.

With real investment, by contrast, your gain can accrue without someone else's loss, because what you are doing in holding the investment instrument is benefiting from the asset's fruitfulness. At least, you are if the asset is genuinely fruitful. The returns from equity derive from the profitability of the company, current or future. When the value of an equity gets detached from this simple anchor, all hell breaks loose. This is exactly what happened in the dot-com boom: assets that were not genuinely fruitful were traded as though they were.

The business of investment

The business of investment is due for a shake-up. There are too many people employed in financial services, earning too much money, and delivering too bad a service for their clients. This situation has arisen as a result of centuries of restrictive practices, decades of mystique, and the long bull market. I hoped that the weakness of the equity market after the bursting of the dot-com boom would see the Augean stables cleaned out, but that didn't happen on any scale. I am hopeful, though, that the Great Implosion will do a better job.

A frequent criticism is that fund managers fail to "beat the index." I think that this criticism is unfair. On average, investors cannot beat the index. Obvious ways of making huge amounts of money without huge risk are not thick on the ground. I have criticized the efficient markets hypothesis, but in this respect it has something to offer.

As John Kay has put it, "The efficient markets hypothesis is 90% true and you will lose money by ignoring it. The search for the elusive 10%, like the search for discarded $10 bills, attracts greater effort than the rewards."[12]

Accordingly, the really serious problem with the investment management industry is the huge amount of resources that it uses to such poor effect, and the inordinate charges that it makes to its clients.

Meanwhile, the incompetence of many financial advisers is staggering. In particular, in my experience, financial advisers frequently fall for the most egregious of financial fallacies:

- They don't know the difference between the real sources of wealth and the illusory ones.
- They believe that it is possible for all of us to make money out of financial speculation.
- They believe that it is possible to time entry to and exit from the market, and/or to pick stocks successfully.

- They believe in the idea of star fund managers whose talents will continue to produce excess returns.
- They believe that past excess returns were the result of skill and good decisions, rather than excessive risk taking and luck.
- They overemphasize the attractions of trading and underemphasize the benefits of stability and keeping the expenses down.
- They don't fully understand the difference between nominal and real and the importance this distinction has in explaining the past record of investment performance.
- They do not understand the impossibility of equities rising for ever more, out of proportion to the rise in nominal GDP. They seem to believe in a sort of financial version of the Indian rope trick.
- They know no economic or financial theory and they know no financial history – except the latest bit of data that appears to back up their own pet view on asset markets.

Of course there are exceptions, and really good financial advisers are worth their weight in gold – if you can find one. But so many financial advisers haven't got a clue – except about how to maximize their commissions or other forms of income, which many of them seem to understand all too well. Given this, there is a lot to be said for managing your own investments and taking your own advice.[13]

Doesn't the performance of the so-called star fund managers who are apparently able to select assets to give superior returns argue in the opposite direction? These "stars" are largely a creature of the adman's imagination. Very few have had outstanding returns over a long period. And it is relatively easy to have outstanding returns over short periods just by taking a risk and having some luck. They may not be stars, but we appear to have been star struck.

There are a few exceptional performers. It is very difficult to dismiss Warren Buffett's long run of successful investment as the product of luck. He is probably the closest there is to an investment genius. In the UK, Anthony Bolton of Fidelity also has a long record that speaks of great skill and professionalism. And both Buffett and Bolton are active investors, often taking a keen interest in the management of the firms they invest in, and holding the stock over many years.

But they are a far cry from the ubiquitous firm of investment advisers BSR, otherwise known as Buyit Sellit and Run, not to mention the hedge fund SBR, otherwise known as Sellit Buyit and Run.

Keeping your wits about you

Bit by bit, painful cut by painful cut, I think we will eventually reach a point where the pretensions of finance are cut down to size. Once you have understood what the bankers got up to with subprime mortgage lending, how close they sailed to the wind, and how unprepared for the crash most investment professionals were, it is difficult to take seriously any claim to expertise. The emperor has no clothes – and his courtiers are all naked too.

So how should individual investors behave in the years ahead? There is no magic road to riches. Everything I have written emphasizes this. The idea that thousands of people reading my words on this subject, or anyone else's words for that matter, could become rich as a result of our musings is laughable. The most I can do is to give some general principles that may help save individual investors from making a huge mistake. This is a modest ambition, I admit, but it is as far as I can go. So here are my six guiding principles:

1   This may come as a surprise after the catastrophic events of 2007/9, but avoid being too pessimistic about the future. Things will eventually get better. Indeed, if Phase 2 is characterized by a significant recovery in both equities and property, it will be possible, for a time, to make some super investment returns. Indeed, this was true for much of 2009. But remember, strong economic recovery could bring a bloodbath for bonds, and for the investor in these it will be easy to make substantial losses, both absolute and relative.

2   This will seem contradictory, but don't be too ambitious. The world does not naturally permit sustained annual returns of 20% per annum – at least not for everyone. In Phase 3, returns will drop back to a more pedestrian norm.

3   Be patient. Trading costs money and in aggregate yields nothing.

4   Pay close attention to the level of charges and commissions and do your best to minimize these.

5   Beware of investments with cascading structures, which put your money into funds, which then put it into other funds, which put it into other funds, and so on, all the while clocking up more charges and reducing the proportion of your money that is actually invested.

6   Avoid investments that you don't understand. Furthermore, avoid investments that "they" don't understand (which covers quite a lot).

If you stick to these six principles, although you won't get rich quick (except by luck), at least you should be able to survive and prosper in the years ahead – assuming, that is, that the world manages to escape from the clutches of the Great Implosion. As I shall show in the next chapter, although that lies outside the range of things that can be influenced by ordinary folk, it is not outside the range of things that can be influenced by governments and central banks. Indeed, economic recovery, as well as the state of your finances, absolutely depends on what they do – and on what they don't.

8

How the World Can Get Out of this Mess

This notion that the economy is self-stabilizing is usually right but it is wrong a few times a century. And this is one of those times... there's a need for extraordinary public action at those times and that's a clear lesson of today.

Lawrence Summers, senior economic adviser to the US President, 2009[1]

Men occasionally stumble over the truth, but most of them pick themselves up and hurry off as if nothing ever happened.

Winston Churchill[2]

In the aftermath of the Great Implosion, policymakers face two major challenges: how to get us out of the hole in which we currently find ourselves, and how to prevent a repeat in the future. Even as the economy spiraled downwards, there were those who obsessed about the second of these tasks. That is not necessarily wrong. Indeed, as I shall argue in a moment, developing a credibly robust financial structure for the future may help to boost confidence in the present, and thereby bolster economic recovery.

However, it is imperative that designing a new system for the future doesn't stop us from dealing with the more urgent task of strengthening the current beginnings of recovery and preventing a relapse into depression. Although we should avoid dealing with the current disaster in a way that will make designing a new system for the future more tricky, equally, we should not design a new system in such a way that makes dealing with the current situation more difficult. Keynes has been widely criticized for his remark, "In the long run, we are all dead." But there are those who would have us all croaking pretty much straightaway.

The brave new world of stability and robustness, the new normality, is a subject I take up in Chapter 9. Here I confine myself to the more pressing problem of how we can bolster the forces making for recovery. Before discussing practical steps, I must tackle head on some philosophical roadblocks that stand in the way of effective action to bring about an early and full recovery. These roadblocks held back world policymakers as they initially contemplated what to do when the financial system imploded in late 2008, and they may yet temper any further measures that may be needed – or even prompt an early reversal of the measures already taken.

The case for doing nothing

Is there a need to do anything at all? Indeed, is there anything that *can* usefully be done? According to some people, recessions clean things up and sort things out. So, far from complaining about the recession or trying to stop it, we should simply lie back and enjoy it.

I see things differently. Yes, a little bit of recession can sometimes do you good. So too, I am told, can the occasional cold bath. But spending the whole day immersed in freezing water is not to be recommended. The current economic downturn has gone well beyond a short, sharp dip. The fashionable phrase for crisis deniers is "creative destruction," first coined by the economist Joseph Schumpeter. However, remember that this phrase and the associated idea only gained traction from the contrast with their more frequently observed cousin, *destructive* destruction.

There is a variant of the "recession is good for you view" that is more plausible, namely that although financial disasters are manmade, it is *inevitable* that we should suffer from them. While the Great Implosion may not be a good thing, the consequences are simply unavoidable. It is useless, or even counterproductive, to try to find ways of reducing the pain, never mind escaping the clutches of the depression. We should see it as the natural and inevitable consequence of the previous boom.

If you like, we should regard the recession as the equivalent of a fever. There is no treatment; we should just let it take its course. Perhaps the occasional cold flannel on the forehead, but that is all. The victim should rest and we should sit watching patiently. By contrast, if we try to intervene, with bleedings or drugs, we will only make matters worse.

This view, which I touched on in Chapter 2, is often described as "Austrian," after the school of Austrian economists led by Friedrich von Hayek who argued against Keynes in the 1930s, to the effect that the economy should be left to its own devices. It might be better described as Martian. A recession is *not* like a fever. For a start, it can become ingrained and lead to something much worse. Switching medical metaphors, just because the wound was self-inflicted does not mean that we should not treat it. Just because the problem has origins that may be described as "Austrian" does not mean that the solution must be "Austrian" as well. And just because it may be better to let asset prices deflate rather than try to prop them up, that does not mean that we should stand idly by, watching the consequences of such deflation without taking any action to limit them.

It is a peculiar view of the human condition that sees us helpless before fate when our predicament results from our own actions. The Great Implosion was a purely financial event. No productive assets were destroyed; no people were killed; no knowledge was lost. Accordingly, there is no need for penury caused by the economy being less productive. Admittedly, there could, in principle, be some loss of economic capacity because some financial skills have become less valuable, or in some cases even been made redundant, and because finance has become less readily available to support activity in the rest of the economy. This is the line taken by the British government, which, as a direct result of the Great Implosion, has reduced its estimate of the sustainable level of UK GDP by 4% for as far as the eye can see.

But both the reasoning and the estimate are highly tendentious. The reduced provision of finance is a possible source of loss, which I deal with below. But, as I argued in Chapter 5, a good deal of what has gone on in the financial markets has been at best useless and at worst positively harmful. In that case, the release of resources from the financial sector and their re-employment elsewhere will bring no net loss and may even bring a net gain. The only meaningful way in which the Great Implosion can be thought to reduce productive capacity permanently is through the unemployment of resources, and the consequences that this may have for the slower accumulation of capital and the atrophying of skills and motivation. But that is a loss that can be avoided by ending the recession and re-employing the resources.

If we accept that nothing real has changed, why should the destruction of paper wealth cause so much mayhem and threaten a long-lasting reduction in GDP? It needn't – although there are four ways in which it frequently has – and could do so again this time.

The first is that the burden of bad debts clobbers the banks. In some cases it wipes them out completely and in others it leaves their capital so depleted that they are unwilling or unable to lend as much as before. And credit is the economy's lifeblood.

However, if that is the reason for economic collapse, then why cannot bank capital be restored? As long as banks function normally, there is nothing in the new situation that justifies a lower level of production or income than before. And what makes banks not function normally is the burden of past mistakes weighing on the present, rather than anything different about the present or future.

There is an obvious solution: recapitalize the banks with public money so that the weight of past mistakes is removed. Or set up a new bank, or rather several new banks, perhaps with publicly provided capital, in order to ensure that bank lending continues as before.

The "Austrian" reply is that even though such measures might deal with the problem directly at hand, they will cause others that may well be worse – including a repeat of the events that led to the financial crisis in the first place. There is something in this. Indeed, this is the thinking that initially persuaded the Bank of England to be niggardly in its provision of market support in the wake of the Northern Rock collapse.

Nevertheless, the notion that we must all endure years of misery and fear to make sure that people don't repeat the same mistakes in the future is extraordinarily primitive and profoundly defeatist in its attitude to the human condition. The dangers of "moral hazard" mean that we have to be careful in quite how we support the financial system – and once the immediate crisis is past, we have to refashion the system pretty quickly to make sure that there cannot be a repeat of this episode. But that doesn't mean that we should do nothing.

Even if the banks were fixed, in current conditions that would not be enough to bring a full economic recovery, because most of the banks' potential customers will be reluctant to borrow. This is the second way in which a man-made occurrence like the Great Implosion may lead to subdued aggregate demand. The simple point is that now they feel less wealthy, people feel less inclined to spend. Similarly, with lower asset values, they are less able to borrow because they don't have the same amount of collateral. However, both of these factors should be capable of being overcome by normal expansionary policies, monetary and fiscal, about which I have much to say below.

The consequences of fiscal pain

The third factor that may cause this purely financial crisis to have major real effects is the sheer scale of government debt and the burden of financing it. The fear of default, discussed below, is one factor, but weighing more heavily in the public's state of mind is the fear of higher taxes to fend off this possibility. Indeed, there is a widespread fear that the burden of financing and then paying down the debt will prolong the recession, and may, indeed, ensure that it is truly a depression.

And even if it doesn't have that macroeconomic consequence, there is widespread fear that for most of us as individuals it implies a penurious future as taxes are bound to be much higher. I will argue below that the fear of higher future taxes is not sufficiently powerful to negate the stimulatory effect of expansionary fiscal policy. But over and above this, I believe that this fear is essentially unjustified and that thinking about this issue is confused.

If you accept the conclusion I came to earlier, namely that there is nothing in the Great Implosion that itself brings reduced economic capacity, then why should the existence of a huge public debt itself threaten future penury? Much of common thinking about this issue confuses the position of an individual's finances with that of society as a whole.

If you listened to the alarmists you would think that the money paid out by the government in debt interest disappears down a black hole, never to be seen again. But in fact it is received by the holders of government debt, who are effectively us, or more accurately some of us. Pension funds, insurance companies, banks, private individuals – a whole host of different investors will receive an increased flow of interest from government. For the public debt, over which there is so much anxiety, is owed to ourselves.

Admittedly, the picture is more complicated looked at from the perspective of individual countries that are net debtors to the rest of the world. This is true for the US and the UK. But even for these countries, net external debt is small in relation to government debt as a whole. More importantly, focus on external indebtedness obscures the fundamental point that, for the world as a whole, there are no external debtors. From a global standpoint, all of the debt, unambiguously, is owed to ourselves.

Depression psychology

The fourth factor that stands in the way of recovery is linked to fears about the fiscal position. It is distinctly Austrian, but in a rather different way to the one encountered earlier. Cue not so much the economists Schumpeter and Von Hayek as the psychologists Freud and Jung.[3] Bubbles are an aspect of mass psychology. Nor is it accidental that *depressions* are so termed. Bubbles develop when a whole society permits itself to be taken in by an illusion. As they inflate they become difficult to stop because the illusion appears to be validated by the facts on the ground: asset prices are higher, fortunes are made, and the Cassandras are proved wrong.

A rational analysis of the situation facing a society in the aftermath of a bubble might conclude that, if the banks are fixed and monetary and fiscal policy is relaxed so as to offset the destruction of wealth, there is nothing to worry about. Or, in the words of President Roosevelt in the 1930s, "We have nothing to fear but fear itself."

However, in such circumstances is it rational to be rational? The whole of society has just passed through a period when normal yardsticks of belief and behavior have proved useless and have therefore been discarded. Is it humanly possible simply to return to a normal position as though nothing had happened? After all, institutions and the people both within them and outside them, in which investors might previously have had complete trust, have just been exposed as men of straw, or worse, incompetent charlatans or crooks. How can you ever trust them, or their like, again?

Accordingly, there is a deep psychological pressure for "depression" to follow a boom, even if the narrow demand management and institutional factors are straightened out. In essence, if they wish to prevent a depression, the authorities have to battle against a mass mood. This mood of depression may be as stubborn as the earlier mood of euphoria, and for related reasons. Nevertheless, it needs to be contrasted, rather than passively submitted to.

Spending and recovery

Thus a recovery from the current mess must involve four vital components:

◆ Rebuilding the banking system and its ability to lend.
◆ A boost to income, wealth, and liquidity.
◆ Stabilization of the public finances without imposing a big cut in overall personal incomes.
◆ A recovery of confidence.

On the basis of these four pillars, increased spending – the *sine qua non* of recovery – can begin to take place. Yes, more spending. You often hear the mantra "we cannot spend our way out of recession." But how else is recession to be brought to an end? A recession is a situation in which output, spending, and income are all below normal or below potential. It has to be all three because these are three aspects of the same thing. They are an identity. If output and income are to go up, *someone* must spend more. There is simply no other way – as a matter of logic.

It is easy to fall into the trap of thinking that the problem facing society as a whole is the same as the problem facing individuals. If we as individuals wish to improve our financial position, we can either increase income or reduce spending. But for society as whole, aggregate spending equals aggregate income. If we all seek to improve our position by spending less and saving more, each person's income will fall as result of someone else's reduced spending.

The idea that the act of saving may make other people worse off is bad enough, but what is really devastating is that it may not even end up creating any extra saving at all! For when people who are on the receiving end of your "nonspending" confront their reduced circumstances, they are likely to cut both their spending *and* their saving; similarly for those people who suffer reduced income as a result.

Even though the shape of a healthy future economy will surely involve higher personal saving in the Anglo-Saxon countries, this is absolutely *not* the way in which they can escape from recession. In the current environment, trying to boost saving is the economics of the madhouse. So the only sensible debate is about who should spend more and on what – and how they can be persuaded to do so.

If spending is to increase, thinking in terms of aggregates, there are only four candidates for the job: consumers, companies, the government, and foreigners. For some individual countries, such as the UK, getting foreigners to spend more on your output – that is, enjoying a boost to net exports – is a viable proposition. But for the world as a whole there are no foreigners. So we are down to only three candidates. If we say that governments cannot be allowed to borrow more, because they are too much in debt already or because they waste the money, we are left with only two.

But do we really want to encourage more borrowing by western consumers, who in many countries are heavily indebted already? Perhaps we could encourage increased spending by those members of society who are currently net savers or who have substantial accumulated deposits. Mind you, even if this route were followed, the result would be the same for the west's aggregate saving ratio, namely it would stay at its very low levels, whereas stability in the medium term seems to require that it rises. However, at least this would have the merit of reducing reliance on credit and reducing the extent to which bank balance sheets had to expand again to accommodate reflationary spending.

Yet how could western societies achieve such an outcome if they wanted to? I suppose they could end certain subsidies to saving, such as favorable tax treatment for pension contributions, thereby encouraging people to spend rather than putting money aside for their old age. But this hardly seems desirable and it would give exactly the wrong message for the medium term.[4] So more spending by consumers will almost certainly entail more borrowing by consumers.

If we also say that consumers cannot be expected to borrow more because they need to repair their financial position, there is only one candidate for increased spending left standing: companies. If companies could be prodded into increasing their spending on investment, that might be a good thing. The result of eastern savings provided to the west would be an increased capital stock, rather than increased consumption. In this way the west would not be impoverishing itself relative to the rest of the world as a result of eastern saving. Indeed, if the capital investments were really productive it could be doing the opposite.

Eventually, such an outcome is both desirable and feasible – once reforms to the financial system and to corporate governance encourage businesses to focus less on short-term increases in share prices and more on profitable long-term investment. However, it is going to be a really tall order to make much progress on this in the short term.

That's it, then. We are stuck with the recession and we had better learn to live with it. After all, we brought it on ourselves, didn't we, so it is only right and proper that we should suffer now. It was thinking such as this that put the "Great" in the Great Depression.

We need to go back to the four candidates. The solution will have to involve more spending by a mixture of governments, consumers, companies, and foreigners, the mixture varying with the circumstances of individual countries. In some cases it may be possible to persuade some or all of these candidates to increase their spending by running down their savings, but in many cases this will not be possible. Accordingly, if they are to increase their spending, that automatically means that they will have to increase their borrowing. And that automatically gives rise to another objection. If too much borrowing got us here in the first place, how can encouraging more debt be the route out of our troubles?

How can more borrowing be the answer?

Too much borrowing got us into this position in the sense that it got us to a state of near financial collapse, with the result that we are now in danger of spending *too little*. The answer to this can hardly be to spend even less!

Although in many countries the Great Implosion has resulted in government borrowing soaring to previously uncontemplated levels, in general it is not government borrowing that has got us into this mess. Admittedly, it has got us into other messes, but it is easy to confuse two issues here. In my view, in most developed countries, especially in the UK, government spending is too high. I believe that we would be better off if spending were reduced and taxes cut commensurately. However, in itself this would do nothing to end the recession. In fact, cutting government spending and *not* giving the money to taxpayers (in order to cut the public deficit) would reduce aggregate demand and worsen the recession. (More on this in a moment.)

I know that to some people this realization is both startling and offensive, but wasteful government spending on the creation of nonjobs boosts aggregate demand. Diversity awareness coordinators go shopping too. (I will qualify this radical conclusion below.) Accordingly, it is not contradictory to acknowledge the waste implied by the current level of government spending and yet to advocate a policy of increased government borrowing to deal with the current crisis.

The moral imperative

A related vein of criticism comes from a moral angle. Pope Benedict XVI has emphasized this aspect of the crisis, even going so far as to publish in 2009 an encyclical entitled "Charity in Truth." According to the Pope, the economy is marked by "grave deviations and failures" and is an area of life "where the pernicious effects of sin are evident." The Archbishop of Canterbury, Dr. Rowan Williams, has argued that the near-collapse of the system is the result of a moral failure, associated with excessive credit and too much materialism. Thus, it would be wrong to try to fix matters by administering more of the same. It would be like giving more drugs to a drug addict.[5]

Both religious leaders are right to argue that there is a moral aspect to the economy and indeed in its restructuring, which I will turn to in Chapter 9 and the Conclusion, there is a vital role for moral and ethical questions to play. But that still leaves the field wide open as regards what should be done to revive the economy now. Would it be moral to allow the economic system to implode, putting millions of people out of work and causing misery to them and their families? Avoiding that means encouraging spending and, as

I argued above, in practical terms more spending will probably entail more borrowing, by someone or other; if it doesn't involve more borrowing, it will certainly require less saving. You cannot endorse the objective of maintaining full employment while opposing increased spending. There is no escape from the identity of aggregate spending, income, and production.

Admittedly, society might be healthier and happier if more people were interested in basket weaving and learning to play the harp and less interested in working hard to acquire the latest car or electronic gizmo before someone else. In that case, "full employment" would not mean the same thing. An economy would be operating at maximum capacity at a lower level of output and employment.

Nevertheless, let us not delude ourselves. Although it might put any number of people off debt and materialism, an extended economic downturn would not increase the sum total of human happiness. In fact, as happened in the 1930s, a deep and prolonged economic downturn could lead to consequences that undermine the very stability of society itself. The result would be untold human misery. Basket weaving and learning to play the harp will have to wait.

Accordingly, although there is much to be debated about the legitimate ends of economic activity and how society might be reshaped to achieve them, in what follows I take it as given that the task ahead is to keep people spending and to keep the economy growing. The question is what measures need to be taken to achieve this result.

What should be our objectives?

There is a prior matter to be resolved. In seeking to bring a recovery from the current gloomy state, what should our objectives be? The immediate task has clearly been to prevent the collapse of the world's banking system and the associated shattering of confidence from sending the global economy into a depression. Then, as far as possible, to return aggregate demand to normal, and with it employment, spending, and output.

However, assuming that such expansionary policies are set to work, how far should they be pushed? If they really worked, you could envisage an outcome where credit was back to the previous level and bank balance sheets were expanding at the previous rate. Full employment had returned. It would be back to business as usual.

Yet that is an outcome that we should *not* want, even if it were possible. It would place the financial system back in the vulnerable position it was in before. Moreover, such a strategy would still involve many countries in the west, including the US and the UK, relying on the savings of other countries, with the adverse consequences that I highlighted in Chapter 6.

We cannot sensibly aim to go back to the financial and economic structures that got us here in the first place. That was about the most abnormal of all possible normalities. Accordingly, unless something else happens, our policymakers' ambitions will have to stop short of returning the system to full employment. Something else *could* happen, namely a change in the behavior of the super-saving countries, resulting in a rebalancing of the world economy and permitting full employment in the west, without rebuilding a grossly unstable financial structure. I will come to that in a moment. Let me start, though, by leaving China *et al.* to one side and first address the steps necessary to get the western countries' economies moving, beginning with the supply of credit.

Dealing with the banks

The banks have been at the center of what has gone wrong and they must be at the center of any attempt to put matters right. Without banks being able to supply credit to the system, there can be no hope of getting back to normal.

Fortunately, by the autumn of 2009, it seemed as though the worst of the banking crisis was over – largely as a result of some of the measures that I discuss below. But there may well be further bank weakness to come and criticism of the actions to save the banks has been mounting. A backtracking on bank support packages is perfectly feasible – as is the failure to provide new support if it is needed. Accordingly, it is right to try to establish the principles of government intervention in the banking system.

Faced with a banking collapse, there is a compelling case for collective action, sponsored or organized by the state. An individual bank, looking to the interests of its shareholders, is bound to be cautious about lending when what it sees is falling asset prices and a failing economy. But if all banks refuse to lend they will create the very result they fear. By contrast, if all banks stepped up their lending, that would bolster asset prices and support the economy. This is a clear case of a dichotomy between the interests of the individual and the collective.

So we have a vicious circle of a problem and a virtuous circle of a solution: all we need to do is to break in somewhere and get the circle working virtuously. There are two points of entry: persuade the banks to lend more, thus making the economy stronger; make the economy stronger, thereby making the banks more inclined to lend. We need to do both. Let me start with the measures necessary to get the banks prepared and able to lend, beginning with the issue of bank capital.

In the abnormal financial conditions that obtained in 2008, there was little prospect of banks acquiring sufficient capital from the private sector. Accordingly, with the public interest in banks' recovery and a return to adequate levels of lending, governments and central banks had to step into the breach. In the US, the eurozone, and the UK, this they did.

But you ain't seen nothin' yet. The losses, collapses, and enforced mergers of 2008 occurred before the economies of the west had gone into freefall and before the full consequences were felt on the perceived quality of banks' assets. By the time this crisis has run its course, to keep banks' capital bases at a level that could sustain lending at the rate of 2007, never mind higher, it is quite possible that they will need further massive capital injections. In the more optimistic climate of autumn 2009, there were grounds to think that a good part of what might be needed could come from private sources. But if the economy were to suffer a relapse, I am sure that much, if not most, of the extra capital required would have to come from governments.

Public ownership and control

Given the risks to the system and the consequences of a systemic collapse, governments have been right to supply capital – and they will be right to provide more, if needed. However, the form of their support has been very much second best. The first best solution would have been temporary, outright nationalization of most of the banking system.

It has been bizarre to see governments inject hundreds of billions of dollars of taxpayers' money into banks while having little or no direct control over their behavior – including both their lending policy and how they pay their staff. The solution in which the state owns the banks and directs their activities is purer and simpler, and more likely to yield results. Under full public control, the banks could be set lending targets, covering both the total amount of lending and its distribution across broad groups such as corporate, consumer, mortgages, and trade finance.

Governments have *effectively* nationalized significant parts of the banking system in the US, the eurozone, and the UK. However, they have done this reluctantly, messily, and in piecemeal fashion. What has held governments back? First, a horror of the political reaction. In the US the idea of state ownership and control is a complete no-no. In the UK, the Labour Party has spent a generation escaping from the advocacy of nationalization. Its leaders are terrified of being pilloried as turning the clock back to the bad old days.

On top of this there is still a lingering respect for "the market," and a belief that the problems are best sorted out by the private sector. This reflects an appalling intellectual failure. The market can only "sort it out" when there is no macro problem. However, the situation of 2007/9 presents a macro problem in the extreme.

Moreover, there is an anxiety about the sheer amount of money that would be needed to nationalize the banks, thereby adding to the stock of government debt, and limiting the scope for stimulatory, Keynesian fiscal action. Instead, in both the US, the UK, and much of the eurozone, the authorities have believed that the cheapest solution for the public purse is a piecemeal one of buying "toxic" assets, guaranteeing some of the banks' assets and some of their liabilities, as well as intervening in an ad hoc way to support ailing banks.

In reality, although this strategy may appear to be cheaper in the short run, it breeds uncertainty and a lack of confidence, which inhibit eventual recovery and leave the taxpayer effectively holding all of the banks' liabilities yet not placed to gain fully from any recovery. In the words of the British MP Vince Cable, "The proposal for asset protection is a disgrace and a betrayal of the taxpayer's interests. It is a classic case of privatizing profits and socializing loss."[6]

A recovery of interbank lending

Just because banks have enough capital to lend does not mean that they *will* lend, even if urged to by the government. Many bankers themselves say that the essential problem has been "liquidity." In particular, they blame the drying up of the interbank market. (This is the market where banks lend to each other at the drop of a hat in huge amounts for periods varying between one day and a few years.)

When the interbank market was functioning normally, banks did not need to think about where the money would come from to fund lending. If they lent in excess of the deposit money they had available, they simply borrowed the extra amount in the money markets. The money would always be there in the system because the act of lending creates a deposit somewhere; the lending bank, if you like, ends up borrowing the money it has created. (I know! It sounds like make-believe. And it is liable to make one jealous: if only we could all behave that way.)

The interbank market enables deposits to be spread around the system. Some banks are more strongly placed as lenders rather than deposit takers; some the other way round. Accordingly, some banks tend to be takers of interbank money and some givers, but all banks do a bit of both from time to time. The knowledge that the funding is always available puts the lending decision in the driving seat.

Why did the interbank market dry up? There are two reasons: reasonable doubt about other banks' solvency and self-justifying fears. The first needs no more explanation. Who wants to lend to an institution that may go bust, whether that institution is called a bank or anything else? The second factor, however, does need some elaboration. If each bank cuts back on lending to other banks because it feels the interbank market has dried up, the interbank market will indeed dry up, even if all banks are solvent and are believed to be solvent.

It is difficult to believe that this second part of the problem is beyond the wit of man to solve. The self-justifying part of the problem can be put into reverse. Once a few banks start lending, others will follow. The market can reliquify itself as readily as liquidity collapsed. Again, outright public owner-ship would help, by easing solvency fears. What has one nationalized bank to fear from lending to another nationalized bank? Indeed, nationalized banks can be *instructed* to boost interbank lending. By the middle of 2009, the interbank market had indeed started to revive, and this part of the explanation for soft bank lending to customers had begun to weaken.

Interest rates and the zero bound

Yet getting the banks in a position to increase their lending will not be enough. You cannot force people to borrow. In order for the willingness and ability of banks to lend to convert into increased lending, people have to be prepared to borrow. But this will not readily occur of its own accord. It will largely depend on an improvement in the state of the economy. Success here will not only increase the preparedness to borrow, it will also increase the safety of lending, hence boosting the supply of credit.

Again, this is an instance of the collective interest being different from the individual interest. It therefore calls for collective action orchestrated by the state. There are two avenues to pursue: monetary and fiscal policies and measures to boost confidence.

The first resort for economies in need of a stimulus to aggregate demand is lower interest rates. In normal circumstances lower rates would increase the desire to borrow by creditworthy borrowers and thereby present banks with more profitable opportunities to lend. In today's circumstances, however, the demand for funds will be pretty much insensitive to any stimulus from lower rates. Moreover, banks are inclined to keep much of the benefit of lower funding costs to themselves by failing to cut lending rates commensurately.

So what hope is there from the plunge to zero or near-zero rates, which has now been effected by central banks more or less everywhere? There are four reasons it is right to pursue the zero policy. The first stems from one of the apparent limitations of the policy, namely to help the banks to rebuild their profitability through wider margins without causing lending rates to rise. The second, in so far as lower official rates bring any reduction at all in bank lending rates, is to minimize the pain for a particularly vulnerable section of the economy, the heavily indebted. This is particularly important if inflation threatens to turn negative, as it does now. Under conditions of deflation, the burden of servicing debts increases.

The third is to reduce the yields on government debt and thereby reduce the cost of servicing that debt. This is particularly important at the moment because, as I shall argue shortly, in many countries the sheer scale of the debt is so great that we are not far off the point at which investors may start to get worried about the solvency of governments. At that point, governments will have reached one of the limits to fiscal action. Zero interest rates put back the point at which this limit is encountered.

The fourth is that low interest rates, and the low government bond yields they support, tend to boost the price of assets, including both residential and commercial property and shares. This increases the stock of wealth and hence may tend to boost consumption, and makes increased corporate spending on real investment more attractive.

For these reasons, the right thing to do when facing a deflationary slump is to get rates down all the way to zero and keep them there for an extended period.[7] While this is a necessary condition for escape from the slump, it is unlikely to be sufficient. As we saw with Japan in the late 1990s and early 2000s, once confidence is shattered, on their own zero rates will not get the system going again. So what can central banks do then?

Quantitative easing

The answer is that they can buy assets and expand their balance sheet, as the central banks of the US, the eurozone, and the UK have been doing. As Ben Bernanke, chairman of the US Federal Reserve, put it, "The US Government has a technology called a printing press, that allows it to produce as many US dollars as it wishes at essentially no cost."[8] In the jargon, the policy of buying assets paid for with central bank money goes by the ghastly name of quantitative easing (QE), but in reality this is no more than the classic policy of open market operations advocated by Keynes in the 1930s.

Nevertheless, as I explained in Chapter 3, in abnormal times such as the present this policy may not work very well. It may be difficult to force down yields by very much, even through gargantuan asset purchases – especially when governments are issuing so much debt to fund their fiscal expansion (which I discuss below). Moreover, if yields do fall, in depressed economic conditions potential borrowers may not respond much, if at all. Equally, the increase in liquid assets in portfolios may have next to no effect. In depressed conditions, with feelings of fear and even panic predominating, people and firms may be relatively happy to sit with money holdings that are much higher than normal.

It is similar with the supposed encouragement of banks to lend. You can take a horse to water but you cannot make him drink. There is no necessity for banks to lend. In today's conditions, letting reserves pile up at the central bank may seem an attractive option; at least banks will not lose money by doing this.

This is exactly what happened in Japan in the early 2000s and in the US in 2008. Banks simply did not want to lend. In these conditions the central bank can expand its balance sheet by buying assets until it is blue in the face and achieve nothing at all.

In this case, there are two things for the central bank to do. The first is to start to charge banks negative interest rates for holding deposits at the central bank. The second is to carry on pursuing QE until it does have an effect, and to tilt the purchase of assets more toward private-sector paper and less toward government debt. In the textbooks, QE is bound to work in the end because there is no limit to the amount of its own money that a central bank can create. Accordingly, the textbook answer to the question of how much QE to do is "as much as it takes" – all the way to infinity.

In practice, central banks usually have to apply to government or parliament for permission to undertake a definite quantity of QE, and they are loath to push the policy too far. In early 2009, the Bank of England's practical equivalent to infinity was £75 billion now, and *possibly* another £75 billion later. Moreover, remarks made by Bank of England officials made it seem that the Bank was extremely nervous about the policy and wanted to limit, or even reverse, it at the earliest opportunity. This attitude was hardly likely to increase the policy's effectiveness.

Central banks could pursue QE much more aggressively than they have. The key is developing a strategy for reversal – and thereby being able to convince both themselves and the markets that they can continue this policy to the extreme, without undue danger.

Charting a path back to normality

In order to prevent a massive monetary expansion from causing inflation, once demand conditions have returned to something like normal, the central banks have to reabsorb liquidity. Monetary expansion has been likened to sending out a helicopter to drop bank notes on the populace. Because of his advocacy of monetary expansion to counter deflation, Ben Bernanke is known as "Helicopter Ben." After a program of QE, to get banks to normality, the central banks have to send the helicopter out with a gigantic hoover, sucking up all the extra notes they have dispensed. In practice, they do this simply by selling assets from their holdings and thereby contracting their balance sheets.

In principle, this is easy. In practice, it is likely to be extremely difficult. Imagine the circumstances when this would be necessary. The economy has turned and the market can see an end to deflation and the beginning of inflation. Equally, it can see the end of zero interest rates not far off. These factors alone would cause market operators to sell bonds, with the result that yields would rise sharply. But into this difficult environment for bonds come the central banks, selling squillions of bonds from their holdings. As I pointed out in Chapter 7, the result could be very nasty for bonds. Heavy bond-holding institutions would register massive capital losses and some could go under. Who knows what mayhem this would bring? It would be ironic if the undoing of the support operation that had stopped the previous financial crisis ended up by causing another one, just as the economy was starting to recover.

Faced with these problems, what are central banks to do? One possible response is to underdo the bond purchases, consistently hoping that what has been done already will prove to be enough. Another is to underdo the subsequent mop-up operation in order to minimize the disturbance to the bond market. The first is likely to cause deflation to rumble on. This is what happened in Japan and I suspect that this will be the ECB's approach, proceeding cautiously, little by little – and too late. However, the second approach risks allowing inflation to resurge. This is what many in the market fear will happen in the US and the UK.

The solution is to rely on other instruments to neutralize excess bank liquidity. Central banks could raise interest rates, including those payable on reserves, and thereby make it more attractive for banks to hold the reserves rather than lending them out. Or they could simply freeze excess reserves, by moving them into nonoperational accounts or by imposing minimum cash requirements well above operational needs; or they could absorb them by issuing new short-term bonds or central bank bills.

In these ways they could soak up the excess liquidity and prevent a surge of lending, without having to offload boatloads of bonds from their books. Indeed, this would give them time to offload their portfolios of bonds, combined with a relaxation of the restrictions on banks' cash holdings, at a time, and at a pace, of their own choosing.[9]

Fiscal expansion

Given that monetary policy isn't exactly plain sailing, even with the QE spinnaker, there is surely a major role for fiscal policy, just as Keynes envisaged in the 1930s. When the private sector won't spend, even when poked and prodded to do so, the answer is for the government to step in and increase its deficit. It can boost its spending or it can dish out money to benefit recipients or to taxpayers. From a crude, purely macro standpoint, it doesn't matter which, as long as it finances the shortfall by borrowing. The result will increase purchasing power in the hands of someone or other, and at least some of this will be spent, thereby raising aggregate demand.

Many governments acknowledged their responsibility for boosting demand when announcing significant fiscal packages in 2008/9. Nevertheless, the critics of this policy have been vociferous and there are strident calls for an early reversal. This is nothing new. When Keynes advanced the argument for increased government borrowing in the 1930s, it was attacked by the establishment of the time on the grounds that it would not work because increased borrowing by the government would simply displace borrowing by the private sector. Productive spending by the private sector would therefore be replaced by wasteful spending by the state, with no net effect on aggregate demand.

Many people still believe something like this – even some distinguished economists. Eugene Fama, the man who developed the efficient markets hypothesis, said, "The problem is simple: bailouts and stimulus plans are funded by issuing more government debt. (The money must come from somewhere.)"[10]

As the Keynesian economist Paul Krugman has put it, "it's deeply depressing to find, not that people like Eugene Fama disagree with Keynes's conclusions, but that they're obviously completely unaware of the whole argument."[11]

This argument against Keynesian expansion was always very weak, because if extra spending by the government would "crowd out" spending by the private sector, why would extra private sector spending not do the same? In that case, how could there ever be a recovery?

Keynes proved the establishment argument wrong by a brilliant piece of imaginative reasoning about the way the monetary economy works. Extra issues of government bonds would not wholly displace other spending, because some of the money drawn into purchasing them would come out of idle bank balances. Moreover, once the first round of increased spending financed by government borrowing had got under way, increased saving from the resulting increased incomes would provide the finance. The economy would be pulled up by its own bootstraps.

In any case, if, for whatever reason, the bond market would not easily provide the finance for an increased deficit, it should always be possible to increase the money supply by getting the banks to buy the debt – or even the central bank. This is effectively what happens under the policy of QE. As long as the economy is underemployed, the idea that increased government borrowing will not work because it will crowd out other borrowing is a red herring – albeit one with a lifespan longer than any other fish I have ever encountered, real or imaginary.

It is striking how difficult it is to keep a bad idea down. Not only are there still some adherents to the "crowding out" view, even in depression conditions, another version of the idea has sprung up. It is as though what the Keynesians are fighting is one of those creatures of Greek mythology that, as soon as you cut off its head, sprouts another one.

The version of the "do-nothing school" the really smart academics espouse today is so-called Ricardian Equivalence. The idea is not that increased government borrowing to fund increased spending today is bound to crowd out other borrowing, but rather that it will not produce any extra demand because people will realize that increased government borrowing today implies increased taxes tomorrow to pay for it. Anticipating this future loss of disposable income, private saving will rise to offset the *dis*saving of the public sector, so there will be no net effect.

There are times when something like Ricardian Equivalence may apply, but for much of the world today is not one of them. As a theory it has two holes in it. First, it is not reasonable to expect people to act in such a "rational" way, both knowing what the future implications of higher government borrowing are and acting on these implications today. Even if people understand what is going on, they may be sufficiently myopic that they decide to spend the current handout. In view of the uncertainty surrounding the future, far from being irrational this would be a perfectly legitimate response.

Second, and more tellingly, it is by no means obvious that it is rational to save in response to increased government borrowing. For a start, if a program of increased public borrowing succeeds in boosting the economy, public debt may end up no higher and there may be no need for taxes to rise in future anyway.

Moreover, even if there is such a need, *when* will taxes rise? In a world where people have finite lives (an assumption that will doubtless seem unnecessarily demanding to many a theoretical economist) it makes a huge difference if you think they are going up next year or in ten years' time.

Suppose that the change that is going to happen to correct excessive government borrowing is not a rise in taxes but a cut in public spending. What is the rational response to that? I suppose that will depend on what sorts of things are going to be cut. If it is spending on health then perhaps increased saving becomes rational, given that perhaps you should prepare to make more personal provision for expenditure on your health. But if it is spending on defense what are you supposed to do: increase saving in order to buy off the enemy, or club together to buy a new nuclear submarine?

The solvency question
There *are* limits to a Keynesian expansion, nevertheless. In the extreme, there is the limit posed by fear of default. Moreover, the problems may not wait

until the point of default but rather may emerge well before then, as the markets come to fear default, and thereby force the yields on government bonds higher. Thus, a big deficit may end up causing higher bond yields, even though the crude "crowding out" view is wrong.

There have been umpteen sovereign defaults even in the recent period. Russia defaulted in 1998, Argentina in 2001, and Ecuador in 2008. Going back further, Germany defaulted in 1932. Even the UK, supposedly a paragon of reliability when it comes to its public debt, sort of defaulted in 1932 when it unilaterally cut the coupon (interest payment) on one of its substantial bond issues (War Loan) from 5% to 3½%.

If you go back before the modern era, defaults by sovereigns were a frequent occurrence. Sometimes a king might decide to renege on his obligations, and if he did, there was usually little that the lender could do about it. Or he might die in battle or be overthrown. By contrast, a great banking house like Fuggers would go on and on. Accordingly, it was not uncommon for sovereign borrowers to pay a higher rate of interest than top-quality private borrowers.

There is a combination of circumstances when outright default becomes almost inevitable – unless it is avoided by resort to implicit default – through inflation. Running a public deficit implies that the stock of public debt is rising. This implies that interest payments are rising. Unless the government squeezes other parts of the budget or the deficit falls back naturally, this means that the gap between spending and revenue will get bigger, and so the debt will increase, and so on and so forth.

In normal circumstances, with the economy growing, debt reasonably low, and interest rates modest, it is perfectly possible to live with this. For most of the postwar period western economies lived with it easily. However, there is a combination of factors that can make the debt situation explosive, known in the economics literature as the "debt trap." Essentially, when the rate of interest exceeds the growth rate of the economy in nominal terms (that is, the real growth rate plus the inflation rate) – which for most western countries in normal times would be 5–6% – the debt starts to increase exponentially. What is more, as markets see this tendency developing, they force the cost of government borrowing higher, thereby speeding up the deterioration.

At low levels of debt it is relatively easy for governments to stabilize the situation by budget tightening. But at higher levels, the amount of necessary tightening gets larger and larger, until it eventually exceeds the capacity of any democratic government to enact. As the markets see this coming, they push bond yields higher and higher, or even refuse to lend to the government at all, which then makes the thing everyone fears – default – inevitable.

Until recently, it would have seemed incredible that any leading western government could find itself in this position. Now it is conceivable for almost all of them, and some are already perilously close to it. In the US, the budget deficit is already likely to reach 13% of GDP. In the UK it may reach 15%. In most of continental Europe it is heading for close to 10%.

Admittedly, in both the US and the UK at the end of 2008, the ratio of government debt to GDP was about 40%. But when the budget deficit is running at more than 10% of GDP, the cumulative level of debt rises very quickly, even without a big rise in the interest rate at which markets will lend.

The upshot is that in both the US and the UK the scope for Keynesian fiscal expansion is limited. Indeed, the UK needs to implement a policy of significant fiscal tightening. While similar reasoning applies for the governments of Ireland, Italy, and much of eastern Europe, these constraints certainly do not apply to many governments in Asia, particularly China. There the Keynesian logic remains compelling and they are in a position to launch a large Keynesian expansion. (I will deal with the options open to China and other Asian countries in a moment.)

Avoiding fiscal pain

Bearing in mind the fact that, as I explained above, the public debt is owed to ourselves, I believe that the greatest threats to economic wellbeing arising from the size of the public debt are posed not by the debt itself, but rather by how we might react to it; that is, by excessive early tax rises, which could have the effect of prolonging the depression. That really would provide real reason for penury – lower output of goods and services and lower employment.

Now, there are circumstances where such an outcome could be forced on us, by the desire to avoid a default. But once that danger is dealt with, there is no reason to seek to reduce the public debt rapidly. The key strategy for dealing with the debt is to allow economic growth to do most of the work, just as happened in the nineteenth century and in the half-century after the Second World War. The secret is to ensure that most of the burden of tightening falls in future years when the recovery should have begun, and to offset the impact of immediate tightening with looser monetary policy.

This itself provides a very strong argument why, subject to the need to fend off fears of default, fiscal tightening should be postponed. When interest rates are already at zero, there is no scope to offset the effect of fiscal tightening by a loosening of conventional monetary policy. All that central banks can do is to extend QE still further. But since this itself has its problems and limitations, and is likely to be only modestly effective at best, this offers a slender reed to lean on.

Accordingly, it makes sense to postpone fiscal tightening until the point where the economy can take it and when, other things being equal, interest rates would otherwise be going up. At that stage the fiscal tightening can be offset by interest rates not going up. The implication of all this is that in all likelihood, most western economies facing the need to improve the public finances in conditions of continuing economic fragility will need to extend the period of near-zero interest rates. In several countries, it also implies the need to step up and extend the QE program, which I discussed above. This is a marathon, not a sprint.

Restoring confidence

So we come to the last of the four things the authorities can do to increase aggregate demand – boosting confidence. However, this is about the most difficult of the tasks facing policymakers. Without it, all the stimulatory policies in the world will have next to no effect. Yet governments cannot simply issue announcements saying: "Be confident!" What can they usefully do?

◆ They can "do the right thing" and explain to people what they are doing. Here my earlier message about expansionary Keynesian fiscal policy needs to be nuanced. Where the state sector has become bloated, it makes sense to try to reduce the deficit by cutting government spending rather than by increasing taxes. People can more readily believe that cutting government spending will bring long-term benefits, and this may serve to bolster their confidence about the future. In the same vein, where increased public deficits are feasible, using them to finance sensible real investment projects with a recognizably positive return to society may have more impact on aggregate demand than the equivalent amount of money spent on make-work schemes of no value.

◆ Governments can coordinate policies internationally and, again, demonstrate to people that they are doing this. In particular, the governments of the advanced countries can develop a new partnership with China.

◆ The authorities should develop a new financial architecture to ensure that nothing like this can ever happen again. This is the sense in which the fashioning of the new normality, the discussion of which I am putting off to the next chapter, is not entirely separate from the more pressing task of bringing about recovery.

◆ Without being bombastic or making overconfident forecasts, the authorities can point out where recovery might reasonably come from. It is not true that a prolonged depression is inevitable. As I have argued here, what it is perverse to believe is not that the economy can recover, but rather that a period of suffering and misery is inevitable, given that nothing real has been impaired. Governments need to get across the message that just as the depression is man-made, so the recovery can be also.

The fifth cavalry, Chinese detachment

Although there are policies to drive western domestic demand higher, as I have shown, they are all problematic, and prudent governments would not push them far enough to generate a full recovery. That would land us back where we were before. The missing link is increased demand from China and the other super-savers. If these countries can be persuaded to increase their domestic demand substantially, thereby eliminating their structural current account surpluses, the countries of the west can hope to return to full employment on a sustainable basis.

From the point of view of the west, it doesn't much matter whether Asian countries allow their currencies to rise or boost their domestic demand. More demand for western output is the requirement, no matter how that is achieved; although the inflationary implications would be different, as stronger Asian currencies would automatically imply weaker currencies for the west, which would drive up the western price level, for all the usual reasons.

However, which route is followed does matter greatly for Asia, and for the growth of the world as a whole. Allowing Asian currencies to rise would merely redistribute the benefit of a given level of aggregate demand around the world – more for the west and less for Asia. For this reason, for the world as a whole it offers no solution at all, and the countries of Asia are highly unlikely to embrace it.

What the countries of the west should be pressing for, therefore, is a policy of Asian currency appreciation, *combined* with domestic expansionary measures. The expansion of demand is much the more important of these. The result, if the policy were successful, would be full employment and continued strong growth in the east, combined with full employment without excessive credit creation in the west. If the east didn't run large surpluses, the west would not be running large deficits. In the countries of the west, the financial position of companies, households, and governments would improve.

The options for China

It will not be easy to persuade China to take further action. When asked recently whether China bore any responsibility for causing the current financial crisis, Chinese premier Wen Jiabao replied, "It is a ridiculous view."[12] Yet in Chapter 6 I showed how this stance fails to take into account the interdependence between deficits and surpluses.

Mind you, refusing to accept some responsibility for what has happened is one thing, acknowledging a role in putting matters right is another. And there are some encouraging signs of movement, not least the package of fiscal measures announced by the Chinese government in the wake of the economic slowdown of 2008. As I argued in Chapter 6, China is in a very strong position to relax fiscal policy and hence boost aggregate demand. It is impossible to be sure how much of the package represents genuine increases in public spending rather than the reannouncement of measures that were going to take place anyway. The IMF estimates that this package amounts to a net stimulus in 2009 of about 3% of GDP. The good news is that Chinese leaders recognize that the economy has become dangerously unbalanced. According to Wen Jiabao, the structure of the economy is "Unstable, Unbalanced, Uncoordinated and Unsustainable." The bad news, though, is that he said that in 2007. Indeed, rebalancing the economy away from exports and toward consumption has been a policy priority since 2004. At top-level consultations between the Chinese and American governments in Beijing in 2009, while the US reiterated its promise to lower its budget deficit by 2013, China reiterated its pledge to rebalance toward domestic demand-led growth.

Some commentators in the west criticize China for not having a generous social security system, modeled on western lines. This meets with well-deserved Chinese skepticism, bordering on incredulity. From an Asian perspective, overgenerous state handouts given for nothing in return are responsible for many of the ills of western society. However, there are plenty of other things the Chinese government could do to stimulate domestic demand:

◆ Accelerate spending on healthcare and education. Even after the recent expansionary package, China spends less on health or education than most of its neighbors.[13] In 1992 the Chinese government committed to spending 4% of national income on healthcare, yet in 2008 spending still languished at just over 2%.

◆ Issue shopping vouchers.[14]

◆ Give every resident a share in the state-owned asset management company.

◆ Increase income subsidies to low-income families.

◆ Force state-owned enterprises (SOEs) to pay bigger dividends to the state, which could then be distributed to the people.

◆ Continue with financial sector reform so that private firms have easier access to bank loans and equity and bond markets. This would discourage corporate hoarding of profits and encourage payments of dividends and spending on investment.

Elsewhere in Asia, many other governments are also in a strong financial position. Just about all the countries of the region, except the Philippines and India, have low debt ratios. With the exception of Malaysia and India, cyclically adjusted budget deficits are very small, or even negative; that is, a surplus. Accordingly, they are in a position to engage in a Keynesian expansion. They also have the scope to allow their exchange rates to appreciate considerably.

I do not think there is much the Middle Eastern oil producers, or Russia, can or should do to boost domestic demand, although some token measures could usefully be put in place as part of a global solution. However, substantive measures could be taken by the governments of Germany, Switzerland, and Norway.

While it is true that Germany is now running a large fiscal deficit, which is forecast by the OECD to reach 7% of GDP in 2010, the deficit is also forecast to fall to 2% in 2012. In 2008, the ratio of net public debt to GDP was only about 45%.

The numbers are much more striking for Switzerland and Norway. In 2008, the Swiss budget was just about in balance and the net debt to GDP ratio was about 10%. In Norway, the government was running a huge surplus of about 18% of GDP, and because of the funneling of its huge oil surplus into a national savings fund, its net debt was negative; that is, its government had net financial *assets* to the tune of about 125% of GDP. All of these countries could plausibly expand their budget deficits somewhat, and in the case of Switzerland and Norway by a considerable amount.

A solution made in China?

Although my charted path involves policy prescriptions for many countries, there is no doubting the pivotal role to be played by China. We used to think there was a struggle going on for the world's savings. Now there is a struggle going on for the world's spending. The countries of the west cannot look for a purely domestic solution to the current crisis, they must engage with China. This does not mean browbeating her, which would be futile. It does mean helping her to see her own self-interest and convincing her of the dangers of allowing current imbalances to continue. These dangers include a lapse into protectionism, which would cause havoc in the world economy but disaster for China.

So much of what we buy in the shops is now made in China. I have argued that in one sense the financial crisis of 2007/9 was also made there. It would be fitting if the solution to it, which allows western countries to resume prosperity without undue pain and suffering, could be made there also.

This idea that China holds the key to the west's salvation – and that the Chinese authorities will actually use it to open the door to a prosperous future for us all – will strike many people as absurd. But then all along, most people in the west, including most of the supposed experts, have failed to see the significance of China for the world economy.

For most of human history, China has been the world's largest economy. The exception is the period since the Industrial Revolution, which it missed out on, leading to two centuries of sharp relative decline. By the 1970s, China had become almost irrelevant in global economic terms and was widely ignored, by both ordinary people and experts alike. So when it embarked on its own version of the Industrial Revolution in 1978, launching its $1\frac{1}{4}$ billion people into the world economy, it was not generally perceived quite how revolutionary this was going to be for the rest of us.

Although the experts missed it, this was bound to have an enormous effect. Phase I of this effect was the boost to the west's prosperity and the sharp reduction in its inflation rate made possible by the burgeoning flow of cheap manufactures. Phase II was the challenge for western financial structures and economic policy posed by China's huge surpluses. Phase III still lies in the future. It is the opportunity created by China's emergence as a huge consumer, and as the destination for vast quantities of western exports. It wouldn't surprise me if the "experts" missed that too.

However, unless a credible world financial architecture can be built from the current wreckage, it is unlikely that the various key players, especially the Chinese, can be persuaded to make the radical changes to policy necessary to deliver the west's salvation: increased Asian demand. Accordingly, the way to enable a solution to our immediate problem must include designing a system that addresses our fundamental, underlying difficulties. Getting out of the current mess will require a refashioning of the whole world monetary order. The sooner we get on with it the better.

9

Saving Capitalism from Itself

There is one and only one social responsibility of business – to use its resources and engage in activities designed to increase its profits so long as it stays within the rules of the game, which is to say, engages in open and free competition without deception or fraud.

Milton Friedman, *Capitalism and Freedom*, 1962

Never before in the field of human conduct has so much been filched from so many by so few.

With apologies (again) to Winston Churchill

It has long amused me that the doctrine of efficient markets, and the much looser but wider endorsement of free markets in general, find their strongest supporters in university economics and finance departments, by and large peopled by individuals who, protected by their tenured appointments at not-for-profit institutions, never come face to face with the capitalist system in action. They are the ones who blithely assert the case for free markets, even to the point of arguing the merits of allowing the whole financial system to be allowed to implode, confident in its later resurgence, stronger and healthier – and presumably in the resilience of their own pension schemes. They would not last five minutes on a trading floor before being eaten alive.[1]

Yet unfettered financial markets are not the be-all and end-all of capitalism and the market economy. On the whole, within the restraints and with the modifications that we have learned to impose on it, the real economy of production, distribution, and exchange works pretty well; certainly far better than any other economic system ever invented.

So the test that lies before us is to reconstruct, and *reconstrict*, the financial system to act again in the public interest, without losing altogether the impulse toward financial innovation – and without threatening the competitive, market economy outside the realms of finance.

The world is now awash with proposals for re-regulation of the financial system from both official bodies and outside commentators. It would not be helpful for me to burden the reader with my blow-by-blow assessment of those suggestions, nor to put forward a competing detailed agenda of my own. Rather, I will confine myself to discussion of the central ideas behind a reformed financial system and to the general principles to be followed in fashioning it. Some of my suggestions are already in active discussion in policymaking forums; some are decidedly not.

The workings of the market

In thinking about a new system for regulating the financial system, the first priority should be to avoid overdoing the restrictions. Markets do work – in the end. It is just that the end may be a long time coming. If they worked perfectly, checks and balances would have come into play to stop the excesses of the credit boom. Bank managements would have been conscious of the risks of excessive lending and would have put the brakes on. If they hadn't, the banks' shareholders would have seen what was going on and imposed their will on bank managements. But we always knew that markets weren't perfect, didn't we? Well, if you didn't, you do now!

Now we will see the checks and balances that should have operated before, but didn't, put in place with a vengeance. The air will be thick with the sound of stable doors being shut. Banks will severely restrict trading activities; they will be extra cautious about holding complex financial derivatives that are difficult to understand; they will be wary of excessive exposure to asset classes that could be caught up in a bubble; they will closely examine their remuneration structures to make sure that they do not richly reward excessive risk taking; and they will ensure that they pay out rewards to bankers over a long time horizon, comparable with the longevity of the real economic and financial cycles. Committees will meet regularly and report back. Audits will be conducted. Reports will be written. Boards will discuss. In short, the last war will be fought, and refought, over and over again.

Meanwhile, outside the banks themselves, the supervisory agents of the capitalist system will wake up to their responsibilities. The accountants will crawl over their activities with a fine-tooth comb. The ratings agencies will scrutinize their clients' activities for any hint of excessive risk taking. Bank managements will be grilled over how well they comply with the new norms. And the institutional shareholders will do all of the above all over again. Excessive risks, dodgy lending, or risky remuneration structures will be penalized where it really hurts – in the share price.

As if this were not enough, the financial press, no longer supine and star struck by the glitter of our financial superheroes, will crawl over all of the above to ensure that everyone is doing their job, exposing excessive risk taking and bad management, ever watchful for the next bubble or financial disaster. Finally, finally, the market will work.

The do-nothing option

Given this, why interfere with the market at all? Isn't there a case for leaving it well alone? There is. Indeed, I suspect that in the next few years the greatest danger lies in over-, rather than underregulation. That is to say, there is a real risk that, over and above the restrictions placed on financial activities by banks themselves and their scrutiny by shareholders, auditors, ratings agencies, and the press, pressure by regulators will constrain them still further. We will end up with a shackled and crippled financial system that is unable to provide support to the real economy – just when it needs it most. It would be galling if restrictions put in place to prevent a past bubble, already burst, stopped in its tracks the recovery yet to come.[2]

It is very striking, moreover, that the urge to curb and regulate extends to institutions that were not directly implicated in what has gone wrong. Many European political leaders, for instance, want to restrict the activities of hedge funds and private equity businesses. There may or may not be good reasons to do this, but if there are, trying to prevent a repeat of the crisis of 2007/9 is not one of them. The agents of this crisis were banks, which were heavily (though incompetently) regulated.

Nevertheless, extra restrictions on financial markets will be necessary, for two reasons. First, it will be impossible for confidence to recover fully without them. The world has undergone a shock to its central nervous system. Its faith in people, institutions, markets, practices, and regulations is shattered. The idea that we can simply go back to the *status quo ante* is unthinkable. People will not wear it. They need reassurance that things are different, that they are controlled. Above all, they need to believe that someone is looking at the system as a whole, and thinking of the interests of the system as a whole – not merely their own profit.

Second, something like the Great Implosion could happen all over again. Periodic bouts of irrational exuberance are endemic to the financial system. Indeed, believe it or not, in mid-2009 there were signs of the bad old banking habits returning. In London, big bonuses were being paid again and several banks were going on a hiring spree. To have believed the guff about efficient markets, and in the process allowed the world to have become vulnerable to a systemic financial collapse, is just about understandable *once*, but twice would be unforgivable.

So action is needed, and in several areas. I will start with the regulation of banks and financial institutions, then consider macroeconomic policy, and conclude with a discussion of the international monetary regime.

The shape of banking regulation

If the Great Implosion was partly the result of a failure of the banking system, it was also partly the result of a failure of regulation. Given this, it is far from obvious that what a reformed financial system needs is more regulation. It may need *less*. Such regulation as it has, however, needs to be more effective. The aim should be to work with the grain of the market, not against it. Much of what needs to be done is about not restricting but rather improving the workings of the markets in financial services.

I will turn to my suggestions in that regard in a moment. First, I concentrate on the aspects where the market, even if it works efficiently, will not produce an outcome that will generate stability, and therefore needs effective regulation. There are four areas where banks need to be subject to enhanced regulation. If these areas are adequately dealt with, the banking system can be largely left to get on with its business – and ours – much as before.

Reforming capital requirements

The pure free market approach to capital holding would be that this is some-thing that banks, like other businesses, can be left to sort out for themselves, in their own, or rather their shareholders', best interests. But this argument will not stand up to close scrutiny. First, there is the problem of myopia, which I discussed in Chapters 4 and 5. Bank executives, and even bank shareholders, have a natural tendency to underestimate the amount of capital they need to hold as protection against future losses. Given that banks are systemically important and that their failure imposes severe costs on the rest of us ("exter-nalities," in the jargon), this tendency to operate with too little capital needs to be corrected, in the public interest.

The second flaw is that in practice, as we have seen in recent events, ulti-mately the state will provide protection for banks. That alone should give the state a legitimate say in how much capital banks hold. Moreover, once it is quite clear that the state will ultimately provide protection, if the banks were left to their own devices there would be a natural tendency to carry less cap-ital than they otherwise would.

Accordingly, the state has to regulate bank capital holdings. But how? Bearing in mind the risks to the economic system and the extent of the may-hem unleashed when the financial system breaks down, the arrangements with regard to capital need to err on the side of caution. The aim should be that at the very least a normal recession should be withstandable without renewed access to outside shareholders, let alone public support. Capital requirements need to be calculated with regard to the whole gamut of bank liabilities, not just those shown on the balance sheet.

Moreover, these capital requirements need to be variable across the cycle so that, as the economy gathers steam and bank balance sheets expand rapidly, cap-ital requirements rise. The *quid pro quo* for this is that as the cycle turns down, banks should be allowed to operate with lower capital ratios, thereby reducing the pressure on them to cut back on lending when the economy is weak.[3]

Imposing liquidity requirements

Similar considerations apply to liquidity requirements. Left to their own devices, banks will tend to hold fewer liquid assets than the public interest would dictate. Liquid assets yield a lower return. Accordingly, having higher holdings of liquid assets costs money – at least in the short run.

The need for liquid assets has undergone a reassessment as a result of the apparent nonfunctioning of the interbank market. We now know that there is much in common between the workings of the interbank market and the availability of umbrellas. When the sun is shining, umbrellas are available in abundance. When the heavens have opened, you have a job securing a single umbrella for either love or money.

One suggested defense against the unreliability of interbank funding is for all banks to rely on retail deposits. Taken to an extreme this would effectively end the interbank market for good and all. This would do something to reduce the risk of liquidity crises, but in my view not a lot, and the loss of efficiency would be considerable.[4]

A more robust defense is for banks to attract *long-term* money, whether retail or wholesale. However, there are limits on how far this is likely to go. At present the wholesale markets are wary of lending to banks beyond the very short term. Until confidence is restored this won't change. Moreover, the essential job of banks is *maturity transformation*; that is, borrowing short and lending long. They cannot sensibly be encouraged to match the maturity of all assets and liabilities; that is tantamount to opting for extinction.

The solution is surely that banks must hold a good proportion of liquid assets, those that can be realized "at short notice and without loss." The leading candidate for this role must be marketable government debt.

Public regulation of remuneration structures

The idea of the state setting pay or bonus levels in banking, or anywhere else for that matter, seems ridiculous. Furthermore, as I indicated above, I suspect that capitalism's natural recuperative processes will come into play to restrict overall remuneration in banking and to reform its structure.

Nevertheless, given what we have been through, public confidence and a sense of justice will demand some outside scrutiny of pay structures. Moreover, if banks and other financial institutions are to have access to public funds in times of trouble, about which I write in more detail below, it is right that the state should have a say in how pay incentivizes risk taking.

Furthermore, as I argued in Chapters 4 and 5, how pay is set involves considerable elements of externality. It is difficult for one individual bank, or indeed a nonfinancial firm, to exercise pay restraint while others are not. If pay needs to be restrained, some outside agency needs to restrain it.

For institutions that qualify for government support in time of trouble, there could be a requirement that they conform to certain remuneration practices. These need not lay down limits to pay, but they could reasonably require that bonuses be paid in stock rather than cash; that they can be reduced over time if the subsequent performance of the bank, the business unit, or the individual concerned so merits; and that they are accessible to the beneficiaries only after the elapse of a considerable period of time. Something along these lines has already occurred in the US, imposed by Congress. And in the UK the government has exercised influence over the pay policies of the banks in which it holds a considerable stake. At its meeting in London in September 2009, the G-20 made proposals along the lines of my suggestions, also going so far as to limit the size of banks' bonus pools, while not attempting to limit bonuses for individuals.

My suspicion is that together a package of such reforms would bring about a revolution in the levels and structure of remuneration in banking. The reformed bonus structure sketched above would significantly inhibit the processes that cause the upward ratchet in bankers' pay, not least by making it difficult for bankers to threaten to leave in search of higher rewards.[5] Nevertheless, absurdly high pay in banking is a symptom of a deeper problem; namely, as I analyzed in Chapter 5, a lack of effective competition. Accordingly, a large part of any effective attempt to drive down pay in banking must focus on competition issues, to which I turn in a moment.

Restrictions on some financial instruments

Warren Buffett called derivatives "financial instruments of mass destruction." The events of the last few years seem to have vindicated his judgment. There is a case for reviewing whether some of these instruments should be banned or restricted.

No less a market figure than George Soros has called for credit default swaps (CDSs) to be banned, calling them truly toxic. Referring to the case of

General Motors in America, Mr. Soros said that as a result of their credit default swap positions, some bondholders had stood to gain more from bankruptcy than from reorganization. He said: "It's like buying life insurance on someone else's life and owning a license to kill him."[6] On other occasions he has called into question the use of commodities as investment vehicles, and has challenged the activities of commodity index funds. It seems to me that they played a major role in the huge run-up in commodity prices in 2007/8, which proved to be highly destabilizing. In my view, there could be a case for restrictions to be placed on their activities.

Eligibility for public support

It was not pretty watching the world's monetary authorities deciding on the spot which institutions were worthy of government support and which were not, effectively making financial strategy on the hoof, and in the process making some key mistakes. In Martin Wolf's words, they were "caught between the elite's fear of bankruptcy and the public's loathing of bailouts."[7] In the economy of the future, the structure of the financial system needs to be radically rebased, with a clear understanding of which institutions are eligible for public support and which are not, and on what terms.

In essence, in the memorable expression coined by the distinguished British economist John Kay, modern banking has represented a union between a utility and a casino. What is more, the casino has been wearing the trousers. A key part of the reform of the system will be ensuring a divorce between these two ill-starred partners. Whatever the precise form of the restrictions, the aim will surely be to ring-fence the boring, essential functions of the banking system – such as money transfer, simple savings accounts, and plain vanilla lending – from the racier bits. There would be strict limits on what a banking utility could do. Its functions would be to administer the payments system, and to provide simple deposit and savings products and simple loan services.

There are two leading versions of the vision for this "utility." One is that it is merely old-style "commercial banking" without the "investment banking" frills. In other words, it represents a return to the separation between commercial and investment banking imposed in America by the Glass Steagall

Act, repealed in 1999. The idea is that commercial banks would be both heavily regulated and have access to public support in the event of trouble, while investment banks would be left to get on with whatever they found profitable, but would not have access to public support and would accordingly be allowed to go bust as and when trouble arose.

The other vision is of so-called narrow banking, where banks are obliged to hold onto the deposits entrusted to them, rather than lending them out at risk. Their assets would be heavily dominated by holdings of government bonds.

The second is a much narrower vision than the first, although they share the same philosophical starting point. Actually, I am not sure they are mutually exclusive; that is, there could be a three-tier system of banks: narrow banks, closely limited to basic services and closely circumscribed in what assets they could hold; wider, commercial banks, with more freedom to operate but still not allowed to engage in "investment banking"; and investment banks. In such a structure there would be room for mutually owned institutions to be narrow banks, or wider commercial banks, under certain restrictions.

No complete solution

Such a structure has much to recommend it. I am concerned, though, that it would still not allow governments to wash their hands of the rest of the financial system and allow investment banks to "get on with it," even to the point of undertaking activities that caused them to go bust.

For a start, it is surely instructive that the event that set off the financial crisis in 2008 was the collapse of an *investment bank*, Lehman Brothers. The new world would have to be structured in such a way that a similar collapse in the future would not excite such an extreme panic. Nor was this the only example. According to Alan Greenspan, the near-collapse of the hedge fund LTCM in 1998 had the potential to cause a systemic crisis.

Accordingly, under the new dispensation even investment banks might need close supervision. However, at least the separation of ultra-safe narrow banks and closely constrained commercial banks should minimize the extent of any panic emanating from the failure of an individual investment bank.

Moreover, the emphasis of macroeconomic policy on preventing macro bubbles, to which I will turn in a moment, should discourage a situation developing in which a whole series of investment banks, as well as many counterparts in the rest of the financial system, are simultaneously exposed to the same risks. Furthermore, following the reforms to both the financial system and overall corporate governance, which I also discuss below, investment banks should be smaller and less significant in the economy. In such a world it might be perfectly feasible for the authorities to let an individual investment bank go bust without turning a hair; although I suspect that they would always be wary of allowing this.

Restrictions could go further still. It has been argued that banks that are too big to fail are *ipso facto* too big. In that case, public policy should place a limit on the size of banks or, more plausibly, impose increased capital ratios as banks get larger.

I have my doubts about such a policy. It isn't that size doesn't matter, but rather that size isn't all that matters. If you broke the banking system into umpteen small pieces and changed nothing else, the Great Implosion could still have happened. Swimming in the same waters and imbued with the same objectives and subject to the same illusions, banks would still have engaged in the same madcap exposure to toxic assets. And it is not obvious to me that 100 small banks going bust is preferable to 10 big ones. Moreover, supervising a system of umpteen small banks, and keeping track of their interlinkages, could be more difficult.

That said, I suppose that if there were umpteen small banks this might reduce the likelihood of a single approach to lending and financial activity dominating the whole industry, although I wouldn't rely on it. It would, however, also serve to boost competition in the industry and thereby help to contain the level of fees and charges for financial services.

In that regard, as well as, or instead of, limiting the size of investment banks, there is a case for splitting up their functions and restricting which of these an individual bank can perform. This would amount to a partial reversal of the 1986 "Big Bang" reforms in London and earlier similar reforms in the US. The aim would not be to return to the cosy environment of the old City, but rather, by restricting the functions that an individual "bank" could perform, to limit conflicts of interest and the power of banks over their clients. The functions of market making, broking, corporate advice, and investment research could take place in separate institutions – as they once largely did.

Wider financial reform

Restricting banks in the way I have described should make a big difference to how financial markets behave, to how important financial markets are in the economy, and to how well financial market operators are rewarded. But will these effects go far enough?

As I argued in Chapter 5, there is a tendency for financial markets to expand beyond their social usefulness. This is because the rewards from outwitting others are so great, and because of the human urge to gain great riches quickly, with minimal effort. Ensuring a prosperous and secure future for us all will involve the financial sector being cut down to size.

The approach most friendly to the libertarian attitude to markets would be to rely on the above measures to achieve this – or not. After all, although a large part of the bloated level of financial activity derives from excessive trading that collectively brings no benefit, if people want to engage in this activity arguably they should be allowed to do so. Also, if banks, and other financial institutions, wish to employ too many people and pay them too much, that is up to them. Nevertheless, there are huge dangers involved in this, and heavy costs. These argue for further action.

One possible strategy would be for society substantially to cut back the scope of financial markets. In many countries in the west, the prevailing trend has been to increase this scope by putting more pension provision on a funded basis and by privatizing large numbers of previously state-owned businesses. This could be reversed – although I would not recommend it. Quite apart from the disruption involved in another sharp change of structure, there are other problems arising both from pay-as-you-go pension systems and from large amounts of the economy being owned and operated by the state. Nevertheless, for countries in the emerging world that have not yet gone fully down the path of relying on financial markets, the revelation of the weaknesses of financial markets should give them pause for thought.

Instead, my favored approach for the developed countries of the west is a set of interventions that will make market forces work better in financial services. The challenge is to find forms of intervention that legitimately sit within the public realm and yet still leave markets essentially free to pursue profit.

The Tobin tax

There is one overarching radical idea for reform: to tax financial transactions. The Nobel Prize-winning American economist James Tobin once advocated a tax on foreign exchange activity, which would serve to reduce trading.[8] The Tobin tax could be extended beyond foreign exchange trading and applied to financial trading more generally, including in shares. In the 1930s Keynes argued for just such a tax.[9]

At the time that Tobin suggested it, the idea of a so-called Tobin tax, as it became known, immediately came in for widespread attack from all the usual suspects – the "leave the market well alone" brigade. Then, in the heady days of enthusiasm for markets in the 1980s and 1990s, it suffered the worst fate of any idea: it was totally ignored. In August 2009, Lord Turner, the head of Britain's Financial Services Authority, resurrected it – and was immediately embroiled in a raging controversy as he was vehemently attacked by financial market practitioners and those who see their role as defending either the financial services industry, or free markets, or both. He was branded naive, leftist, and dangerous. Most tellingly, he was accused of endangering the health of Britain's financial services industry, which contributes roughly 8% of her GDP, employs millions of people, and is a substantial generator of net external income for the UK.

Yet, with some qualifications, which I will emphasize below, Turner was right to say that the Tobin tax may have something to offer. How much the financial services industry contributes to GDP or employment is beside the point. Would the critics of the Tobin tax approach the provision of health services in the same way? Although I must admit that I don't see how it can make much of a contribution to the balance of payments, the UK's National Health Service "contributes a huge amount to GDP" and is reputedly western Europe's largest employer. Does this mean that it is immune from criticism or that we should not question both its efficiency and its role in the economy?

Or what about the tobacco industry or the arms industry? These are not only large and successful but are also major net earners of external incomes for the UK.

The real issue is what an economic activity contributes to overall human welfare – and that can be negative even when the usual metrics of economic assessment involving GDP and such like appear to show it making a major positive contribution.

In the case of an individual country, such as the UK, though, there is a further complication. There is the scope for making a substantial national loss from the curtailment of financial market activity just because this is an area where the UK has a comparative advantage. Accordingly, a country like the UK would need to proceed with application of the Tobin tax with extreme caution. Indeed, there would be next to no point in proceeding with it unilaterally, since other financial centers would take the business, thereby producing no curtailment of the financial sector overall, but a substantial loss for London.

Nevertheless, the Tobin tax would have a clear intellectual rationale. I argued in Chapter 5 that financial markets are subject to liquidity fetishism. Frantic trading takes up massive resources, generates volatility, and adds nothing to human welfare. As Tobin once said, "every financial market absorbs private resources to operate and government resources to police. The country cannot afford all the markets that enthusiasts may dream up."[10] A Tobin (or Keynes) tax would reduce the level of such frothy activity and in the process restrict the rewards of all those institutions – and individuals – actively involved in it. The beauty of the tax is that it would not do much to discourage long-term investment, but it would discourage – without preventing – short-term speculation.[11] Its intention would be to throw some sand in the well-oiled wheels of finance.

Apart from the usual objections to any proposal that interferes with the market, the main argument against the Tobin tax has been that it would not work because financial markets would find ways round it, rather in the way that a stream finds its way round a rock lying in its path. In particular, even if the major financial centers all agreed to implement it, market activities would shift to offshore centers where the tax did not apply.

Yet this point can easily be overdone. The rate of the tax would be set pretty low, such that the extra costs/disadvantages of diverting activities from New York or London to the Cayman Islands or Liechtenstein could easily outweigh the cost of paying the tax. More importantly, as part of the new global settlement that needs to follow from the Great Implosion, the position of offshore tax havens and centers with minimal regulation is up for discussion anyway. With both regulators and the regulated under pressure from both shareholders and the public, and the prevailing mood being to seek safety and security, even respectability, it should be possible readily to discourage such diversion, perhaps by taxing transactions between mainstream centers and offshore havens at a penal rate.[12]

My main reservation about the Tobin tax is quite different. Although it might make a valuable contribution by penalizing a great deal of socially useless activity, it would do next to nothing to affect serious speculation and the build-up of bubbles. When it really matters, it seems that what needs to be thrown into the wheels is not sand but boulders. After all, the Stamp Duty, which applies in the UK to transactions in shares and many other assets, is itself a form of Tobin tax. It certainly hasn't stood in the way of bubbles developing in UK asset markets. In this regard there is a good deal to recommend the idea that capital gains tax be levied on a sliding scale, with very short-term gains taxed at high rates, and gains on assets held for many years taxed at low rates. (Limited exemptions could be granted to specialized financial entities such as those acting as market makers.)

Over and above this, I have another radical suggestion for consideration. Entitlement to receive a dividend could be restricted by law to those who have held shares for a certain minimum period, say two years. Care would be needed in the design of such a system to ensure that it wasn't circumvented, for example by trading in depository receipts. However, if it were successful, the result of such a measure would be a much reduced level of trading activity.

Perhaps more importantly, since institutional shareholders would typically now hold their shares for a longer period, they would be encouraged to exercise their responsibilities as owners, rather than behaving like the temporary holders of so many gambling chips. Meanwhile, restrictions could be placed on the ability of corporate executives, as well as bank employees, to enjoy the benefit of share options, share awards, and special incentive schemes before some specified minimum time limit, say ten years. Interestingly, my proposed measure on entitlement to dividends would closely mirror the proposed delay for executives – and for similar reasons. It is appropriate that both capital and labor should have to wait for their full reward.

Other possible reforms include increasing the responsibilities of institutional shareholders in relation to the remuneration levels and structures of the companies in which they have a stake of more than a certain percentage, and tightening up legal restrictions on the ability of one company to acquire another in a contested takeover. The aim should not be to stop such activity but rather to make it more difficult to conduct, so as to align the private interests of the executives involved more closely with the public interest.

Reforms to foster competition

In addition, there are several more possible reforms that could make parts of the financial services industry more competitive and more responsive:

- The payment of "trailing commission" (money paid to a financial adviser each year an asset is owned) could be made illegal.
- Pension funds and insurance companies could be legally obliged to facilitate the movement of clients' funds without financial penalty, much in the way that banks are obliged to facilitate the switching of bank accounts.
- If the functions of integrated banks and brokerage houses are not split up, as described above, the Spitzer reforms to banks and brokers in the US could be extended internationally. Market-making institutions could be obliged by law to offer their services free of any add-ons for research and other functions, which must be offered, and charged for, on a separate, take-it-or-leave-it basis.
- The state could organize the establishment of professional guilds for different parts of the financial services industry, funded by the constituent firms, where the prevailing ethos would be the promotion of customer service.

Shrinking public debt

Besides regulation and reforms to promote competition and discourage excessive trading, there are two aspects of macroeconomic policy that need reform
in order to add greater robustness to the financial system. The first is policy
over debt and deficits. It was deeply shocking to see major western governments inhibited in their actions to support the banking system and their use
of fiscal expansion to counter the depression by worries about default risk.
During the Great Implosion, how far the governments of the US, the eurozone, and the UK went in increasing government borrowing was effectively
restricted by the realization that if they ran a deficit of 10% of GDP for a very
long period, their debt-to-GDP ratio would rise into dangerous territory and
before long investors would worry about default.

Preventing a recession from turning into a slump is one of the key roles
of government in the modern age. It requires the ability to deploy massive
fiscal expansion if necessary. Accordingly, in good times the debt-to-GDP ratio
has to be kept so low that it would remain at reasonable levels even after
many years of running a budget deficit of 10% of GDP, in order that fear of
default never rears its head.

Opinions can reasonably differ on what number constitutes the appropriate level, but it is surely much lower than the figures obtaining on the eve
of the Great Implosion. I suggest that 20% is a reasonable number. This
would allow almost five years of public deficits of 10% of GDP before a ratio
of debt to GDP of 70% was reached. To help ensure that governments stick
to a path of fiscal virtue and resist siren calls for relaxation emanating from
short-term political pressures, it would be helpful to have an independent
Fiscal Policy Committee, modeled on the lines of the UK's Monetary Policy
Committee, to set the course of overall fiscal policy, with the Treasury or
Finance Ministry deciding on the overall level of government spending (and
hence the tax burden) as well as the choice between various sorts of expenditure and the level of particular taxes.

When viewed from this perspective, the fiscal laxity of the postwar years
amounts to a gross dereliction of duty. It is the equivalent of a government
leaving a country undefended against its enemies; in this case undefended

against itself. It is all very well racking up huge debts as the result of a war for survival, as Britain did three times in the last 200 years – first in the Napoleonic wars, then in the First World War, and again in the Second – but the amassing of huge debt as the result of peacetime fiscal incontinence, especially to finance burgeoning welfare spending, is unforgivable.

Inflation targeting and asset prices

The second reform concerns the regime for controlling bubbles. It could have two parts: micro and macro. The micro part concerns the limiting of lending behavior.[13] I have doubts about such an approach. It would be regrettable if regulations put in place to ensure macro stability entailed substantial micro inefficiency.

In this regard, I am dubious about the restrictions on the multiple of incomes on new mortgage lending being proposed by the UK's Financial Services Authority. There can be circumstances when it is good business, and good for both borrowers and the economy at large, that lending at high multiples does take place. In a reformed and macro-regulated financial system, within the context of a regime of macroeconomic management that gave the prevention of bubbles serious weight, detailed regulation of such things as mortgage multiples can be avoided.

Moreover, quite apart from these considerations of efficiency, I doubt that on its own micro regulation would be enough. We need a system that is robust – belt and braces. Accordingly, whatever happens with micro regulation, I suspect that we must look to macro policy for a good part of the defense against bubbles.

One way of doing this is to add some sort of "macroprudential" instrument to the policymakers' toolkit. The most favored candidate is variable capital ratios. If these did their job effectively, arguably the framework governing pure macroeconomic policymaking could be left pretty much untouched. In particular, those countries that set interest rates in pursuit of an explicit inflation target, such as the eurozone and the UK, could continue, much as before.

Although, as I argued above, variable capital ratios have some merits, I am highly dubious that they will solve the problem on their own. Perhaps the next bubble will not depend on much increased lending by banks; at least not domestically regulated ones. Or perhaps increased capital ratios will be less effective in discouraging excessive lending than the regulators originally envisaged.

In fact we have a test case to go on: Spain. Since 2000, Spanish banks have had to make provisions for latent losses; that is, those that are likely to emerge but are unrecognized by conventional accounting. It seems as though this model has enabled Spanish banks to withstand the current crisis pretty well. But strikingly, it did not prevent Spain from undergoing a massive property boom. Whatever restraint was felt as a result of these provisioning arrangements was swamped by the effects of low interest rates imposed by the ECB.

Accordingly, I do not believe that such "macroprudential" instruments will be enough on their own and that the monetary policymakers can simply carry on setting interest rates as before, confident in the belief that prudential control of the system is being carried on by someone else. On the contrary, I believe that the objectives of monetary policy will have to be reformed in order to give greater prominence to asset prices. This is not the same thing as *targeting* asset prices. That is something central banks should *not* do, even if they could. But it does mean accepting that bubbles can happen, that when they do, the effects on the economy can be devastating, and that interest rate policy can and should play a part in preventing them.

Moreover, far from being a diversion from the modern central bank's concentration on inflation, this would be a refinement of it. The point is that money can be in the process of debauch even while the current rate of consumer prices index (CPI) inflation is nugatory. This is what happened in the mid-1990s. Rates of consumer price inflation were very low, but asset prices, particularly for residential property, were rampant. Yet the policy regime centered on CPI inflation, and on that score there was no sign of any problem on the horizon. Accordingly, central banks cut interest rates to low levels and left them there.

But rampant asset price inflation is not consistent with monetary stability in the medium term. Accordingly, if asset prices are rising strongly for a persistent period, it is otiose for a central bank to argue that all is well, as long as the rate of CPI inflation is benign.

As I argued in *Money for Nothing*, central banks need to give greater prominence to asset prices as part of a new focus on financial stability. This need not necessarily replace inflation targets – or the Fed's joint mandate – but rather would modify the way in which they operate. In the new regime, central banks would give greater prominence to asset prices simply by emphasizing their link with price stability in the medium term. In many cases this would not even require a change in the wording of their objectives, let alone new legislation. Rather, it would require a reinterpretation or, at most, some minor rewording.

Forecasting misleads

Under the present policy regime there is too much emphasis on forecasting, especially in the UK. The Bank of England forecasts inflation, concentrating on the period up to two years out, looking at a range of indicators including asset prices, and, on the basis of this forecast compared to its inflation objective, sets interest rates. However, asset prices will tend to exert their influence on consumer prices over periods longer than two years, and in an unpredictable manner. So, under this approach, the role of asset prices in regard to inflation is automatically downplayed.

In fact, it is not that easy to forecast inflation even up to two years. Equally, the costs to business and individuals of inflation being marginally above or below the target over this short period are pretty low as well. Yet this is what monetary policy has concentrated on!

By contrast, the importance of a bubble building up in the most important asset class of all is enormous. The distortions this creates threaten to waste massive amounts of resources in the real economy: as it builds, it could readily unleash inflation; and when it bursts, it will certainly unleash huge disinflationary forces that could easily produce deflation in the short term, possibly leading to inflation shortly afterwards.

Admittedly, if the central banks are to continue with only one instrument, namely short-term interest rates, then they can only have one objective. This is the mantra repeated over and over again by consensus-hugging central bankers everywhere, as though it absolves them from responsibility for serious thought. (In practice, it looks as though they will soon have at least one more instrument, countercyclical capital ratios, which I briefly discussed above.)

The issue is not about trying to escape the one-instrument, one-target logic, but rather to debate the form of the target. I am suggesting that this should continue to be some sort of inflation or price-level objective, but that this should be interpreted flexibly, with asset prices accorded a key role. The mistake has been to focus narrowly on the rate of inflation year by year. We all know where that policy has got us.

The alternative approach that I am supporting is a focus on price stability over the medium term. In my suggested regime, if house prices are increasing strongly then, even if the current rate of CPI inflation is very low and looking likely to remain so, this constitutes a major argument for not cutting interest rates, and perhaps even an argument for raising them.

The result of my suggested regime would be greater variability in the inflation rate, as central banks do not react to every twitch of the recorded consumer price statistics. Depending on the target for inflation in the medium term, this could even be consistent with the toleration of occasional dips into negative territory; that is, deflation.

What is the right level for the inflation target?

In the UK the objective is explicitly to hit a target of 2% on the CPI; in the eurozone the objective is CPI inflation of less than but close to 2%; in the US, although there is no formal inflation target, it is believed that the Fed's implicit objective is an inflation rate of 2%. But is 2% the right level? It is sufficiently high that the price level moves up considerably over time; an inflation rate of 2% results in a doubling of the price level in 35 years. Yet it is also low enough to make occasional dips below zero fairly likely. After the experience of 2007/9 and the intensity of the deflation scare, there will be arguments for raising the inflation objective to 3% or even higher.

This would be a mistake, however. What made the deflation scare of 2007/9 so scary was that the financial and economic system, including the policy regime, was so unprepared for it. After that experience it will now be a different kettle of fish. It would be unwise and unnecessary to give up a regime that offers us something close to price stability over time in a hurried reaction to circumstances that will not be repeated.

Rules and discretion

The chief objection to a regime such as the one I have described is that it gives too much discretion to central bankers. The great benefit of the current system, it is alleged, is the easy measurability of the central bank against its objectives, and hence the much closer accountability for its actions.

There is something in this. Under my proposed regime, by contrast, a central banker being grilled by a parliamentary committee on why inflation was currently so far below the declared long-term path could simply say that he would get it back to that path in good time, perhaps even in his own good time. This sounds as though it gives central banks – and central bankers – far too much rope.

There are some possible ways round the problem that would keep precision and accountability but would enable more focus on the medium term and thereby allow central banks to pay more attention to asset prices. For instance, central banks could seek to achieve a specified average inflation rate over a period of, say, five years, or, which comes to much the same thing, to keep the price level rising on a specified path.[14] As it happens, I think that such a regime could easily land us in deep water again. The complexity of the real world demands that central banks have some discretion.

If this means a diminution of precise measurability then so be it. It is typical of the modern age to place so much store by precision. A regime of precisely specified inflation targets was what allowed the Bank of England, among others, to think all was well while the greatest bubble in financial history was inflating. The target was measurable all right, and the central bank was accountable all right, but you might as well have been measuring rainfall in Peru or average car speeds on the Michigan freeway. There is more to life than measurability.

Golden illusions

It may be tempting to believe that the way to escape from the precariousness of financial structures is to return to a system based on gold. After all, it is only comparatively recently that the world financial system broke its tie to that precious metal. To be precise, this happened in 1971 when US President Nixon ceased the convertibility of paper dollars into gold.

Up to that point, the fixed exchange rate system known as Bretton Woods, which had been the basis of the world's financial system since the end of the Second World War, had involved national currencies maintaining fixed but adjustable rates of exchange to the dollar, which was itself exchangeable into gold. So although the Gold Standard proper had broken down in the 1930s, the post-1945 system still had gold at its heart.

And look what the world has experienced in the 40 odd years since that link was broken: massive inflation, exchange rate instability, a series of destabilizing bubbles – and now the Great Implosion. You can see why it might be tempting to believe that paper is the problem and gold is the solution.

There are two aspects to this issue, which are related but sufficiently distinct to deserve separate consideration: the prevention of inflation and the maintenance of financial stability. On the first, it is easy to see that a system based on gold should be less subject to inflation over the long term, and for that reason looked at in isolation, preferable to the current system of fiat, or credit, money. Indeed, as a real asset of finite amount, not subject to government control or manipulation, gold should hold its real value pretty well over long periods. The long-run history of the gold price bears this out. Accordingly, a system in which money either was gold, or was tied to gold, should preserve rough long-run price stability. For all those who wish to banish inflation for good and all, gold is immensely seductive.

In fact, though, matters are not quite so simple. Even under the classical Gold Standard in the nineteenth century, the gold supply varied. Moreover, it was possible for bankers to create credit money on a given base of gold in the system. Profit maximization would naturally urge them to do so. Partly because of this, although the overall US price level under the Gold Standard did stay reasonably stable over a run of 90 odd years from 1821 to 1910, there were enormous fluctuations within this period. In 1835, the inflation rate was over 13%. In 1840, however, there was *de*flation of over 15%. This is not a definition of stability that modern markets – or modern voters – would accept.

Furthermore, this hints at a more profound difficulty. It is all very well saying that operating some sort of Gold Standard takes the politics out of money, but how does a society stay on the Gold Standard? The answer can only be through an act of political will, supported by the people. It might have been possible to have believed in the nineteenth century that the Gold Standard would endure forever and that there was no viable alternative to it. But having witnessed the abandonment of gold in the 1930s, and the abandonment of the gold–dollar standard in the 1970s, modern man – and modern governments – will not believe this. It is impossible to destroy our knowledge of how to operate a fiat currency, so paper is always there as a possible replacement for gold. And that possibility – the option of going off gold – diminishes the attraction of relying on gold in the first place!

The second aspect of gold's allure – the idea that a return to a system based on gold would end *financial instability* – is a delusion. Even if a new Gold Standard stabilized the consumer price level over long periods, it would not end the precariousness of financial structures, nor make them necessarily less given to instability.

The whole point about a system based on gold is precisely that: it is *based* on gold; that is, there is a financial superstructure built on it and that superstructure can expand or contract, just as at present.

This is not mere theoretical surmise. Just look at the financial and economic fluctuations experienced by Britain while it was on the Gold Standard in the nineteenth century, which I referred to in Chapter 2. Or, more tellingly perhaps, remember that the Great Crash of 1929, and the boom that preceded it, both occurred while America was on the Gold Standard.

In so far as financial market instability is greater in the modern world than it used to be hundreds of years ago, this is *not* because paper has replaced gold. Rather, it is because financial markets are bigger – that is, there are now more and larger markets; because they are more fragile; because the future may itself be more uncertain (because the economy is dynamic); and because there is a much higher capital stock (where value is determined by views about the future) in relation to current output.

Like it or not, we must face up to the reality: money is a social phenomenon. Accordingly, we must learn to manage it collectively, not retreat to the illusory protection of the "barbarous relic." After the Great Implosion, surely it is clear that this must mean managing it globally.

A global money

In the early twentieth century, the rise of America led to the displacement of sterling as the world's currency. In the twenty-first century, one way or another, the rise of China is going to lead to the displacement of the dollar. However, I very much doubt that its replacement will be the renminbi, or any other national money. There is an enormous amount at stake and the world could get stuck into a slump marked by rampant protectionism and a return to nationalism – including in monetary policy. But if the world manages to escape this fate, then I suspect that the development of a *global* money and an effective framework of *global* financial governance will be part of the reason.

This is much less otherworldly than it sounds. When thinking about the foundations of prosperity in the postwar world in 1944, at Bretton Woods, and in reaction to the monetary chaos and economic misery of the 1930s, Keynes wanted to establish a new international money, named bancor, which was to be at the center of the IMF's operations. In the end, the Americans overruled him. Instead, they established a regime that put the dollar in pole position. Interestingly, the governor of the Chinese central bank, Zhou Xiaochuan, recently advocated a reform to the international monetary system, explicitly modeling his suggestions on Keynes' ideas about bancor.[15]

The solution to our present predicament is not a return to gold, nor the emergence of another national money as a reserve currency, but rather the evolution of a globally managed, fiat money, just as Keynes envisaged back in 1944 and as China's central bank governor is advocating now. The aim would be that countries would tend to hold their reserves in such money and make settlements between each other in this money, as well as doubtless continuing to hold and use both national currencies such as the dollar and gold.

This global money would have to be issued and managed by a global institution – a global central bank. Such a bank would have enormous power and prestige. Accordingly, how such a bank is established and how it would operate go right to the heart of international politics.[16] If the world manages to establish such a bank, this would recast the balance of power and shape international relations for a generation or more.[17]

If such a bank were to be formed, at the same time it would surely be right to reform the membership of the world's various international bodies, which is an anachronism, reflecting the interests of the victors in the Second World War.[18] Under this structure, when the world comes to discuss its problems some of the most important countries are cast as mere observers from the outside, like impoverished characters from a Dickens novel, looking in from the outside through frosted windows, at a sumptuous Christmas feast within.

Pressure on the surplus countries

The process by which a world money was issued could be used to cure one of the endemic weaknesses of the present international economic system: the tendency of some countries, led by China, to run persistent large current account surpluses, which puts other countries in a difficult position. Within my proposed new global framework, this could be discouraged by tilting the distribution of the new global money toward those countries that did *not* run large, persistent surpluses, or by taxing their reserve holdings.

Naturally, getting the existing large-surplus countries to agree to such a radical reform would be difficult. It would involve them either directly losing out financially or being forced to change strategy to avoid losing out. Nevertheless, the prize for them, especially for China, would be their assured place at the global top table, the end of dollar domination, and, as discussed below, a possible solution to the problem of huge dollar reserves. At the very least, China and other Asian countries will need to feel secure in the international monetary system and not see themselves as potential victims of self-interested, cowboy financiers, allowed to run free in an American economic imperium.

For the Americans, of course, the advantages and disadvantages would stack up in exactly the opposite way. The advantages of running the world's money would be attenuated – but they would gain the benefits of China *et al.* pulling their weight in the generation of world aggregate demand. This is the grand bargain that China and America should make for their own sakes, as well as for the rest of us.

As part of this bargain, these two countries might negotiate a solution to the problem of the vast stock of dollar assets in Chinese hands. This represents a timebomb – for both sides. For the Chinese, the problem is the potentially huge losses on its dollar holdings if it seeks to diversify them by selling dollars in the markets. For the Americans, the problem is the destabilizing effects that might follow from a huge fall of the dollar if China does dump its dollars.

It might be possible to arrange a solution in which China swapped a good proportion of its dollar holdings for the new world money, held at the new global bank. That could provide a suitable way out for both parties.

Doubtless this scheme for a new global money and global bank will strike many as far-fetched. It is certainly ambitious, but today's circumstances call for nothing less. At times, the world can make large bounds. America didn't have a central bank until 1913. The world didn't have the United Nations until 1945. Why can't we have a global central bank now?

Putting it starkly, a large part of what has gone wrong in the financial world in 2007/9 is the result of the contrast between globalized finance and national financial governance. In the future, either governance will have to become more globalized or finance will have to become less globalized.

Reforming economics

So far my proposals for reform have left untouched one of the key villains in the piece that I identified early on, namely the subject of economics itself. Of course, governments cannot reshape academic subjects or remake whole fields of study, yet there needs to be a radical reshaping of the way economics and finance are studied and taught. What has gone wrong has long historical roots and will doubtless take a long time to correct – but correct it must.

Academic economics has become a disaster and a disgrace. In a recent lecture, Nobel Laureate Paul Krugman said that much of the past 30 years of macroeconomics was "spectacularly useless at best, and positively harmful at worst."[19] He is right. Not only did most academic economists fail to see the Great Implosion coming, but they weren't even looking in the right direction. And having been surprised by its arrival, they have little to say about its implications – the greatest event to have befallen the capitalist system since the Second World War.

This is not the first time that something like this has happened. Much the same was true of the fall of communism, which broke on an unsuspecting academic community that had written virtually nothing about how a society should move from communism to a market system. It is as though the average economist considers such questions beneath him (or her). One wonders what questions they would think worthy of their study.

Although there are shining exceptions, most academic economists, while clinging to the idea that their subject is relevant and of interest to the wider world, in fact practice a modern form of medieval scholasticism – of no use, or interest, to man or beast. The output of this activity consists of articles entombed in "scholarly" journals, usually about questions of startling irrelevance, badly thought out and appallingly badly written, littered with jargon and liberally dosed with mathematics, destined to be read by no one outside a narrow coterie of specialists, and increasingly not even by them.

It hasn't always been like this. Adam Smith, Ricardo, Malthus, John Stuart Mill, and Marx saw economics as part of a study of the human condition and human society – what we might today call political economy. Nearer to the present, the same was true of Keynes. Interestingly, although he was a mathematician by training, he largely eschewed the use of mathematics in writing about economics and communicated brilliantly to both his peers and a wider audience in plain English.[20]

Although the first half of the postwar world saw the triumph of Keynesian ideas, it also witnessed the progressive decline of the Keynesian approach to doing economics that, by the 1970s, was in wholesale retreat. Its adversaries were mathematical models, econometric testing, and the supposed elevation of economics to the status of a science. This was a direct response to the scientism that had emerged in the late nineteenth century. Supposedly, if economics was to have status as a subject it had to be scientific, and that meant being rigorous and mathematical. Economists suffered from *physics envy*.

What a shame that it wasn't engineering envy! Gerald Holtham, who is both a fine theorist and an excellent applied economist, has put his finger on what is wrong with the training of economists and with the mindset that usually holds them in its grip:

> *It's as if an engineer were to try to build a structure using Newton's laws of motion and nothing else. Friction, air pressure, elasticity of materials etc. are all assumed away. There is no equivalent of engineers in economics. No one wants to be Brunel, everyone wants to be Einstein and produce a "general" theory.*[21]

And in trying to tackle economic problems that were of the sort that might yield to the "Brunel approach," instead economists tackled them the Einstein way. Out went the qualifications, the judgment, and the doubts, and in came the simplistic assumptions, the mind-numbing equations dressed up in Greek letters, and the conclusions of staggering banality. Meanwhile, the emergence of huge amounts of economic *data* and, more recently, the advent of computers allowed economists relentlessly to test their pet theories against the evidence – or, more truthfully, to torture the data in pursuit of support for the theories.

In the process, ideology had been written into the new subject's DNA. The models the mathematicians slaved over embodied simplistic assumptions about issues over which earlier generations of economists had wrestled: the nature of human motivations, the structure of costs, the nature of firms, the behavior of the macro system as opposed to individual elements, and the path of the system, and its parts, when it is not "in equilibrium."

What has emerged is a set of beliefs – and an accompanying set of knee-jerk reactions to almost any issue – which hardly bears at all on practical matters, yet which unthinkingly favors free markets as the solution to almost any problem. Ironically, in seeking so assiduously to become a science, modern economics has turned itself into a religion. The god to whose worship this religion is dedicated is "The Market." Some of the greatest names in modern economics have been in thrall to this religion. According to Paul Samuelson, a Nobel Laureate in Economics, Milton Friedman, the high priest of monetarism and the free market, as well as being supremely intelligent and remarkably gifted as a persuader, "was a libertarian to the point of nuttiness. People thought he was joking, but he was against licensing surgeons and so forth."[22]

Finance theory is an offshoot of this poisoned plant. It is mathematics applied to human affairs – with the humanity taken out. Scarce wonder, then, that when one of the greatest challenges ever posed for the modern capitalist system arose, modern economics and finance theory were both at the center of what had gone wrong and were powerless to put it right. A whole generation of economists, bankers, regulators, accountants, central bankers, journalists, analysts, and plain old Joe Soaps had grown up knowing nothing about financial and economic history but everything about "efficient markets theory."

How was it that so few economists questioned what had happened to the subject? Robert Waldmann has supplied a good part of the answer:

I have a view of how people can devote so much effort to working out the implications of assumptions which almost no ordinary people would find other than nonsensical if they understood them. Freshwater economics (i.e., the sort taught at the University of Chicago) uses difficult mathematical tools. Students in freshwater graduate programs have to learn a huge amount of math very fast. It is not possible to do so if one doesn't set aside all doubts as to the validity of the approach. Once the huge investment has been made it is psychologically difficult to decide that it was wasted. Hence the school gets new disciples by forcing students to follow extremely difficult courses.[23]

In fact, it turns out that, in the memorable phrase of Paul Krugman's, all this intellectual capital was invested with Bernie Madoff.

The way ahead

What needs to happen is pretty clear. Just as in financial markets, the Augean stables need to be cleaned out: of people and ideas.[24] The study of economics – and finance – needs to be restored to the position of humble practical subject that it once held: a sort of mixture of dentistry and the law, but without the painful drilling of the one and the hidebound pretensions of the other.

As well as knowing *some* mathematics, students of economics must be numerate and have a real sense of magnitudes. They need to master the abstract reasoning of theoretical economics. But in addition, they need to have a sound knowledge of history, both political, social, and economic; know how to read a balance sheet; be familiar with the issues of the present and the controversies of the past; be able to draw the right conclusion from a table of numbers; and be able to marshal an argument, backed up by numbers, to reach a practical conclusion.

They do *not* need to master the pyrotechnics of higher mathematics that baffle the intelligentsia and even many fellow economists, never mind the *hoi polloi*, while simultaneously leaving anyone with serious mathematical ability speechless at the vacuity of the subject. Economics must be rooted in an acknowledgment of what it is to be human, both as regards how human beings can be assumed to behave and the values by which their activity should be judged. *Homo economicus* needs to be laid to rest – for good.

This process has already begun with the rise of "behavioral economics," which makes links between economics and psychology.[25] This marks a major advance and it should carry the subject a good way along the road to relevance and usefulness. Nevertheless, although it might be rigorous in method, it will take the subject away from the apparent certainties and the status as a science to which it aspired. Perhaps economics will become more like medicine, with some universal truths established but much scope for variation between individuals, and with the thrust of the activity being toward the overall "wellness" of human beings.

In the reformed subject, at the macro level, out must go all the ludicrous pretense that the economic system is a finely tuned, economic machine. At its center must be a recognition that Keynes was fundamentally right. It is, I suppose, noteworthy that the high priest of the New Classical school of economists who originated the idea of "rational expectations," Robert Lucas, has said: "I guess everyone is a Keynesian in the foxhole."[26] The point is that the economic terrain is simply littered with foxholes and if we aren't careful we are liable to spend a considerable amount of our time in one or other of them.

Keynes was right in three major respects:

◆ Economic activity is permeated by fundamental uncertainty.
◆ As a result, many of the major factors that affect the economy are psychological and depend critically on the state of confidence, which is not readily analyzable or predictable.
◆ Consequently, the modern economy is inherently unstable and fragile.[27]

These realizations will also have consequences for the study and practice of finance. The idea that the risk of an asset is adequately measured by the variability of its returns over some limited past period will have to go. Even Alan Greenspan seems to recognize this. In October 2008, he told a Congressional Committee: "The modern risk management paradigm held sway for decades... The whole intellectual edifice, however, collapsed in the summer of last year... To exist you need an ideology... The question is whether it is accurate or not. And what I'm saying to you is, yes, I have found a flaw. I don't know how significant or permanent it is. But I have been very distressed by that fact... A flaw in the model that I perceived is the critical functioning structure that defines how the world works, so to speak."

After this failure, those who seek to minimize the risk and ensure the stability of institutions and portfolios will have to stop measuring and computing quite so much and start thinking and imagining rather more.

There will still be a place for some people to approach economics from a highly mathematical standpoint and to study and develop the intricacies of general equilibrium theory – but only a few. Some societies have financed a priestly class to perform ceremonial activities and to preserve the knowledge of what life was like in bygone times. Something similar may be nice for us. But it isn't very useful to have hundreds of thousands of people doing this – let alone pontificating on the basis of such expertise about how society should be run today.

Interestingly, some individuals with a high capacity for abstract and mathematical reasoning have taken very different attitudes to economics. Max Planck, the eminent physicist, decided not to study the subject because he thought it was too difficult. On the other hand, Bertrand Russell, the eminent philosopher and logician, gave it a miss because he thought that it was too easy. In a sense they were both right. Keynes spelled out what a good economist should be like. He wrote:

> *The study of economics does not seem to require any specialized gifts of an unusually high order. Is it not, intellectually regarded, a very easy subject compared with the higher branches of philosophy or pure science? An easy subject, at which very few excel! The paradox finds its explanation, perhaps, in that the master-economist must possess a rare combination of gifts. He must be mathematician, historian, statesman, philosopher – in some degree. He must understand symbols and speak in words. He must contemplate the particular in terms of the general, and touch abstract and concrete in the same flight of thought. He must study the present in the light of the past for the purposes of the future. No part of man's nature or his institutions must lie entirely outside his regard. He must be purposeful and disinterested in a simultaneous mood; as aloof and incorruptible as an artist, yet sometimes as near the earth as a politician.*[28]

I am far from confident that this is how economics will develop in the years ahead. Largely insulated from its beloved market forces, the economics "profession" could easily meander on into genteel irrelevance, if not oblivion, leaving the field clear for – who knows what? Nevertheless, this need not happen. Hopefully, a period of much needed soul searching will lead on to renewal and revival.

So there is a viable, prosperous, and secure future for us all, even for economists, given vigorous reforms designed to save capitalism from itself, and economics from the failed rocket scientists. However, it will need to be a different capitalism that emerges from this process – one more suited to the realities and challenges of the twenty-first century. I have a few ideas about what that capitalism might be like.

Conclusion: The Future of Capitalism

All happy families are alike; each unhappy family is unhappy in its own way.

Leo Tolstoy, 1873

Tolstoy's dictum about the nature of family relations, with which he begins his great novel *Anna Karenina*, has some close parallels in economic affairs. Successful economies are all characterized by the harnessing of individual effort to the creation of wealth, to the benefit of all. Unsuccessful ones are characterized by individual effort being devoted to the distribution of wealth away from others.

However, there are umpteen ways in which this may happen. Throughout much of human history it has happened through wars over territory and treasure; in much of Africa today it happens as a result of the activities of corrupt and kleptocratic governments; in southern Italy through the activities of the Mafia; in the UK in the 1970s it happened through the antics of militant trade unions, each effectively trying to secure a larger share of the national cake. In advanced, western societies now it results from the activities of finance capitalism. In my view, the Great Implosion was the result of a financial sector grown too big, too greedy, too easily drawn to the fabrication of illusory wealth, and too devoted to the distribution of the proceeds, rather than the financing of wealth creation. Making the economy bombproof against a repeat of the events of 2007/9 will involve the imposition of considerable restraints on the financial system, as well as wider reforms of corporate governance.

The defense of the free market

This is far from being a universally accepted diagnosis – or prescription. The free market vigilantes are already rushing to defend the unfettered market system.[1] Their defense is based on one or other of three arguments. First, the market solution is to let failing financial firms fail. If the state intervenes to stop this, the blame for the resulting mess cannot be laid at the door of the market system. Second, and relatedly, banking has been a heavily regulated activity. The regulators have failed in their job. Third, the monetary policy authorities should have paid more attention to the growth of money and credit and the resulting inflation of the property market bubble.

In this way, they try to argue that what seems on the face of it to be a failure of markets is in fact a failure of government. So the solution, they say, is not less freedom for markets but more.

These people are dangerous. The idea of letting the financial system implode and then waiting for the market to bring spontaneous, healthy revival out of the wreckage might read well on the pages of a book, but in the real world it would bring human misery on a gigantic scale. In today's society, people simply will not tolerate it. If that is what the market system is about then they will have none of it; and rightly so. This is exactly the way millions of people in Germany saw matters in the 1930s.

There certainly were mistakes made over regulation, but the answer surely involves not lighter regulation but tougher and tighter. Similarly, on monetary policy major mistakes were made, but that was because not enough allowance was given for the ability of the markets and private financial institutions to get things horrendously wrong! That redoubles, not reduces, the weakness of unfettered financial markets. As the former Chairman of the Fed, Paul Volcker, said in a speech in 2008: "Simply stated, the bright new financial system – for all its talented participants, for all its rich rewards – has failed the test of the marketplace."

Different types of capitalism

That said, what is needed now is not a rejection of capitalism but rather a radical reform of some of its institutions and practices. In a way, this is nothing new. What we now think of as capitalism did not emerge fully formed in an act of creation, but rather evolved. So why should it have stopped its process of evolution now? There is no reason. Nor is there a sense in which change in the economic system must inevitably be a process of development toward an even purer form of capitalism, yet to be revealed in its final state, and after the realization of which no further development will be necessary or possible.

That would represent a peculiar view of human society and of human history: a teleological view. The fact that such a view of the economy shares this teleological quality with many religions – and especially with the latest big religion to have burst on the scene in the last 200 years, namely communism – perhaps tells you something about the state of mind of the market fundamentalists who believe this stuff.

If the teleological view is rejected, an interesting question is highlighted: What *sort* of capitalism will dominate in the immediate future? After all, there are so many types of it around:

- The part free-for-all, part heavily regulated capitalism of America.
- The finance-dominated, open capitalism of the UK.
- The bureaucratic capitalism of France and Germany.
- The welfare state capitalism of Scandinavia.
- The robber baron capitalism of Russia.
- The managed capitalism of Singapore.
- The state capitalism of China.

Perhaps all these different types will survive. I suspect, though, that some new type, or a new melding of these existing types, will emerge and rise to dominance.[2] After all, the modern market system is a completely different animal from what existed for most of the time since the Industrial Revolution. The economy has become more complex, more integrated, and more financially dependent, and therefore more fragile.

Not that the nineteenth-century market economy was all sweetness and light. As I pointed out in Chapter 2, it underwent umpteen crises. Moreover, in the Great Depression the system was brought to its knees. It was rescued not by some innate recuperative power but by the onset of war. After the war, the financial system was then bottled up and restricted. Once those restrictions started to be released in the 1970s, it suffered a series of ground-shaking crises of which the Great Implosion has been the most severe.

We have been trying to live comfortably in a completely new era with a system of controls – and a set of ideas – fashioned for an age long past. This is not the end of capitalism but the beginning of a new phase of it, a phase in which it is not controlled or suppressed, but channeled and marshaled, rather like a great river whose course is managed and whose boundaries are banked and buttressed.

Such a thought will offend those who tend the flame of the free market ideal. But the market was made for man, not man for the market. An effective market system is like democracy: how it operates in practice can be very different from how it works in theory. Effective market systems and effective democracies are fuzzy. In both cases there is a theoretically pure version that appears to embody the essence of the thing, whereas in practice the presence of this thing alone often sees the essence escape.

The essence of democracy, you might think, is free elections. Yet it is comparatively easy to establish elections that are free in a system that is democratic in only the most tenuous sense. This is true of contemporary Russia. Although the country is nominally democratic, there is no doubt that the current Prime Minister, Vladimir Putin, exercises an influence way beyond what would be normal in a western democracy.

Once elections are over, what really counts in ensuring democratic government, and a free election next time, are a free press, an independent judiciary, and sources of making a living independent of the patronage of whoever holds the levers of state power.

For markets, it is a similar story. According to the theory, free markets deliver an optimum result for society, given perfect information and a large number of competitors (and a whole load of other near-unrealizable conditions). In practice, an effective market economy is a mish-mash of less than perfect facts on the ground that rarely even approximate the conditions of the textbook model. The saving grace (as well as one of its major bugbears) is change, and the dynamic that is set up by the progress of technology and continuous economic growth. This factor ensures that apparently cosy positions can be upset and transformed. Even so, markets still need the state to keep them on the straight and narrow. They even need the state to keep them competitive. In the words of the economist Edmund Phelps, "Capitalism is not the 'free market' or laisser faire – a system of zero government 'plus the constable'."[3]

The extremes of finance capitalism

Financial markets take the problems created by market failure to a new pitch – including in the international dimension. The trouble with markets does not appear to account for the contribution to the bubble and the subsequent Great Implosion from excessive saving by China and other large surplus countries. But why do China and other countries save so much? A good part of the answer is because of the experience of the Asian crisis in 1997/8, which revealed to them how perilous it was to be at the mercy of financial markets. In many ways their contribution to the bubble came as a direct response to an earlier burst of finance capitalism gone mad, when western investors poured money into the region – and then promptly took it out again.

The unresponsiveness of capital investment

Why did the countries of the west not respond to the availability of cheap "eastern" finance by sharply increasing their real investment in plant, machinery, and new businesses? In most western countries investment has been sluggish; in some it has been downright weak. I wonder what the great Victorian entrepreneurs would have done with so much capital available so cheaply. The answer, I suspect, is that they would have rebuilt the world.

Nothing like this happened because it didn't seem profitable to do so. But why not? I suggest four reasons, three of which derive from failings of the financial markets. The odd one out, the nonfinancial explanation, is the way the pace of technological change and the spread of globalization have heightened risk in the economy. Even though, until the Great Implosion at least, the macroeconomy seemed to be pretty stable, at the micro level it was anything but. Companies felt very insecure about their competitive position and consequently the risk factor applied to assessing investment projects became unusually high.

The other explanations are all financial in nature. A commonly used method of assessing the attractions of an investment project has centered on comparing its returns with the "cost of capital." However, the cost of capital is judged by reference to what sort of returns equity investors have been accustomed to make on their shares. With equities having until recently been in a long bull market, many corporate managements would interpret this as meaning a return of 10%, or even more. And corporate executives are not content with projects that merely match the cost of capital, they want projects that exceed it by a comfortable margin "to cover risk." Yet in an economy where the sustainable growth rate is 2–3% and the returns to ordinary savers are pitifully low, even 10% is an absurdly high rate. Scarce wonder that not many projects get through.

Over and above this, the motivations of corporate decision makers have been not solely about the prospects for their companies but heavily influenced by the prospects for themselves. Managers' time horizons are often pretty short compared to the payoff period of investment projects. Their natural risk aversion will have been increased by the experience of the dot-com boom, when substantial investments were made in the telecoms sector and many subsequently were shown to have been bad. Moreover, this period was followed in America by a web of regulations and controls on executives that will have made them even more than usually risk averse.

There is another factor emerging from the split between owners and managers that may well hold back real investment: the increasing tendency toward revenue sharing; that is, senior employees creaming off a large proportion of any incremental rewards in the form of higher bonuses and stock options. Where this occurs on any scale, although the incentives of senior executives to push projects through may be increased, the ability of a project to produce a return to the shareholders above the "cost of capital" is correspondingly reduced.

More generally, though, the modest level of real investment in the west reflects a Keynesian communications failure in the macro economy. Large-scale saving by the rapidly growing countries of Asia, the oil producers, and even Japan and Mitteleuropa can be partially justified on the grounds that they are saving now in order to be able to spend later. In that case, large deficit countries in the west, such as the US and the UK, should be preparing for this future surge of foreign consumption, and hence demand for their exports, by investing in real equipment and real businesses now.

But when will the surplus countries spend? And what will they spend their money on? These messages are not communicated. Just as Keynes argued in the 1930s in the context of a national economy, the increased desire to save is simply transmitted as decreased consumption now and the message about implied future consumption gets lost.

In fact, corporate managements, in thrall to the imperative of quick returns and cowed by the insecurities of the new globalized economy, just carried on as before. Accordingly, they left the field open for the bankers to recycle the money to those who definitely *did* want to take advantage of it: the consumers. So the assets the west piled up to match increased liabilities to China *et al.* were increasingly dodgy loans to increasingly dodgy, mainly consumer, borrowers.

New problems, new solutions

Capitalism always throws up problems and failings. This is neither surprising nor a fatal criticism. Society has to find a way of either living with them or correcting them. However, as capitalism evolves, so the nature of its failings and problems changes. So too must be the way in which society copes with them.

The Great Implosion has laid bare several different sorts of failing. First, it has revealed just how fragile the financial system is. Second, it has demonstrated the markets' excessive risk taking. Third, it has shown how bloated the financial sector has become. Fourth, it has exhibited a failure of the market with regard to the setting of executive remuneration in general, and pay in the financial sector in particular. Fifth, it has uncovered a deep-seated failure of the corporate system, arising from the separation between owners and managers and the weakness of institutional shareholders in influencing corporate policy.

The result has been the revelation of a financial sector hell-bent on pursuing its own profit, while undermining, not promoting, the public good, and a system of corporate governance where managers have been pursuing either their own interests or the short-term performance of the share price – which often came to the same thing. Even Jack Welch, the former CEO of General Electric who is often thought of as one of the originators of the shareholder value movement, has said recently that "focusing solely on quarterly profit increases is 'the dumbest idea in the world'. Shareholder value is a result, not a strategy." He added: "Your main constituencies are your employees, your customers and your products."[4]

More widely, even in these apparently most capitalist of times, millions of ordinary folk need to feel that people in positions of power and authority are concerned with the public good, not just with lining their own pockets. That includes business executives. The revelations of the Great Implosion have delivered a profound shock that has left people anxious, bewildered – and angry.

It is no wonder that these problems have emerged only recently, since it is only since the early 1970s that the financial markets have grown to such size and importance in the economy, that markets have been given free rein, and that large-scale institutional shareholders have become dominant.

Moreover, during most of the postwar period, the values and motivations of senior executives both inside and outside finance were influenced by a different set of social values and experience. There was a large hangover of Victorian values and a still strong influence of Judaeo-Christian thinking. Furthermore, the Second World War was surely the greatest expression of the importance of collective effort and public purpose. Its influence lingered for decades. The result was that for a long time, the serious problems for society that would be unleashed by blatant self-interest remained latent. They only burst forth once the combination of deregulation and the doctrine of "greed is good" released them in the 1980s.

But now we know. Greed is dangerous, and the encouragement of it is stupid. In order for society to work efficiently, never mind fairly and cohesively, there has to be a balance between the competitive and cooperative parts of the system. This balance goes right to the heart of human nature and human society.

The free-for-all that rules in the financial markets does not promote such a balance. Worse than that, as I argued in Chapter 5, because of their high profile and apparent success, the values of the financial markets spill out into the wider business world and poison its values. Society cannot live by greed alone. Even if it can cope perfectly well if some of its members are motivated in this way, it needs millions of people to be motivated by duty, responsibility, and a sense of public purpose. These are feelings that the triumph of unbridled greed in the financial markets threatens to overwhelm.

The thinking that has allowed this situation to develop goes back to the origins of economics. The defenders of naked self-interest often quote a classic passage from Adam Smith's *The Wealth of Nations*:

It is not from the benevolence of the butcher, the brewer, or the baker that we expect our dinner, but from their regard to their own interest. We address ourselves not to their humanity, but to their self-love, and never talk to them of our own necessities, but of their advantage.[5]

It is less well known, however, that in *The Theory of Moral Sentiments* Smith wrote that although "prudence" was "of all the virtues that which is most helpful to the individual" yet "humanity, justice, generosity, and public spirit, are the qualities most useful to others."[6] He also argued the importance of mutual trust in society and for a mixture of institutions and motivations. Although he trumpeted the virtues of markets, this did not amount even to the advocacy of a wholly market economy, let alone a market society.

Moreover, it is even less often acknowledged that being born a few years after the collapse of two spectacular bubbles, the Mississippi Scheme and the South Sea Bubble, Smith was well aware of the phenomenon of rampant speculation, which he termed "overtrading." He called the promoters of excessive risk in search of profit "prodigals and projectors."

The evidence is that he would not have been taken in by the housing bubble that led to the Great Implosion. In 1776 he wrote: "A dwelling house, as such, contributes nothing to the revenue of its inhabitant. If it is lett (sic) to a tenant for rent, as the house itself can produce nothing, the tenant must always pay the rent out of some other revenue." Therefore, although a house can make money for its owner if is rented, "the revenue of the whole body of the people can never be in the smallest degree increased by it."[7]

It would be easy for someone reading this book to see it as being "antimarket." It is most definitely not. The trouble with markets is that some of them work better than others. When all are left to their own devices, the interaction of the ones that do work well with those that don't produces a dog's breakfast.

In order to save capitalism from itself, we need to recognize something that Smith knew full well but many modern economists, especially those who liberally invoke his name in support of their views, often seek to deny: markets have limits. We need to use markets where we can, not worship them. That may include bringing markets to bear in areas where they are not currently in extensive use, including road pricing and the deterrence of pollution. But it also includes imposing limitations in areas where markets have encouraged activities or sectors to grow too large and to become distorted. More generally, as well as placing restrictions on the activities of financial markets, somehow we have to put the idea of public purpose back into business – including finance.

While this may sound a tall order, it isn't really. It is all about structure and expectations. Once it is widely understood that the purpose of business is to deliver the goods (and services) for society and not to enrich cowboys on the make, business executives will more readily behave with restraint and responsibility, with an eye to public purpose. Duty and honor will be back where they belong. Confirmation of real success will come from a society-wide decline of the bonus culture and the return of a sense of pride in doing a good job.

If we don't do this, the future is bleak indeed. By the middle of 2009, as the financial markets seemed to settle, the feeling that we had lived through momentous events appeared to subside. Many defenders of the old system, with its rampant greed and ludicrous levels of executive and trader rewards, might reasonably have felt that nothing fundamentally had changed. They should beware. In the days after Russia's Bolshevik Revolution in 1917, the comfortable middle classes didn't think that much had happened either, and on the Petrograd stock exchange prices held their ground.[8]

If the *status quo ante* is allowed to continue, then in the painful conditions caused for everyone by the Great Implosion, I wonder which trees will be left standing in the hurricane of righteous indignation that will sweep through our society. It isn't only the institutions of the market economy that would be vulnerable but also those of democracy and freedom.

Markets and government

In order to save capitalism from itself, we need to deal with the capacity for financial markets to create havoc. This will involve *better* regulation, to be sure, although it needn't necessarily involve *more* regulation. Much of what needs to be done involves making markets work better.

However, at the root of this intervention must be the recognition that:

◆ Support for market principles does not necessarily imply support for laisser-faire.
◆ Interventions are more likely to be successful and to be efficient if they work with the grain of the market rather than against it.

Nor should it be assumed that the measures advocated in this book would constitute a return to "big government." The restrictions and reforms I advocate for domestic financial systems are designed to make the market mechanism more effective, while laying bare the protective, guaranteeing role of the state, which provides a public good.

The proposed system of global money and a world central bank is not so much aimed at creating another level of governance as at replacing one narrowly focused and heavily constricted player, the US Fed, with an institution focused on, and empowered to pursue, the global economic interest.

Nor does the thrust of the book endorse heavy state borrowing. On the contrary, once the need to support aggregate demand in the current downturn is over, it argues that governments should tighten fiscal policy gradually to bring the public debt-to-GDP ratio down sharply – and to keep it down. In principle, this could be achieved either by increasing taxation or by cutting spending. In my view, however, it should overwhelmingly be done by the latter.

Although this book has discussed aspects of the market system that do not work very well, its fundamental stance is that markets, and not governments, are best at allocating resources. Individuals – and their families – need to be left with control over the fruits of their labors.

Who got it right?

Toward the end of a book like this, of all the questions that must press in on the reader, the author is profoundly conscious of one in particular. If the ills of the financial system, and the general shape of what must be done to correct them, are as I describe them, then who "got it right"?

Among thinkers now deceased, I would strongly advance the claims of John Maynard Keynes, John Kenneth Galbraith, and Hyman Minsky. Among those still alive, Joseph Stiglitz and Nassim Nicholas Taleb have serious claims. Among political leaders with good claims are Dr. Mahathir Mohammed of Malaysia and Lee Kwan Yew of Singapore.

Among the nations of the world, China has a decent claim, for resisting the market fundamentalists who argued that to allow capitalism to deliver prosperity you had to liberalize everything instantaneously. In 2000, at the time that Alan Greenspan, then Chairman of the US Federal Reserve, was waxing lyrical about the economic value of derivatives, Gao Xiqing, an adviser to China's premier, said: "If you look at every one of these (derivative) products, they make sense. But in aggregate, they are bullshit. They are crap. They serve to cheat people."[9] Meanwhile, China's economic progress has been a triumph. Nevertheless, China's place among the vindicated comes with a serious caveat: its apparent view that surpluses of 10% of GDP are both desirable and sustainable. They are neither.

On the matter of pure insight and understanding, I would advance the claims of France. Yes, the *French*. Most members of the French establishment, both the intellectual and policy elites, have always been suspicious of finance capitalism and of the wisdom and stability of the Anglo-Saxon "free-for-all." Their suspicions have been proved right. What a pity, though, that they have simultaneously squandered so much by being suspicious of markets in general and embracing a regime of high personal taxation and a government reaching into every nook and cranny of economic life. Accordingly, their victory in the world of ideas has been only partial. It would be a gross error – and a great shame – if the vindication of France's traditional attitude to financial markets also led people, not least French people, to conclude that traditional French attitudes to markets in general, as well as to state spending, personal taxation, and protectionism, had been vindicated as well – especially when the facts so clearly support the opposite conclusion.

Getting it right for the future

Regardless of who "got it right" in the past, it is now imperative that the world "gets it right" for the future. The failures and excesses of finance capitalism have coincided with the rise of Asia to produce a time fraught with danger. The plunge of much of the world into depression coincides with the rise of new powers needing to be accommodated.

However, there are ways out of our predicament, which I described in the previous chapter. Once we are free from the grip of the present crisis, there is a new world order waiting to be constructed. I have argued that much of the job of regulating financial activity will now be done by the markets themselves. But, over and above this, I have put forward several ideas for measures that would radically alter the shape and behavior of the financial system and make it robust against a repeat of 2007/9. More importantly, in my view, in explaining how and why the Great Implosion took place, this book has made it clear that the failure of finance capitalism does not suggest that capitalism is finished. It has also sketched a more humane, rounded vision of the market system with which modern humanity can feel comfortable.

Despite the obvious dangers, this time is also pregnant with positive possibilities. Suppose that the reform and restraint of finance capitalism coincide with the advent of roughly balanced international trade brought about by expanded domestic demand in Asia. There would then be the scope for a new confidence about our economic future, leading to a take-off of real investment expenditure in the west. Meanwhile, in China and the emerging countries, living standards could continue to rise, and indeed to rise at an even faster pace than before. Who knows what problems – economic, political, social, and environmental – could not be solved in such a world?

So from where we stand, the way ahead forks. One path leads to further economic and fiscal disaster and a rerun of the 1930s. Another leads to future prosperity, stability, and a new era of close international cooperation.

I cannot pretend that I am confident we will take the decisions that will lead us down the right path, although I am certain that we could do so. Those who argue that we are helpless before the steamroller of disastrous events are as wrong as those who argue that although we could do something, we will be better off by doing nothing. Theirs is a counsel of despair, leading to disaster. It is as weak in theory as it is poorly grounded in history. It betrays an ignorance of human nature as much as an insouciance toward human suffering. Given both the will and the understanding, we can do so much better.

Facing similar threats, our parents and grandparents tried and failed. We owe it to them both to try and to succeed. We owe this even more to our children.

Notes

Chapter 1

1 A fine account of these events and many of the people involved is to be found in Gillian Tett's *Fool's Gold*, London: Little Brown, 2009. See also Vince Cable's *The Storm*, London: Atlantic Books, 2009.

2 In the immediate aftermath of the Lehmans collapse and the seizing up of other credit markets, bank lending increased dramatically because banks were forced to honor pre-arranged lines of credit to firms shut out of the commercial paper and bond markets.

3 I owe this quip to the distinguished economist Willem Buiter.

4 One of the best analyses of the contribution to the crisis from the fragility of the banks and the complexity of financial instruments is to be found in the Turner Review, published by the UK Treasury in March 2009.

5 Berger, A., Herring R., & Szego, G., "The role of capital in financial institutions," *Journal of Banking and Finance*, 1995, pp. 399–430.

6 Haldane, A., "Small lessons from a big crisis," remarks at the Federal Reserve Bank of Chicago 45th Annual Conference, *Reforming Financial Regulation*, 8th May, 2009.

7 Greenspan, A., *The Age of Turbulence*, London: Allen Lane, 2007, p. 507.

8 For a compelling exposition of the case against the widely employed methods of risk assessment, see Nassim Nicholas Taleb's *The Black Swan*, London: Allen Lane, 2007.

9 Quoted in an interview with the *Guardian*, 1st May, 2009.

10 For an analysis of the underlying causes behind the current crisis, as well as advocacy of reform of the international monetary system, see Martin Wolf's *Fixing Global Finance*, New Haven: Yale University Press, 2009.

11 For an excellent account of London's rise as an international financial center, see Philip Augar's *Chasing Alpha*, London: Bodley Head, 2009.

12 Reported by John Authers in the *Financial Times*, 12th May, 2009.

13 Basel II sought to broaden and refine the risks assessed under the Basel I framework in order to make capital requirements more sensitive to the risks that banks face in their operations.

14 I revealed a glimpse of what would happen in my book *Money for Nothing*, first published in 2003. I wrote: "The bursting of the late 1990s bubble did not have more serious effects because it isn't all over yet. There is a second shoe to drop. What is happening in the real estate market is the second leg of the bubble." Bootle, Roger, *Money for Nothing*, London: Nicholas Brealey Publishing, 2003, p. 3.

"Just as in the share boom, hundreds of millions of people have thought that money would cascade to them from rising house prices, without effort or desert, merely by sitting there – money for nothing. But a society can no more get rich through rising house prices than it can through everyone agreeing to take in each other's washing. Even so, this illusion has enabled measured wealth levels to recover, and for all those people worried about their pensions it has provided a soothing balm. The bursting of the house price bubble will puncture this illusion and bring people face to face with the sober realities of their financial situation." Bootle, *op. cit.*, p. 3.

"For society as a whole the increase in wealth created by soaring house prices has been a financial fantasy; albeit one that has had major real consequences, not least the boost to consumer confidence and consumer spending... The irony is that the immediate health of the economy in the US, UK, and several other countries depends on the illusion continuing for a while longer. In my view, it is now only the continuation of the housing illusion that stands between us and a world slump." Bootle, *op. cit.*, p. 58.

"In the end, this bubble may be more serious than the primary bubble in shares. When it bursts, the world will tremble." Bootle, *op. cit.*, p. ix.

15 In an interview with Conor Clarke, theatlantic.com, 17 June 2009.

16 The prime critic of Keynes in the United States was Chicago's Professor Jacob Viner. The "neo-classical synthesis" that, following the way first laid out by Sir John Hicks in 1937, sought to marry Keynes' thought with classical economics, and in the process smothered it, was forged by many people, but prominent among them was Chicago's Don Patinkin. The originator of the efficient markets hypothesis was Chicago's Eugene Fama. Mind you, Chicago's contribution wasn't all on one side. Chicago's Frank Knight, alongside Keynes, emphasized uncertainty, as distinct from risk. My good friend Robert Z. Aliber, who has adapted and effectively cowritten the classic work on bubbles by Charles Kindleberger, hailed from Chicago. Hyman Minsky, the champion of Keynes' ideas, was educated at the University of Chicago, as was the Nobel Laureate and avowedly Keynesian Paul Samuelson, and the great Professor Ronald Coase, whose ideas I make much of in Chapter 4, spent many years there. Moreover, Richard Thaler, one of the fathers of behavioral finance, is a professor there.

17 See Fox, Justin, *The Myth of the Rational Market*, New York: HarperCollins, 2009; and MacKenzie, Donald, *An Engine, Not a Camera*, Cambridge, MA: MIT Press, 2008.

18 Black, F., "Noise", *Journal of Finance*, vol. 41, 1986, pp. 529–43.

19 The study was by the Center for Public Integrity, reported in the *Financial Times*, 6th May, 2009, p6.

20 Simon Johnson, "The quiet coup," *Atlantic Online*, May 2009, www.theatlantic.com.

Chapter 2

1 Herbert Hoover, Address at the annual dinner of the Chamber of Commerce of the United States, 1st May, 1930.

2   In the preindustrial era, there must, though, have been occasional demand-led fluctuations caused by the changing intensity of government-financed activities. Building the pyramids, for instance, is unlikely to have taken place with exactly the same intensity year after year. Similarly, the money to pay for various royal activities or public projects may well have been raised in bursts, rather than steadily year after year. Accordingly, there could have been variations in the sovereign's budget position, thereby giving rise to fluctuations of a straightforward Keynesian nature.

3   It is very difficult to believe in the notion of a single "cycle" over this whole diverse period, which includes among other things the age of empires, the rise of industrialization and urbanization, a technological transformation involving steam power, electricity, the motor car, aviation, and the computer, as well as two devastating world wars, the rise of communism and its subsequent demise. The idea that all of this, including the technological and sociological elements, can be subsumed in some overarching theory of society – political, economic, technological, and sociological – is one of the worst examples of nineteenth-century determinism taken *ad absurdum*. The truth is surely much more difficult to theorize about, mathematize, and manipulate. In other words, it is much more historical. The state we are in at any point in time is part of a complex historical process in which ideas, institutions, technology, and accident interact. Admittedly, there are similarities between one period and the next, but there are individual characteristics of each period that mark it out from its predecessors. There are processes at work, to be sure, but they are not mechanical.

4   See Eichengreen, B. & O'Rourke, K., *A Tale of Two Depressions*, June 2009, www.voxeu.org.

5   Galbraith, *The Great Crash, 1929*, London: Penguin, 1992, p. 3.

6   For data see Maddison, A., *Historical Statistics of the World Economy: 1-2006 AD*, 2009, available at www.ggdc.net/maddison/; and Mitchell, B.R., *International Historical Statistics, Europe, 1750–2000*, Fifth Edition, London: Palgrave Macmillan, 2003.

7   Maddison, *op. cit.*

8   See Kindleberger, C., *The World in Depression 1929–1939*, Berkeley: University of California Press, 1973.

9   There is an enormous literature on the Great Depression. The following represents a sample of sources that I have found most helpful: Bernanke, Ben S., "Deflation: Making sure 'it' doesn't happen here," remarks by the Federal Reserve Governor before the National Economists Club, Washington, DC, 21 November 2002; Fisher, Irving, "The debt–deflation theory of great depressions," *Econometrica*, Vol. 1, Issue 4, New York, 1933; Friedman, Milton & Schwartz, Anna, *A Monetary History of the United States, 1867–1960*, New Jersey: Princeton University Press, 1971; Galbraith, *The Great Crash 1929*; Kindleberger, *The World in Depression, 1929–39*; Liesner, Thelma, "One hundred years of economic statistics," *The Economist*, New York, 1989; Maddison, Angus, *The World Economy: Historical Statistics*, Paris: OECD, 2003; Mitchell, B.R., *International Historical Statistics: Europe and The*

Americas 1750–1993, London: Stockton Press, 1998; National Bureau of Economic Research, online database, www.nber.org/data/, 2009; Richardson, Gary, "The Collapse of the United States Banking System during the Great Depression, 1929 to 1933, New Archival Evidence," *Australasian Accounting Business and Finance Journal*, Vol. 1, No. 1, pp. 39–50, February 2007; Shiller, Robert J., *Irrational Exuberance*, New Jersey: Princeton University Press, 2000; Temin, Peter, *Lessons from the Great Depression*, Cambridge: MIT Press, 1989; Wicke, Elmus, "A Reconsideration of the Causes of the Banking Panic of 1930," *Journal of Economic History*, Vol. 40, No. 3, Cambridge: Cambridge University Press, September 1980; White, Eugene Nelson, "A Reinterpretation of the Banking Crisis of 1930," *Journal of Economic History*, Vol. 44, No. 1, pp. 119–138, Cambridge: Cambridge University Press, March 1984.

10 Galbraith, *op. cit.*, pp. 187–8.

11 See *Newsweek*, 25th May, 1970, p. 78.

12 This speech was delivered at the Conference to Honor Milton Friedman, University of Chicago, Chicago, Illinois, November 8, 2002.

13 Friedman & Schwartz, *op. cit.*

14 Maddison, *op. cit.*

15 According to estimates in Boyer, G. & Hatton, T., "New Estimates of British Unemployment, 1870–1913," CEPR Discussion Paper No. 2814, 2002, p. 31.

16 The speech was delivered at the Democratic National Convention in Chicago on 9th July, 1896.

17 Mathias, P., *The First Industrial Nation*, Oxford: Oxford University Press, 2001, p. 364.

18 Mitchell, B.R., *International Historical Statistics, Europe, 1750–2000*, 5th edn, Palgrave Macmillan, 2003, Table 1.

19 Bordo, M., *Stock Market Crashes, Productivity Boom Busts and Recessions: Some Historical Evidence*, Rutgers University, 2003, p. 11, www.cfr.org/content/thinktank/Depression/Bordo_2.pdf.

20 Richardson, H., *The National Banks*, New York: Harper & Brothers, 1880.

21 Bordo, *op. cit.*, p. 4.

22 Markham, J., *A Financial History of the United States*, Armonk, NY: M.E. Sharpe, 2002, p. 202.

23 Bordo, *op. cit.*, p. 11.

24 Schwartz, A., "Financial Stability and the Federal Safety Net." In Haraf, S. & Kushmeider, M. (eds), *Restructuring Banking and Financial Services in America*, Washington, DC: American Enterprise Institute for Public Policy Research, 1988, pp. 34–62.

25 For a discussion of the Nordic crisis see Honkapohja S., "The 1990s Financial Crises in Nordic countries," speech at the Global Interdependence Center, Philadelphia, 30th September 2008; and Moe T.G., Solheim, A.J., & Vale B., "The Norwegian Banking Crisis," Norges Bank Occasional Paper No. 33, 2004.

26 Quoted by Ambrose Evans-Pritchard in the *Daily Telegraph*, 26 August 2009.

27 Fukuyama, Francis, *The End of History and the Last Man*, London: Penguin, 1993.

Chapter 3

1 All it needs to do is to lend money to the banking system (injecting liquidity) or buy some asset in the market. Traditionally, such assets have been government bonds or bills, but there is no reason in theory why the central banks should not buy any sort of asset in the system.

2 Banks don't make much of a return by holding deposits at the central bank. Indeed, in many monetary systems it has been normal for banks to earn no return at all on their central bank deposits. So they have an incentive to minimize such deposits, subject to regulatory requirements and their need for liquidity.

3 Moreover, whereas an individual bank can reduce its holdings of central bank money in this way, in fact it only moves the deposits around the system so that some other bank ends up with excess reserve holdings. The system overall is only in equilibrium again when commercial banks' assets and liabilities have risen sufficiently to justify the increased holdings of central bank money. In this way, analysts have spoken of central bank money as "high-powered money" and of the "money multiplier." Inject some extra central bank money into the system and you will get an expansion of the money supply several times the original injection.

4 I first put forward this idea in *The Death of Inflation*, London: Nicholas Brealey Publishing, 1997, p. 210.

Chapter 4

1 A. Gowers & D. Buchan, "EU action over unfair trade urged by Balladur," *Financial Times*, 31 December, 1993.

2 What Churchill said was: "No one pretends that democracy is perfect or all-wise. Indeed, it has been said that democracy is the worst form of Government except all those other forms that have been tried from time to time." Speech in the Chamber of the House of Commons; see *Hansard*, 11 November 1947, Vol. 444, c. 206–07.

3 Of course, there are textbooks and textbooks. And even in economics there are some heretical economists who question received wisdom. But in general the textbooks that form the basis of most teaching stick closely to a narrowly conceived, received orthodoxy.

4 Heilbroner, Robert, *The Worldly Philosophers*, revised 7th edn, London, Penguin, 2000, p. 24.

5   In many other countries, the market economy was even more rudimentary for much longer. In Russia, for instance, serfdom was only abolished in 1861, and even after this, countless millions of people remained rooted to the spot where they were born.

6   Polanyi, Karl, *The Great Transformation: The Political and Economic Origins of Our Time*, Boston, Beacon Press, 1944.

7   Tanzi, Vito & Schuknecht, Ludger, *Public Spending in the 20th Century: A Global Perspective*, New York: Cambridge University Press, 2000.

8   America and most of continental Europe followed policies that protected home industries and favored exports. Britain's economy, however, was essentially open from the mid-1840s until the 1930s.

9   Maddison, *op. cit.*; and Bradford DeLong, J., "Estimating world GDP, one million years B.C.–present," http://econ161.berkeley.edu.

10 Greenspan, A., *The Age of Turbulence*, London: Allen Lane, 2007.

11 Smith, A., *The Wealth of Nations*, Book 1, Chapter 10, Part II, p. 144.

12 It is possible to imagine this problem being dealt with in a free society without the intervention of the state. The sufferers from pollution could band together and pay the polluter to stop. Or, in a society infused with concern for the environment, the polluter might voluntarily desist, under moral pressure. In practice, however, it has been widely recognized since the 1970s that the practical barriers to successful combination by the sufferers from pollution are so great, and the powers of self-restraint so weak, that some form of state intervention is necessary – either in the shape of a law limiting the polluting activity or a tax on it that forces the polluters to confront a cost that more nearly reflects the overall cost to society.

13 This is not to say, of course, that public goods cannot be promoted and public bads prevented, except by government. Rather, they must be promoted/prevented by some sort of collective rather than individual effort. Such effort can, and often does, emerge spontaneously in society without government intervention. The key point is that the market cannot deal with these issues.

14 This point is argued forcefully by Michael Sandel in the 2009 BBC Reith Lectures.

15 Indeed, in the nineteenth century and earlier, the people doing the saving were often the same as the ones doing the investing, so no communication had to take place at all.

16 Most standard textbooks still don't present the Keynesian case correctly. In the years after the Second World War, in the controversies that raged about what Keynes really meant, attention came to focus on various "rigidities" – in particular, fixed money wages, or interest rates that were stuck in a liquidity trap. These may or may not have been reasonable assumptions for the 1930s, or for some other period, but they cannot be said to be general. Accordingly, it came to be believed by the academic consensus that, as a matter of theory, Keynes' contribution was trivial. This view was overturned in the 1970s, in particular as a result of a book by Axel Leijonhufvud, *On Keynesian Economics and the Economics of*

Keynes, New York: Oxford University Press, 1968. Leijonhufvud successfully argued that Keynesian economics was about a money-exchange economy. You could not usefully analyze the problem by thinking about workers receiving their "marginal product" as wages, as though they typically received this in kind. The whole point is that they didn't – they received money. And in order for their employers to be able profitably to pay them this money, they had to be able to sell the products. In depressed conditions, this is what they could not do. So if you analyze the economy in real terms without money, or if you confine money to the realms of an asset and forget about its role as a medium of exchange, then the Keynesian problem is assumed away. Admittedly, something less than perfect flexibility of prices and wages is required for the economy to get into a state of depressed demand, but once in that state the amount of flexibility required to get the economy out of it is much greater. Indeed, in an economy dominated by imperfect competition (i.e., just about any economy in practice) it may be next to impossible for the workers in an individual firm or industry to bargain themselves into employment through accepting wage cuts. Indeed, it is not wages that are the problem. It is the level of effective aggregate demand. So far from being trivial, Keynes' insight into this issue was revolutionary.

17 It cannot be said that he left this area completely undisturbed because with regard to the behavior of financial investors and entrepreneurs and industrialists, his theories emphasized "animal spirits" and confidence above rational calculation. Indeed, his point was that in the conditions of outright uncertainty that surrounded most economic and financial issues, a purely rational decision was often impossible.

18 See, for example, the book by Richard Layard, *Happiness*, London: Allen Lane, 2005.

19 One riposte to these examples is that such people are still "maximizing their utility," for reasons that would readily admit of a Darwinian explanation. It is simply that an individual's utility sometimes includes the welfare of others. However, this is a fatuous answer. If everything can be automatically reconciled with the "utility-maximizing" view of human nature, it is empty of all content. It ceases to be a testable, falsifiable hypothesis about human nature and behavior and becomes instead a mere tautology. If the utility-maximizing view has any insight and content, it must be capable of being disproved by observation. The real questions are about what items appear in the utility that the individual is apparently maximizing – is it merely narrow self-interest or does it include some altruistic content? And is the objective best described as maximization or satisfaction?

20 See Newlyn, D., *Other Lives*, York: Dorne Publications, 2008.

21 See Norwich, John Julius, *A History of Venice*, Harmondsworth: Penguin, 1983.

22 One simple reason is that the efficient size of capital equipment is usually way beyond the needs and the finances of an individual, or an individual family. In theory, arrangements could be made for sharing such equipment and there are some examples of this in practice. In many parts of the world, for instance, viniculture is the province of individual families but these share access to expensive wine-making equipment, which is often owned

collectively. However, for anything other than simple activities, such sharing arrangements are impractical. Moreover, access to capital equipment is just one aspect rather than the be-all and end-all of the reasons for the inefficiency of atomistic arrangements and consequently for the existence of firms.

Chapter 5

1   Galbraith, *op. cit.*, p. 27.
2   The only real economy events with such concentrated effects on a person's economic well-being are the loss of a job (which is typically the source of the majority of a person's income) or the destruction of a home.
3   Keynes, J. M., *General Theory of Employment Interest and Money*, London: Macmillan, 1936, p156.
4   New York Times, www.nytimes.com/2006/06/26/business/02grasso.html.
5   BBC News, http://news.bbc.co.uk/2/hi/business/3119030.stm.
6   Mishel, L., Bernstein, J., & Allegretto, S., *The State of Working America 2006/2007*, Ithaca, NY: ILR Press, 2007, Fig. 32.
7   The vast bulk of the pay growth was seen in the late 1990s, when CEO compensation sky-rocketed as more firms offered sweeteners, such as stock options, in an attempt to align the incentives of management with that of shareholders. According to data from Forbes and ExecuComp, between 1995 and 1999 total remuneration for CEOs employed by S&P 500 firms trebled in real terms. This pattern of rapid CEO pay growth was mirrored across the world. Between 1988 and 2005, CEOs' basic salaries grew in real terms by 6% p.a. in the US, 5.8% p.a. in the UK, 6.6% p.a. in France, and 6.4% p.a. in Germany. But still the multiples in the US were much higher. In 2005, the ratio of CEOs' basic pay to workers' basic pay stood at 39:1 in the US, compared to 32:1 in the UK, 23:1 in France, and 20:1 in Germany.
8   Cuomo, A., *No Rhyme or Reason*, August 2009.
9   Group of Ten, "Report on Consolidation in the Financial Sector," Bank for International Settlements, January 2001.
10 Cetorelli, N., Hirtle, B., Morgan, D., Peristiani, S., & Santos, J., "Trends in Financial Market Concentration and Their Implications for Market Stability," Federal Reserve Bank of New York, *Economic Policy Review*, March 2007.
11 On the structure of the financial industry and its practices, see Philip Augar, *The Greed Merchants*, London: Allen Lane, 2006.
12 The insurance industry is an interesting case. Large incomes are made by a host of intermediaries operating in the sector. You would think that competition would bid market rates down, but the incidental and opaque way in which much insurance is sold, combined with the, for most people, difficult nature of the product, means that this doesn't happen effectively.

13 US Department of Commerce, Bureau of Economic Analysis, GDP by industry data, available at www.bea.gov/industry/gdpbyind_data.htm.

14 Quoted by Martin Wolf in the *Financial Times*, 15th April, 2009, p. 13.

15 In order to gauge the size of an industry in the economy, you simply tot up the value of its production, whether goods or services, as determined by "the marketplace," and express this as a share of GDP.

16 See Wojnilower's comment in *Grumpy Old Bankers: Wisdom from Crises Past*, London: CSFI, 2009.

17 www.forbes.com/2009/04/08/wall-street-highest-earners-business-wall-street-earnings.html.

18 *Financial Times*, 25 August 2009.

19 *Wall Street Journal*, http://blogs.wsj.com/deals/2008/03/14/where-in-the-world-is-bears-jimmy-cayne-playing-bridge/; http://online.wsj.com/public/article_print/SB119387369474078336.html; BBC News, http://news.bbc.co.uk/2/hi/business/7317878.stm.

20 Referred to by Simon Johnson, *Atlantic Online*, May 2009, www.theatlantic.com.

21 Reported in the *Financial Times*.

22 http://oversight.house.gov/documents/20080307101333.pdf.

23 As reported in the *Daily Telegraph*, 7th April, 2009, p. 6.

Chapter 6

1 In an interview with the *Financial Times*, printed on 2nd February, 2009.

2 The classic exposition of this view is Bernanke, B., "The Global Saving Glut and the US Current Account Deficit," Sandridge Lecture, Virginia Association of Economics, Richmond, Virginia, Federal Reserve Board, March 2005.

3 In economists' theoretical language you could say that the behavior of the super-saving countries constituted a shift of the IS curve, but their asset preferences also resulted in a shift of the LM curve. But because the net effect of both moves still threatened to depress demand and to push inflation to excessively low levels, the authorities cut interest rates. It is extremely difficult to capture this move in the IS/LM framework, unless you posit a horizontal LM, fixed at whatever interest rate the authorities choose. In that case, the interest rate on the Y axis has to be short-term official interest rates, whereas in order to capture shifts between money and bonds, as in the portfolio preferences as discussed above, it really has to be something like the interest rate on long bonds. It is very difficult to capture both in the same formulation.

4 It is striking that while bond yields were being forced lower, the earnings yield on equities was not. It seems that the equity risk premium had risen. There could be a number of possible explanations for this, but one possible candidate is simply the portfolio preferences of central banks and governments in the surplus countries. For a discussion of this issue,

see Daly, Kevin & Broadbent, Ben, "The Savings Glut, the Return on Capital and the Rise in Risk Aversion," Goldman Sachs Global Economics Paper No 185, 27 May, 2009.

5   His essay, "Reform the International Monetary System," is available in English at www.pbc.gov.cn/english/.

6   The best exposition of this view is by Professor Max Corden, one of my teachers at Oxford, for whom I have the greatest respect. (See "The International Current Account Imbalances: A Sceptical View," *Economic Affairs*, June 2007.) But Corden admits several qualifications to the argument that could undermine the conclusion that imbalances don't matter. In practice, I think that recent conditions in the world economy correspond to these qualifications.

7   There is a demographic argument in favor of China running a substantial surplus now in that, like Japan, its population is aging rapidly and will before long start to fall. But this factor, you would think, should easily be outweighed by its poverty and enormous growth potential.

8   Among the GCC countries (Saudi Arabia, UAE, Oman, Qatar, Kuwait, and Bahrain), Saudi Arabia produced the largest surplus of US$86 billion (25% of GDP), followed by Kuwait (US$47 billion, 43% of GDP) and UAE (US$36 billion, 21% of GDP).

9   There were some exceptions among the trade-oriented economies of East Asia. Singapore and Taiwan have been in surplus since the early 1980s and both China and Hong Kong slipped in and out of surplus through the 1980s and 1990s. But Korea, India, and the other nations of Southeast Asia ran deficits more or less continually from 1980 to 1997.

Chapter 7

1   I found this remark quoted in Stein, R., *The Bull Inside the Bear: Finding New Investment Opportunities in Today's Fast-Changing Financial Markets*, John Wiley and Sons, 2009. However, Stein admitted that he could not find corroboration for the remark, and I have also been unable to do so.

2   American writer and social reformer (1878–1968).

3   I do not agree with those who argue that an inadequate supply of housing, rapid population growth, or lower nominal interest rates support a much higher level of the house price-to-earnings ratio than in the past. In some countries housing shortage combined with population growth can explain, and justify, a part of the rise in house prices. But really big variations in these factors take place only slowly, over long periods, and housing is a very long-lived asset. Consequently, sharp changes in the average price of housing are almost always caused by changes in demand; that is, changes in the ability and willingness of a given number of people to pay the going price for houses.

Lower nominal interest rates have justified some increase in the equilibrium value of the housing market because they eased the burden of initial mortgage payments, and hence the powerful entry barriers posed by high national mortgage rates. However, this effort is small compared to the illusory effect of confusing low national rates with low real rates. This illusion is bound to fade over time.

Nevertheless, I am sympathetic to the idea that the lower current level of real interest rates compared to the past justifies higher real house prices, and higher prices in relation to earnings. But the reduction in real rates has been fairly modest. The rise in house prices justified by this factor might be of the order of 10–15%.

4   There is a possibility that central banks could charge commercial banks for holding reserves at the central bank and, if they did this, this might then establish the basis for short-term rates to be below zero throughout the system. The degree to which interest rates could be set negative would be severely constrained by the ability to hold notes that pay (and charge) no interest. But it might be possible to impose rates of minus $\frac{1}{2}$%, or even 1%, without triggering a stampede into cash.

5   OECD Economic Outlook database, http://stats.oecd.org/WBOS/index.aspx.

6   Thomson Datastream.

7   Shiller, R., *Irrational Exuberance*, New Jersey: Princeton University Press, 2005.

8   Thomson Datastream.

9   Thomson Datastream.

10 It is frequently argued that share values can rise by more than this because of the real growth of the economy and hence the real growth of earnings. This is true for the capital value of all equities. But it is appropriate to assume that new equity will be issued. If the ratio of equity in issue to GDP remains constant, and all earnings are paid out, then real earnings per share, on average, will not rise at all.

11 Kay, J., *The Long and the Short of It*, London: Erasmus Press, 2009.

12 Kay, J., "A fortune built on defying the pull of theory," *Financial Times*, 24 March 2004.

13 For a really useful guide as to how to do this, and for a splendid survey of the investment scene aimed at the general reader, see Kay, *The Long and the Short of It*.

Chapter 8

1   Lawrence Summers made this remark in the course of an interview with the *Financial Times*, 9th March, 2009.

2   Although this saying is widely attributed to Churchill, I have been unable to track down details of time and place. I found the quote on The Quotations Page, www.quotationspage.com/quote/407.html.

3   Jung is best regarded as merely an honorary Austrian. He was in fact Swiss.

4   Nevertheless, this is exactly what happened in the UK in the 2009 Budget, although not because the British government sought to discourage saving, rather because it wanted to raise more revenue.

5   See the Archbishop's article, "Face It: Marx was partly right about capitalism," in *The Spectator*, 24th September, 2008; his lecture, "Ethics, Economies and Global Justice," given in Cardiff on 7th March, 2009; and his interview on BBC's *Today Programme* on 18th December, 2008.

6   Vince Cable, House of Commons, *Daily Hansard*, 26 February 2009, Column 373.

7   It is often argued that a policy of low interest rates is unjust because it helps those people who have been behaving irresponsibly, namely heavy borrowers, and penalizes those who have been doing the decent thing, namely savers. I have some sympathy for this view. I am especially concerned about the plight of older people who have put something by for their old age, believing that the interest on their deposits would supplement their pension.

    But macroeconomic policy cannot be conducted on the basis of such factors. It was partly the influence exercised by pensioners who benefited from a combination of continued deflation and nonzero interest rates that inhibited the Japanese authorities from taking sufficiently vigorous action to get out of deflation in the 1990s.

8   Quoted by Ambrose Evans-Pritchard in the *Daily Telegraph*, 26 August 2009.

9   Admittedly, depending on what the effect was of the original policy of quantitative easing, the policy of freezing bank cash holdings might still leave the nonbank private sector with enlarged holdings of bank deposits, and hence with the liquidity to support increased spending, if that was so desired. However, the effectiveness of just replacing bond holdings with money holdings has always seemed to me to be unlikely to have much of an effect. The potentially more powerful aspect of QE, and the more dangerous aspect if things went wrong, has always been the supply of excess cash to the banks, and the potential impact that would have on bank lending. And that aspect can most definitely be adequately addressed by freezing bank cash holdings.

10 Fama/French Forum, 13 June 2009, www.dimentional.com/ famafrench2009/01/bailout-and-stimulus-plans.html.

11 Paul Krugman's blog, 30 January 2009, http://krugman.blogs.

12 In an interview with the *Financial Times*, printed on 2nd February, 2009.

13 Despite recent increases, education spending is still about 2½% of GDP, which is around half the average for Asia excluding Japan.

14 This would be the equivalent of a tax cut, but with more likelihood of encouraging increased spending rather than increased saving.

Chapter 9

1   There are some exceptions. Long-Term Capital Management (LTCM), the hedge fund that virtually collapsed in 1998, employed the finance professors and Nobel Prize-winners Myron Scholes and Robert C. Merton.

2   For a good skeptical account of both what has gone wrong and what may be done to put

it right, see Lilico, A., *What Killed Capitalism?*, London: Centre for Policy Studies, 2009.

3   This will be trickier than it sounds. It is all very well imposing higher capital ratios as the cycle turns up, but the difficult thing will be allowing lower ratios when things get worse. For as depositors, both interbank, commercial, and individual, see a bank's capital ratio falling during the onset of a downturn, they are bound to get more nervous, thus probably triggering an increase in the bank's funding costs.

4   It was very striking that in 2008/9 the conventional wisdom was that banks that had a larger retail base were in some sense more secure and less vulnerable to a liquidity crisis. This strikes me as rather odd. Individuals may not be as sophisticated as professional wholesale investors and certainly not as fast, but neither are they stupid. If a bank is perceived in the market to be in difficulties, the idea that the average retail investor will stand there idly, just accepting the situation, is bizarre. In the case of the near-failure in 2007 of the British mortgage lender Northern Rock, what finally scared the British authorities rigid, and prompted the lender's nationalization, was not the sight of interbank, or other wholesale, money deserting the bank, but rather the sight of queues of Northern Rock depositors stretching round the block, broadcast on primetime TV. The authorities were worried that this would lead to a widespread panic, causing a run on otherwise sound institutions. The idea that retail funding is "safe" is one of the precrunch precepts that is yet to bite the dust. Whatever the evidence from the past that retail deposits tend to be sticky, they are liable to be a lot less sticky after the Great Implosion.

5   These changes might even serve to strengthen a long-term approach to careers on the part of both employer and employee. In this respect, HSBC, the leading international bank (for which I used to work as Chief Economist), has an interesting culture. Its senior managers are almost all drawn from a cadre of so-called international offices or "IOs" who typically work for the bank for the whole of their careers. They can be sent anywhere in the world at a moment's notice. They are extremely well rewarded, although not excessively so by the standards of modern investment banking. They feel real loyalty to the bank and its customers and in return the bank is loyal to them. It is like something out of the British Army or the civil service during the empire.

   Perhaps it is asking too much to expect something similar for most banks today, but the balance needs to swing in this direction and away from the notion that bank employees are constantly in play in the employment market – just like the financial instruments they may be trading.

6   Quoted in the *Daily Telegraph*, 13th June, 2009.

7   *Financial Times*, 15th April, 2009, p. 13.

8   See Tobin, James, "The New Economics One Decade Older," *Eliot Joneway Lectures on Historical Economics in Honor of Joseph Schumpeter*, Princeton: Princeton University Press, 1972; and "A Proposal for International Monetary Reform," *Eastern Economics Journal*, Vol. 4, 1978, pp. 153–9.

9   The UK, and a number of other countries, already has such a tax in the shape of Stamp
    Duty.

10 Tobin, J., "On the Efficiency of the Financial System," *Lloyds Bank Review*, July, 1984.

11 It can easily be misunderstood. Its intention is not to raise revenue – although it certainly
    would have that effect. The proceeds of such a tax could be deployed in any number of
    ways, but perhaps one of the most attractive would be the funding of an international
    financial institution to take over from the IMF.

12 For a discussion of the Tobin tax see ul Haq, M., Kaul, I., & Grunberg, I. (eds), *The Tobin
    Tax: Coping with Financial Volatility*, New York: Oxford University Press, 1996.

13 There could be restrictions on the percentage of an asset's value that a bank was permitted
    to lend, as well as restrictions on the amount of exposure a bank could have to any partic-
    ular asset class. In this way the authorities could hope to prevent a bubble from building
    up, even if macroeconomic policy were set in the usual way, in pursuit of an inflation objec-
    tive with no special regard for asset values or the prevention of bubbles.

14 There is a good deal to commend a system in which the price objective is cast in the form
    of a target path for the price level rather than the inflation rate. This distinction may sound
    esoteric, but actually it makes a big difference. Under an inflation-targeting regime, such
    as the one that several central banks currently operate, if a shock occurs to cause inflation
    to deviate from the target, in subsequent periods the central bank is not supposed to take
    account of this deviation in setting policy. Its objective is still inflation of 2%, or whatever
    the target rate is. Under a price-level target, by contrast, the central bank pursues a target
    path for the price level. If a shock causes the price level to diverge from that path, the bank
    is obliged to try to get prices back to the path. So, suppose there is an upward shock to the
    price level, say from sharply higher oil and commodity prices, which causes the inflation
    rate to rise well above target in year one, after which it drops down to its previous path in
    year two. Under a price-level regime, however, the central bank needs to take action to
    bring the price level back to its target path, which involves a period of especially low, or
    even negative, inflation.

15 See his essay, "Reform the International Monetary System," available in English at
    www.pbc.cn/english/.

16 It is deeply ironic that the IMF, which was set up, under Keynes' inspiration, to pursue the
    collective good out of recognition that markets could fail, has ended up being a bastion of
    market fundamentalism. See Joseph Stiglitz's *Globalisation and its Discontents*, London:
    Penguin, 2002.

17 Assuming that such a bank were independent and run by monetary professionals, along
    modern lines, then it would nevertheless have to be set objectives by, and be accountable
    to, some political body or other. The natural candidate for that political body would be
    some agency of a grouping of sovereign countries – most probably the G-20, or some vari-
    ant thereof.

18 On the Security Council of the UN, the permanent members include the UK and France, but not Germany and Japan. The voting rights in the IMF, the world's proto-central bank, are similarly distributed. Moreover, the IMF and the other major global financial institution, the World Bank, are located in the US and are effectively under heavy US influence. In the G-7 there are three eurozone members – Germany, France, and Italy – plus another EU member, the UK. Three of the G-7's members are Anglo-Saxon – the US, the UK, and Canada. Meanwhile, China, India, Brazil, and a host of important developing countries hardly get a look in.

19 The Lionel Robbins Lectures at the LSE, 10th June, 2009.

20 For a masterful account of Keynes' contribution and his relevance to today, see Robert Skidelsky's *Keynes – The Return of the Master*, London: Allen Lane, 2009. I have gained much inspiration from both this volume and Skidelsky's earlier work.

21 Quoted by John Llewellyn in *The Observer*, 16 August 2009.

22 In an interview with Conor Clarke, theatlantic.com, 17 June 2009.

23 Robert Waldmann on Angry Bear blog, http://angrybear.blogspot.com, 27 January 2009.

24 I am far from being alone in my excoriation of modern economics and its role in the developments that led to the Great Implosion. See George Soros' *The Crash of 2008 and What It Means*, New York: Perseus Books, 2009.

25 See Akerlof, George A. & Shiller, Robert J., *Animal Spirits*, Woodstock: Princeton University Press, 2009.

26 Quoted in Justin Fox, "The Comeback of Keynes," *Time*, 27 January 2007.

27 At the macro level, Hyman Minsky saw what is needed. He wrote: "Instability is an observed characteristic of our economy. For a theory to be useful as a guide to policy for the control of instability, the theory must show how instability is generated. The abstract model of the neoclassical synthesis cannot generate instability. When the neoclassical synthesis is constructed, capital assets, financing arrangements that center around banks and money creation, constraints imposed by liabilities, and the problems associated with knowledge about uncertain futures are all assumed away. For economists and policymakers to do better we have to abandon the neoclassical synthesis." Hyman Minsky, *Can "It" Happen Again – Essays on Instability and Finance*, New York: M.E. Sharpe, 1982, p. xii.

28 Quoted in Heilbroner, Robert, *The Worldly Philosophers*, revised 7th edn, London: Penguin, 2000, p. 285.

Conclusion

1 Some of the most cogent thinking from this stable is to be found in Booth, P. (ed.), *Verdict on the Crash: Causes and Policy Implications*, London: IEA, 2009.

2 Among the first to recognize the institutional and cultural supports for markets, and that there are umpteen different forms of capitalism, was John Gray. See his *False Dawn*, London: Granta Books, 1998.

3   In the *Financial Times* supplement "The Future of Capitalism," 12th May, 2009.

4   Quoted by Francesco Guerrera in the *Financial Times* supplement, 12th May, 2009.

5   Smith, A., *The Wealth of Nations*, Book 1, Ch. 2, 1776.

6   Smith, A., *The Theory of Moral Sentiments*, Part 4, Ch. 2, Cambridge, UK: Cambridge University Press, 2002.

7   Smith, A., *The Wealth of Nations*, Glasgow Edition of the Collected Works, Oxford: Oxford University Press, 1976, p. 281.

8   According to Chrystia Freeland in the *Financial Times* supplement, 12th May, 2009.

9   Quoted by Kishore Mahbubani in the *Financial Times* supplement, 12th May, 2009.

Index